THE LEI HANDBOOK

Exchange Data's Guide to Financial Codes

Ozren Cvjetic

**With a foreword by Francis Gross,
Senior Adviser, Directorate General Statistics,
European Central Bank**

Chancellor Publications Limited

5 Highgate Road

London NW5 1JY

United Kingdom

Telephone: +44 207 324 0020

Fax: +1 212 214 0825

First edition 2017

ISBN 978-0-9569986-2-0

While every effort has been made to ensure the accuracy of the information contained in this guide, readers should note that it contains only general statements and is not intended to cover all possible situations which may arise. Accordingly, the publisher does not accept any liability for acts undertaken in reliance on the contents of this guide.

Dedicated to my parents, Zdenka and Slobodan Cvjetic

Contents

Foreword

The impact of the technological revolution of the last twenty years on the financial system can be likened to an asteroid striking a planet, viewed in ultra-slow motion. To our senses, the scene can appear quasi-static, perhaps even immobilised – we might not perceive it as the fast, powerful, all-transforming event we know it to be.

This analogy is inspired by the words of the renowned physicist and leading climate scientist Hans-Joachim Schellnhuber. He was, of course, referring to climate change, not the financial world. But the parallel between climate change and today's financial system is clear. Like climate change, shifts occurring in global finance represent an enormous psychological challenge, because their perceived slow speed makes it easy for humans to suppress recognition of the magnitude and profundity of change, and to continue their lives undisturbed.

We realise that in many respects the world has become a village and that information and events can propagate in quasi-real time across that entire village. Yet at the same time, we continue to run established local legacy infrastructures, usually disparate and disconnected, often incompatible, including in fields where new realities would call for a single global infrastructure. The obscure field of identification of financial objects – the subject of this important book — is one such case.

A single web vs national systems

Today, ever more financial organisations and operational processes span the globe, crossing borders and increasing in speed. One could therefore be forgiven for expecting that the identification of financial objects would be globally uniform. Yet, across the world, hundreds of identification schemes for financial contracts, counterparties to contracts and transactions, are in operation. They have been built over the past decades to serve the diverse needs of their respective constituencies, at a time when each constituency could reasonably be treated as a closed system. Indeed, operations and measurements used to be conducted mostly within a single constituency, with cross-border interactions being the exception. But now technology and trade liberalisation have made cross-border interaction so easy and cheap that no constituency can still reasonably be treated in isolation, as a closed system.

In this new context, it might be wise, at least technically, to view the financial system as a single, global web of contracts spanning all constituencies, rather than as a set of closed, national systems with international transactions treated as a perturbation. Yet the financial crisis has revealed that what is in reality an ever-more integrated global network of financial contracts and transactions is not yet reflected in the identification infrastructure, which remains largely fragmented along national, sectoral and market lines.

The crisis has exposed the downside of fragmented, overlapping identification systems where a single object can have a different name in each constituency and many different names across a single operational process that spans those constituencies. Although the owners of a given operational process can, in theory, agree on the language and data they want to use, it would be difficult for them to impose that choice across all parties to that process, especially to parties that also exchange data with others. It becomes even more difficult for any one business, or market authority, to build a picture of even one's own globally connected constituency, which might involve many operational processes, most of which are owned by others, let alone a picture of the broader system.

Towards a single global infrastructure

The recent emergence of the Legal Entity Identifier under the aegis of the G20 signals the beginning of a willingness to progress towards a global identification infrastructure. Yet, not least in view of our heavily entrenched and highly fragmented legacy, we must unfortunately expect a lengthy migration process to such an integrated global identification infrastructure. Progress is also held back by the limited understanding, even by the people most concerned, of the critical nature of a reliable system of single naming. Absent that understanding, the inherent technical and cultural difficulties of the migration towards an identification infrastructure worthy of the digital age could be compounded by an avoidable factor: indifference.

This book offers an essential inventory of existing identification schemes relevant to the financial system that are currently in operation across the world. It is thus very useful as a counterbalance to that indifference, as an early step on the road to explaining the crucial nature and structure of identification schemes. Unfortunately, the venture promises to be a long one. Indeed, one of the first discoveries is that beyond every hill a wider-than-expected landscape meets the eye. Therefore, this book should be considered a living document.

It might easily be thought that global identifiers are not important — with the result that the value of this book could therefore easily be underestimated, even discarded, as the dull drudgery of data. In this foreword, I wish to place this work in context. Two dimensions appear particularly relevant: the emergence of global standards and the roots of data in human language.

Global standards: the case of sports

There are just a handful of human activities that all of mankind has agreed to practice the same way. Sport is one such. In most popular sports, athletes follow the same rules and use the same implements everywhere in the world. We take it for granted that, in every country, football is played 11 a side and that all sprinters run exactly 100 metres. World championships and Olympic Games just wouldn't be possible, and world records would be meaningless, if athletes and teams did not prepare and compete under the exact same rules all over the world. Without such universally applied standards, sport wouldn't be what it is.

Fortunately, the Olympic Games were created before sport developed into a global activity with some political overtones. Because of the Games, countries who wished their best athletes to represent them every four years on the global stage naturally accepted that sports-governing bodies imposed standards on their sports, which became de facto global standards as those sports grew into a global activity.

A second example is telecommunications. Its international standards have emerged alongside its growth and the development of the technologies that enabled its very existence. And it did so very successfully. We take it for granted that we can talk on the phone with anyone, anywhere, and view live video from virtually anywhere on the planet.

Finance hasn't been so lucky. Some of its activities are in the situation sports would be in, had the idea of organising global competitions among 200 countries begun to emerge only once each country already had developed its own sports independently, over generations, fully fledged with national rules and implements. Under such circumstances, the very idea of organising a global sports event might have very quickly been abandoned, suffering from the difficulty of communicating a business case supported mainly by vision and reasoning, with technical and organisational feasibility hard to prove to the most of sceptical minds anchored in daily business and annual budgets.

Deeply global, very fast

Finance doesn't have that choice: globalisation cannot be called off. Moreover, finance has become deeply global very fast, within a single human generation, at a time when – to continue with our sports metaphor – every community had very much consolidated its local game and local rules. Yet, as barriers have been taken away, the world is now much closer to a single pitch on which we all play together. Each player on that pitch tries to find their way the best they can, feverishly searching for game variants that work when football meets cricket bat. The umpires, meanwhile, each coming from their own previous local game, try in the fire of action to come up with agreement on a set of rules that would enable that chaotic situation to converge into a well-oiled global game. The challenge for umpires and players alike is to create, together, a single game with a single set of rules, while play goes on and with the legacy of history and its inertia stacked against them.

Two streams of change are inextricably intertwined in that process: technological and social change. Technological change seems to be the faster and easier one; social change the slower and more difficult one. Accelerating technology gives opportunities to ever-smaller groups of players to rapidly and cheaply build communication and trading systems to do business globally, multiplying the number of channels that cross borders. Those borders have been established, sometimes over centuries, through slow cultural, political, and social processes. The multiplication of channels puncturing those borders renders them increasingly porous; de facto, the homogeneous organisational and cultural groups that slowly matured within their borders find themselves gradually coalescing into a much larger group, like villages coalescing to become a large city.

In finance, as in other areas, we have technically come together much faster than most individuals, let alone a culture, can follow or even perceive. Recent political developments in many countries show how uneasy many people feel about change these days. Yet, the longer we take to adjust our technical infrastructures to the accelerating reality of our faster game on a technically single playing field, the wider the gap to safety will grow, the higher the technical risks will mount and the more reason many might see for seeking safety and certainty elsewhere.

Data as "powdered language"

Just as villagers who grew up knowing everyone in their village could not imagine the anonymity and indifference of large cities, we are gradually discovering what it means to live in a globalised world. By connecting the world, technology has revealed glaringly the profound diversity of human languages. In their diversity, these languages collide when we try to build socio-technical systems that work globally.

This warrants a closer look at what we understand by "data", the condensate of language that we feed into computers. Using another analogy, this time with milk, "data" could well be dubbed "powdered language". Just as, by adding water, we expect powdered milk to be transformed back into milk we can drink, we expect data to generate language that conveys meaning. Unlike the case of milk, however, we don't know how to re-create meaningful language when "powdered language" from diverse, sometimes unknown, sources and of uncertain composition is mixed and processed. The conclusion that data engineering is language engineering comes easily. The word "data" is spoken, typed, printed and read probably billions of times every day across the world, in the many languages we speak. Yet, quite surprisingly, little work has been done on the subject of understanding what "data" actually is and how it relates to human language.

To most of us, the word "data" connotes "IT". Yet, as early as 9,000 BCE, the Minoan and Mycenaean used clay tablets to record counting marks. Ten thousand years ago, long before the first computer was conceived, "data" already existed, as did "data carriers" in the form of these clay tablets. They constituted well-understood, non-arbitrary signs and were ideal for their purpose, which was almost entirely accounting and labelling.

Not only did clay tablets aid in memory and communication, but they established trust and agreement among distant business or trading partners. Those partners had probably agreed about the meaning of signs and counters they would write on tablets; they thus shared at least some of the same culture. They could use clay tablets, sending them to each other alongside goods or money, perhaps carried by third persons travelling separately so that goods could not be stolen without theft being uncovered. The reader could tell from a tablet the language she would have heard from her partner had he been there to tell her in person.

Hand-written paper followed hand-written clay tablets, offering more possibilities, serving an expanded functional scope. Printing, in turn, succeeding handwriting, allowed access by many to the same information, at ever lower cost. Printed content faithfully displays the product of their human author. That changed with computers that actively process content into new content, some of which needs interpretation, i.e. translation into statements in human language to make sense to people – we exclude here the production of sound, pictures or instructions to and among machines. Still, where an isolated computer is fed and programmed by people of the same culture as those who interpret its output, they can likely rely on it. At the point where the sheer volume of content stored and produced by computers outgrows the capacity of any human brain or group of brains, it becomes at first difficult and then eventually impossible for humans to verify the computer's every piece of content and every processing step: we need to be able to explicitly trust the machine and its output.

One object, one name

As computers are networked across many human groups, an even more fundamental change compounds that evolution. Computers networked across human groups are also networked across human cultures that use different systems of signs, e.g. languages and alphabets. These different systems of signs can, in turn, reflect different systems of concepts which different groups use to represent the world as they see it.

Hence networked computers can build their content from many sources, including other computers' content, ultimately fed by people from very different groups and cultures, using different languages and who will likely never know and understand each other.

Conversely, for networked computers to combine meaningfully and process their content into further content, they ideally need to be fed from a single, uniform human language. Alternatively, the computers would need to normalise heterogeneous input content into a single internal language and to translate the output back into the users' language, if it is for human consumption. Whatever the chosen route, the volumes of data, the number of processing steps and of computers involved, and the speed of computers mean that there is no real alternative to full automation and to trusting the data as it comes from the machine.

In the network, the diversity of human languages and cultures collides with the computers' need for uniformity in language. Yet the speed of technical change cannot be matched by the speed of social change. There is therefore no quick solution to what has quickly grown into a profound global problem.

Yet, there is a beginning to a solution. It lies in identification: one object, one name. Globally. Period.

The present work is an important step in the beginning of that beginning.

Francis Gross,
Senior Adviser, Directorate General Statistics, European Central Bank*

* The views expressed here represent the personal opinion of the author, not necessarily the positions of the ECB or the ESCB.

Preface

Exchange Data International (EDI) is pleased to publish this book through its sister company, Chancellor Publications.

EDI is a leading financial data provider with more than 20 years' experience in the sector. During this period, what has been most striking to us is not the lack of information about the financial sector – after all, there are tens, if not hundreds, or thousands of books, magazines, articles, journals, blogs, websites, data feeds, corporate publications and government reports published every year about global finance – but rather the almost total absence of information about the nuts and bolts of the financial sector: how it works, how its various components parts fit together; and the systems that underpin it or make it fragile.

There can be few other major industries where there is such a paucity of information on the "possibly unexciting" but "absolutely essential" basics.

Exchange Data's Guide to LEI and other codes aims to address this deficit in some small way by focusing on the very specific area of security coding. Security coding may well be an arcane subject; however, no trading, settlement and clearing can take place without the use of codes.

As the world found out – to its cost in 2008-coding matters! Many factors caused the financial crisis, among them irrational exuberance, a high degree of leverage and deregulation. The absence of consistent coding clearly exacerbated the situation. Why? Without consistent coding, which allows one to link all the securities issued by an entities and its subsidiaries, Tier 1 investment banking firms were unable to "see", and therefore measure, their entire exposure to Lehmans, and other bankrupt or distressed financial institutions. The result was financial institutions needing to constantly revise their estimates – and, generally, it was a revision upwards – of their dangerous levels of exposure to these institutions.

One solution to this problem, albeit a partial one, was the Global LEI, created in the early 2000s, after the US Treasury Office of Financial Research had called for such a numbering system. However, the implementation of the LEI has been partial at best: The European Union has begun to make its use compulsory in certain instances, and the USA has lagged in this regard.

Regulation of financial markets tends to focus on high profile, "front office activities" such as sales and trading. However, the back office activities also cry out for regulation. The idea that banks and brokerages can regulate themselves is wishful thinking; in the area of financial services, self-regulation often equals no regulation. This is clearly seen in the chaos of back offices exemplified by the absence of standardization and, in its place, presence of a multitude of different codes for entities, sectors and securities.

Whilst this author's view of regulation is currently not the dominant one, and, particularly in the US where there is presently a call for "a bonfire of regulations", we firmly believe that the "bonfire" will certainly not contribute to a more stable financial system.

Jonathan Bloch
CEO

Introduction

The global financial crisis of 2008 focused the world's attention, as no other event in recent history, on the instability and volatility of the financial system. In the wake of the crisis, new regulations emerged with a common purpose: to bring transparency to the financial market.

One answer was the creation of a universal code enabling consistent and accurate identification of all legal entities, including non-financial institutions, taking part in financial transactions. Called the Legal Entity Identifier (LEI), this code allows regulators and financial institutions worldwide to identify efficiently the parties involved in transactions and to aggregate data rapidly from different jurisdictions to get a complete overview of a company's exposure to financial risk.

This guide to the LEI and other financial codes is the only one of its kind. No other financial handbook offers such a comprehensive, up-to-date examination of the codes which govern the financial system and are key to all who work in finance. It provides detailed descriptions of structural tier-level components of the LEI, thus highlighting the different business processes and requirements linked to the implementation of the LEI.

In addition, the book looks at more than 40 identifiers, from international entity to proprietary security codes, including:

Entity codes

International
Global Industry Classification Standard (GICS)
International Standard Industrial Classification System (ISIC)
Business Identifier Code (BIC)

National
North American Industry Classification System (NAICS)
Standard Industrial Classification (SIC)

Proprietary
Avox International Business Entity Identifier (AVID)
Markit codes

Security codes

International
CUSIP International Numbering System (CINS)
International Security Identification Number (ISIN)

National
Exchange ticker codes
Stock Exchange Daily Official List Code (SEDOL)
Valoren

Open Source
Financial Instrument Global Identifier (FIGI)

Proprietary codes
Reuters Instrument Code (RIC)

Miscellaneous codes
Country codes
Currency codes
Market Identifier Code (MIC)

For each code, I offer a detailed description of its structure and meaning; contact details for its issuer; and the entity responsible for it. I explain the code's business context and identify its primary users. I also highlight where duplication lies and the differences between seemingly similar codes. By explaining the nature and background of well-known codes, I hope to clarify the different types of securities related to internationally recognised codes used by financial data professionals across the globe.

An essential handbook

This book is intended for a broad audience: national and international regulators, securities exchange commissions' officials, central bankers, private-sector financial institutions including banks, brokers and fund managers, insurance companies, stock exchanges, depositories, data providers, financial technology companies and financial-sector-related apps developers and other fin-tech software providers. It should help anyone whose job involves financial coding to gain a full understanding of the world's main codes, and inform their decisions about which individual code or combination of codes to use.

I hope that it will be of especial use to people for whom data is central to their responsibilities – professionals such as reference data and market data specialists, operations and back office staff, directors, heads of settlement, IT architects and database administrators. It is designed as a handbook for easy use and reference.

The sources for this book are primarily the institutions which manage the individual codes. References for each can be found, along with the institutions' contact details, at the start of each section.

Because of the rapid changes in the financial world, we will update this handbook frequently. We welcome your comments and suggestions. Email us at mail@chancellorpublication.com

Need to know?

This book is the product of many years of research and work, including my role as a member of the G20 global sponsored Private Sector Preparatory Group for the LEI. Its intention is to provide practical information for people who need to know about data. I also hope that it will help to persuade practitioners and those who have a say in the future of our global structures that, if we want to keep the financial system secure and stable, we must achieve a common language – that is, a common system of global entity identification.

As I was finishing text of this book, I contacted a colleague, a financial-data executive with some 30 years' experience at the top data companies, including a global European bank. I asked him if he could read through the list of all the codes I'd included in this book to see if my list was comprehensive – if it indeed contained all current international and national codes related to securities. My colleague smiled and said something like: "I don't know of any publication that lists all securities codes in use out here. Such a publication with coverage of all internationally recognised codes would be very useful for us data professionals." And so I trust it will be.

About the author

Ozren Cvjetic is an economist with a BA from Seattle University and a Harvard University-trained mathematician, with a background in European Union regulatory finance and emerging market central banks. He is a member of the G20 private sector preparatory group, sponsored by the Financial Stability Board, and an expert on the Legal Entity Identifier. As a member of this group, he co-authored a major report on LEI operations which was adopted at the G20 summit in January 2013.

Mr. Cvjetic is a founder and academic board member of the Masters in Science in Global Financial Data Management at the European Centre for Peace and Development, established by the UN University for Peace. He is also on the board of the European Heart Network's member foundation, the Foundation of Health and Heart, from Bosnia-Herzegovina. As an avant-garde filmmaker, he produced two feature films in 2008 and 2016. Two of his short films were presented at the Festival de Cannes in 2007 and 2015. His feature film, Americana (Love Poem), premiered at the 23rd Sarajevo film festival in 2017.

Section 1
Entity Codes

More than any other development in recent decades, the financial crisis triggered in 2008 demonstrated the urgent need for transparency and regulation in the financial markets. Yet those responsible for carrying out systemic risk analysis, and thereby playing a key role in preventing such a crisis, find themselves ill equipped to do so. Regulators worldwide and financial institutions need to understand the aggregate risks of entities and their counterparties across asset classes and markets. But to do this, they must be able to identify, precisely and accurately, the legal entities engaged in financial transactions.

Until now, the tools for that crucial identification have been lacking. Reference data, in particular business entity data, is a key component in the identification and management of risk exposure. Currently there are many ways of identifying entities in financial transactions: marketplace identifiers, regulatory identifiers, company registration numbers and the SWIFT Business Identifier Code (BIC).

There are also numerous proprietary entity identifiers – such as the Data Universal Numbering System (DUNS) – and the range of codes developed by the financial reference data company Markit. Market participants collect and store reference and entity data in computer systems that include client master and security databases, customer relationship management, financial analysis, risk management systems and more.

Whilst the Global Legal Entity Identifier (LEI) discussed in this book will not necessarily replace these codes in the immediate future, it will become the main entity identifier for regulatory reporting by companies and the reference data vendor community, in conjunction with other codes.

International Codes

Global Legal Entity Identifier (ISO 17442)

The Global Legal Entity Identifier, or Global LEI, is the first global unique entity identifier that enables regulators and risk managers to identify parties to financial transactions precisely. It uniquely identifies any economically distinct entity in a financial transaction by linking to a set of reference data, including information about its ultimate ownership. As such, the Global LEI is pivotal in giving the financial system stability and transparency. Major international financial institutions may have up to three thousand different subsidiaries, each of them a distinct legal entity; the possibilities for confusion are therefore legion, as the Lehman Brothers collapse amply demonstrated. The Global LEI is the first global identifier to uniquely identify each legal entity and give regulators and risk managers the information they need to identify each entity's ultimate ownership.

Global meltdown

Following the global financial crisis of 2008 and the collapse of Lehman Brothers, it became apparent that regulators and private-sector managers could neither assess the extent of their financial market participants' exposure to Lehman nor ascertain how participants were connected to one another. In short, it became clear that, without precise identification of legal entities, they could not measure or manage financial risk.

In the United States, the Dodd-Frank Wall Street Reform and Consumer Protection Act (the Dodd-Frank Act) entered into legislation in July 2010. Dodd-Frank aimed to "promote the financial stability of the United States by improving accountability and transparency in the financial system, to end 'too big to fail', to protect the American taxpayer by ending bailouts, [and] to protect consumers from abusive financial services practices," as well as fulfilling certain other purposes. Dodd-Frank changed US regulatory structures by creating a host of new agencies (while merging and removing others) in an effort to improve the regulatory process. It increased the oversight of institutions seen as posing systemic risk and amended the Federal Reserve Act to promote transparency.

Global Legal Entity Identifier (ISO 17442)

Global standards, global identifier

Two of its most important new agencies were the Financial Stability Oversight Council (FSOC) and its data and research arm, the Office of Financial Research (OFR). Almost immediately, the OFR recognized that creating a global identifier was an essential tool that it would need to aggregate information from all reporting firms regarding activity with their counterparts. As a result, the OFR issued a policy directive in November 2010 citing the criticality of the global LEI and stating its desire to adopt, through rulemaking, a universal standard for identifying parties to financial contracts. According to the OFR, private industry and other stakeholders should establish and maintain this standard through a consensus process.

In May 2011, a coalition of international financial industry associations and their member organizations published the 46-page report entitled "Requirements for a Global Legal Entity Identifier (LEI) Solution" which specified the industry's requirements for the LEI system. It made detailed recommendations for standards and requirements under eight headings: Scope of Coverage; Data Model; Operating Model; Governance Model; Business Model; Implementation; Compliance; and Technical Principles.

By the second quarter of 2016, there were 451,000 LEIs in 199 countries issued by 22 LOUs.

What next?

Although the volume of LEIs issued is accelerating because of the adoption of ISO standards and regulatory mandates, the scope of LEI usage is still in question since only a very small fraction of globally registered legal entities (in millions) have obtained an LEI number and become a part of the legal entity identifier infrastructure.

At present, the LEI is really only fit for one purpose, that of regulatory transaction reporting. Its coverage is limited in types of entities that have LEIs: a mere 15% of companies with listed securities have an LEI. Geographically, too, the LEI is limited in its implementation; not all continents are proportionately implementing it. Unless coverage and usage increases, the LEI will fulfil only one function, and the need for other proprietary identifiers – such as the FIGI, SWIFT's BIC, the Thomson Reuters RIC and other national and international identification systems – will remain. At the same time, however Europe is implementing the Global LEI at the highest level, with the EU making implementation mandatory for all its member states.

Structure of the LEI

Scope of coverage: eligibility for an LEI

Breadth: LEI must apply to all countries globally, all industry types and all asset classes.

Principle of eligibility: Any party to a financial transaction should be eligible to obtain an LEI, providing the entity meets the scope requirements.

Individuals: Only financial entities will be included, not individuals.
Roles: A legal entity playing one or more of the following roles in a financial transaction will be eligible for an LEI: transacting entities, issuing entities, reference entities, reporting entities, parent entities and other participants in financial transactions as deemed necessary in the future (for instance, exchanges, utilities, registrars, regulators and industry organizations).

Materiality: No materiality threshold of any type will apply to the issuance of LEIs (for example, capitalization of legal entity or notional size of transaction).

Data model: data standards and elements

International data standard: The LEI solution must serve as the internationally recognized data standard for the identification of legal entities, provided that standard includes at least the following characteristics: persistent, neutral, singular, unique, extensible, structurally fixed, reliable and interoperable.

Attributes/metadata: The initial data model should include the following attributes and treat them as mandatory: LEI (that is, the identifier itself); exact legal name; address; country of formation; legal form; ultimate parent LEI; LEI status (e.g., available, disabled); and other metadata e.g. date LEI issued; last updated; date disabled. The data attributes noted may be specifically linked to the standard itself, or captured as part of the overall mandatory data model. The data attributes specifically linked to the standard should be

Global Legal Entity Identifier (ISO 17442)

kept as simple as possible to avoid the potential complication of having to update the standard if definitions are modified e.g. a changed status code. Immediate parent will not be mandatory in the initial release but will be available to be populated in the data model.

Ownership test: Ownership shall be defined as greater than 50% ownership. If there is no owner with more than 50%, the legal entity itself is entered as the ultimate parent.

Operating model

Self-registration model: The LEI registration process should be a self-registration model whereby entities eligible for an LEI register, at a minimum, the required information about themselves, and then certify that information periodically (no less than annually), or upon changes to such data. The LEI solution provider over time works with the global regulators and the LEI Governance Committee to require and enforce self-registration.

Extended implementation: During an extended implementation phase, the LEI solution provider has the flexibility to offer both a self-registration process and an alternative mechanism for assigning LEIs to entities that are not required to have an LEI and choose not to self-register.

Data quality: Where required to obtain an LEI, the legal entity itself has the ultimate responsibility for maintaining the accuracy of the data associated with its LEI. The LEI solution provider shall implement a process whereby LEI consumers can challenge the accuracy of the LEI data (for instance, they can request missing data or call for corrections by initiating a "Request for Review"). The LEI solution provider shall implement a comprehensive quality-assurance process to facilitate accurate and up-to-date LEI data.

Data access: Access to LEI data should be unrestricted and freely available to all users (except where prohibited by jurisdictional law, rules or regulations).

Service level agreements: SLAs must be defined and implemented to manage the interactions between the LEI solution providers and all LEI stakeholders.

Governance model

Data governance: A global voluntary consensus standards body.

LEI solution governance: A single global governance committee comprised of global market participants such as trade associations, regulators, supervisors and utilities.

Accountability: The LEI solution provider(s) shall be accountable to the LEI Governance Committee.

Funding: The LEI solution shall be managed on a cost recovery basis. As such, trade associations are agnostic to the overall structure of the LEI solution provider e.g. whether it is not-for-profit or private.

Intellectual property: The LEI Governance Committee shall provide oversight to ensure the appropriate treatment of any LEI intellectual property that is created as part of the LEI solution, including data, data model, industry-facing interfaces, and to protect the openness of the solution, the stakeholders and the solution providers. The LEI Governance Committee shall also oversee contract rights to the services provided by the LEI Solution.

Regional capability: The Governance Committee will ensure that the LEI solution provider has the capability to support regional conventions and regulations and provide local certification while maintaining a single global standard, centralized repository and issuance system.

Local regulatory requirements: The physical location of the LEI database, as well as the access rights to the information contained within it, must comply with local regulations related to data privacy and data access issues.

Business model and fee structure

Financial wherewithal: The LEI solution provider must demonstrate its financial capacity to deliver and maintain the LEI solution, including its ability to meet initial start-up requirements.

Fee structure: The LEI solution shall be funded through an annual fee paid by each legal entity that obtains an LEI as well as fees for customized

Global Legal Entity Identifier (ISO 17442)

services. Fees are intended to cover the cost of issuing LEIs (including the validation and maintenance costs), as well as the interface that makes the data freely available to consumers. The annual fee should also provide for a reasonable reserve fund to cover additional expenses. Given expected varying levels of use and consumption, a reasonable fee structure for consumers requiring customized services beyond the free interface (for instance, a daily feed of newly issued LEIs) should be established by the LEI solution provider. Such a fee structure should seek to ensure that the basic annual fee is kept to the lowest amount possible for LEI registrants that have limited financial market activity and have little or no need of services beyond obtaining an LEI. The LEI Governance Committee will oversee the fee structure to ensure it is being operated on a cost-recovery basis and provides the lowest possible annual fees.

Implementation

Phased implementation: The implementation of the LEI solution should be phased and sequenced according to global regulatory requirements.

Grace period: For each implementation phase (both within and across regions), a reasonable grace period should be implemented during the registration period before enforcement begins.

Implementation management: The LEI solution provider shall create and execute against a comprehensive implementation roadmap.

Compliance

Mandate: To be fully effective and avoid regulatory arbitrage, the LEI solution is explicitly dependent upon global regulators, requiring that in-scope legal entities consistently:

— Register with the LEI solution provider.
— Maintain the accuracy and completeness of their data with such provider.
— Provide their LEI to counterparties with whom they are transacting (or otherwise make the LEI available where required for regulatory reporting by other financial market participants).
— Provide LEI information as required by regulators.

The LEI solution also requires a consistent definition of eligibility criteria for both the issuance of an LEI and in-scope entities.

▬▬ Technical principles

Principles: The technical design, architecture, and support framework of the LEI solution shall be capable of delivering the standards and requirements in this document, including but not limited to, the following:

— Globally consistent technology, operating, and support capabilities.
— The ability to support a single consolidated database in both a centralized and decentralized fashion.
— Interfaces – that is, format of messages, communication protocols – should adhere to non-vendor standards to ensure portability of LEI solutions capabilities.
— Support of a range of messaging formats (such as XML and pipe-delimited formats) and communication protocols (for instance, SFTP and HTTPS) to ensure that all market participants are technically capable of consuming and interacting with the LEI data.
— Current and historical LEI data must be retained and easily transferable to another LEI solution provider; and to meet the bi-directional data collection and data distribution requirements and adopt information security standards commensurate with the global financial and regulatory community, including protection of subscription and feed information (such data implies entities interested in, or transacting with, financial institutions).

Technical evaluation: Criteria identified in the proposal will form the basis for a comprehensive technical evaluation.

Subsequently a solicitation of Interest (SOI) process was initiated to identify potential solution providers for the LEI infrastructure. Final recommendations were made to the global regulatory community in July 2011.

These recommendations were key building blocks towards today's Global LEI. They proposed that:

— The International Organization for Standardization ISO 17442 identifier be used as the legal entity identification standard. Created through the robust

Global Legal Entity Identifier (ISO 17442)

ISO process, this standard meets the characteristics set forth by the trade associations in the report, namely, that the identifier be persistent, neutral, singular, unique, extensible, structurally fixed, reliable and interoperable.

— The Depository Trust and Clearing Corporation (DTCC) and the Society for Worldwide Financial Interbank Telecommunication (SWIFT), along with DTCC's wholly-owned subsidiary, Avox Limited, were recommended as key partners to operate the core LEI utility as the central point for data collection, data maintenance, LEI assignment, and quality assurance. As member and user-owned industry cooperatives, DTCC and SWIFT are user-governed and have non-profit or cost-recovery business models in line with the business model recommendations of the report (See Appendix A).

— The Association of National Numbering Agencies (ANNA), comprising over 110 national numbering agencies (NNAs), was the obvious body to register, validate and maintain LEIs for issuers, obligors and other relevant parties in the countries represented by its members. The NNAs are at the forefront of providing the LEI utility to those markets, while leveraging the functionality of the centralized LEI utility for the assignment, further validation and global distribution of LEIs.

In November 2011, at the G20 summit in Cannes, national leaders, finance ministers and central bank governors considered a global system of identifiers. In its final declaration, the G20 committee stated:

We support the creation of a global legal entity identifier (LEI) which uniquely identifies parties to financial transactions. We call on the FSB to take the lead in helping coordinate work among the regulatory community to prepare recommendations for the appropriate governance framework, representing the public interest, for such a global LEI by our next Summit.

In June 2012 the FSB published a work entitled "A Global Legal Entity Identifier for Financial Markets", which recommended that a three-tier structure be established to meet the broad objectives of the LEI. This structure would comprise the Regulatory Oversight Committee (ROC), the Central Operating Unit (COU) and, at ground level, worldwide Local Operating Units (LOUs).

Together, these bodies comprise the key administrative infrastructure which governs and administers the Global LEI.

Three-tiered structure of the LEI

Regulatory Oversight Committee

The Regulatory Oversight Committee (ROC) was intended to comprise the authorities responsible for overall governance of the global LEI system. The FSB recommended that the ROC's governance principles and obligations be spelled out in an LEI Regulatory Oversight Committee Charter, to be drawn up in the autumn of 2012. It was the endorsement of this charter by the FSB and the G20 that established the ROC. Membership of the ROC was open to all authorities wishing to participate in the global LEI system. An executive committee was also appointed.

Central Operating Unit

The ROC also established the Central Operating Unit (COU), the LEI system's operational arm, led by a board of industry representatives and participants. The COU was to ensure the application of uniform global operational standards and protocols that would deliver seamless, open access to the global LEI and to high-quality reference data for users. It would also develop protocols and methods to allow local systems to connect to the COU, including the support of local systems. The COU would operate as a legal entity in the form of a not-for-profit foundation that would rely on industry participation to develop the most technologically, financially and legally sound methods of implementing the global LEI system as defined by the ROC. In conjunction with the ROC, the COU was also tasked with providing recommendations as to whether to outsource the development of specific functionality and operational elements of the global LEI system or to develop the technology in-house.

Local Operating Units

The Local Operating Units (LOUs) were the third tier in the FSB's recommended structure. Their role was to be LEI system implementers at a local level by providing the primary interface for entities wishing to register for an LEI. The LOUs were to facilitate the use of local languages and recognition of differing entity types. They were also to provide the means whereby registration, validation, maintenance, and protection of reference data could be stored locally. The FSB suggested that LOUs could maximise the use of exist-

Global Legal Entity Identifier (ISO 17442)

ing local infrastructures and services by building on established local business registries or national numbering agencies. In defining the brief for the LOUs, the FSB also recognised that in some jurisdictions it might be appropriate for multiple LOUs to promote competition whereas in others, where no suitable LOU existed, it would be necessary for entities to apply for LEIs across borders or to the COU until the necessary local infrastructure was in place. This obviously meant that if a local LOU was subsequently established, any LEIs assigned by alternative means had to be transferable across jurisdictions.

Beyond 2012

In June 2012, the G20 endorsed the FSB recommendation to implement a Global LEI consistent with the specifications of the International Organisation for Standardisation ISO 17442-2012. The FSB then established the LEI Implementation Group (IG) and an industry consultative group, the LEI Private Sector Preparatory Group (PSPG), to move the global LEI towards the intended launch date of March 2013. Led by legal, IT and other experts from all geographical regions, the IG and the PSPG defined two principal workstreams:

1. Legal and policy work to develop the proposed ROC charter with the necessary documents required for the creation, operation and governance of the ROC and the COU; and

2. Technology work with the private sector to establish the COU.

Legal workstream

The initial objective of the legal workstream was to develop the charter for the ROC as well as other key legal documents such as ROC bylaws and a legal framework for a global LEI foundation charged with developing and operating the COU. The idea was that, once in place, the ROC could then appoint a board to oversee the establishment of the COU according to criteria laid down by the implementation group. Another early task was to come up with the operational business model and practical methods for funding the development of the global system and its long-term maintenance.

Technology workstream

Parallel to the legal side of things was the task of the technology workstream: to identify a range of private industry representatives interested in joining a global LEI foundation consultative group. This group would develop the central platform facilitating the integration of local identification systems into a logically centralised database of unique LEIs based on consistent standards, protocols and procedures that would be seamless for users.

Standard ISO 17442-2012 (Legal Entity Identifier)

ISO 17442 specifies the elements of a legal entity identifier scheme to identify the legal entities relevant to any financial transaction. The term "legal entities" includes, but is not limited to, unique parties that are legally or financially responsible for the performance of financial transactions or have the right in their jurisdiction to enter into legal contracts regardless of whether they are incorporated on constituted in some other way e.g. as a trust or partnership. It excludes individuals but includes governmental organisations and supranationals. Examples of eligible legal entities include:

— All financial intermediaries.
— Banks and finance companies.
— All entities that issue equity, debt or other securities for other capital structures.
— All entities listed on an exchange.
— All entities that trade stock or debt, investment vehicles, including mutual funds, pension funds and alternative investment vehicles constituted as corporate entities or collective investment agreements (including umbrella funds as well as funds under an umbrella structure such as hedge funds or private equity funds).
— All entities under the purview of a financial regulator and their affiliates, subsidiaries and holding companies.
— Counterparties to financial transactions.

Technical structure of the LEI code

An LEI consists of 20 characters comprised of an initial 18 characters without separators or special characters where each character can be either digits 0 to 9 or upper case letters A through to Z, followed by a two-character

Global Legal Entity Identifier (ISO 17442)

numerical check digit calculated according to the scheme defined in ISO/IEC 7064 also known as modulo 97-10. The check digits are used to verify the LEI.

In addition, in order to ensure an unambiguous identification of the legal entities, a set of data attributes is also provided by the entity requesting the LEI. This data set will make up the full LEI data record and will comprise the following data elements or attributes:

— The official name of the legal entity as recorded in the business registry, or with the fund manager for collective investment vehicles, or otherwise in the entity's constituting documents. Where applicable the name of the business registry in which the entity was formed and the identifier of the entity in the business registry will be recorded.
— The address of the headquarters of the legal entity or the address of the fund manager.
— The address and the country of legal formation as represented in ISO 3166 Country Codes.
— The date of the first LEI assignment.
— The date of the last update of the LEI set of information.
— The date of expiry and reason for expiry where applicable. For entities with an expiry date, the reason for the expiry will be recorded and, where applicable, the LEI of the entity or entities that acquired the expired entity.

LEIs and corporate actions

According to the Financial Stability Board-LEI report *http://www.fsb.org/ wp-content/uploads/r_121211.pdf*, an LEI should be persistent; in other words, even if a company moves, merges or changes ownership, its LEI remains the same. An LEI should only become defunct when a company goes out of business. It remains to be seen whether legal differences between one international jurisdiction and another will permit this to be the case.

A corporate action is a change initiated by an issuer. Although some corporate actions, such as stock splits and dividends, will not affect the LEI or its related reference data, others, such as mergers, acquisitions, ownership changes and spinoffs, may affect the LEI or its reference data.

In general, most corporate actions will affect the LEI's reference data but not the LEI itself. For example, if a company acquires or sells a subsidiary, or reorganizes its corporate structure, the entity itself has not changed and therefore its LEI will not change. All that has changed is the hierarchical reference data relating the parent to its subsidiaries. A change in ownership or structure is therefore a corporate action that affects the reference data but not the LEI.

LEI persistence

In the case of a spinoff, in which a company decides to spin off a division or subset of the company to form a new company, persistence is achieved by maintaining the LEI of the original company and assigning a new LEI to the spinoff. Again the corporate action does not affect the LEI of the original entity.

Mergers and acquisitions are more complicated. In most mergers or acquisitions, two or more entities combine to create one entity. Although the legalities can be complex when multiple entities combine, allowing one of the existing LEIs to continue while others become defunct provides continuity and the ability to monitor entities over time. It should be rare that a new LEI is issued as the result of a merger.

In the rare case in which a new LEI must be assigned because of legal restrictions, the corporate action will affect the LEI. When a new LEI is assigned, the recommendation is that a link between the old LEI(s) and the newly created LEI is recorded in the operational metadata to facilitate the tracking of entities over time. It is unclear from documentation as to whether this will be the case from day one.

Corporate actions

A Federal Reserve report from mid-2011 recommends that careful consideration be given to corporate actions that are prompted by external factors, such as accounting or regulatory constraints, but have no effect on the operations of the entity, such as those sometimes found in the banking industry. It says that on occasion, to facilitate the changing of locations or banking charters, it will be efficient to create a temporary legal entity (sometimes referred to as a phantom entity) that exists for less than a day. To effect a change, the existing entity will merge into the phantom entity, resulting in a legal transac-

Global Legal Entity Identifier (ISO 17442)

tion but no change to the entity or within the industry. In these cases, the LEI should not change, but the associated reference data may change.

However, it is thought that the LEI could help eliminate the need for organisations to support complicated cross-referencing of data from different vendors using proprietary security identification codes when processing entity-level corporate actions information such as mergers and acquisitions. There would be fewer practical difficulties when applying and managing entity-level events on a per security basis. For example, an M&A event notification broadcast against a single instrument ID will need to be linked at the issuer level in order to apply it consistently across that issuer's entire global issuance across asset classes, in order to capture against individual positions across the organisation.

LEI Common Data File

Daily reporting of LEI and legal entity reference data is conducted by the using the Common Data File (CDF) formats.

Please use the official GLEIF link from the below, to access the official LEI related daily files.

https://www.gleif.org/en/lei-data/gleif-concatenated-file/download-the-concatenated-file

SWIFT Business Identifier Code BIC (ISO 9362)

In brief

ISO 9362, or SWIFT-BIC, defines a standard format of business identifier codes (also known as BIC code, SWIFT ID or SWIFT code) approved by the **International Organization for Standardization** (ISO). It is a unique identification code for both financial and non-financial institutions. The acronym SWIFT stands for the **Society for Worldwide Interbank Financial Telecommunication**. The ISO has designated SWIFT as the BIC registration authority. When assigned to a non-financial institution, the code may also be known as a Business Entity Identifier or BEI. These codes are used when transferring money between banks, particularly for international **wire transfers**, and also for the exchange of other messages between banks. The codes can sometimes be found on account statements.

SWIFT contact
S.W.I.F.T SCRL
Avenue Adele 1
B-1310 La Hulpe
Belgium
Tel: +32 2 655 31 11
Fax: +32 2 655 32 26
www.swift.com/standards/data-standards/bic

History

SWIFT was founded in Brussels in 1973, and supported by 239 banks from 15 countries. Its aim was the creation of a shared worldwide data processing and communication link and to establish common standards for the transmission of financial information. It became operational in 1977, when the first message was sent over the SWIFT network. In 1979, SWIFT connected to the US for the first time and established an operations center, followed a year later by a connection to Asian countries. In 1987, the SWIFT user base expanded to

SWIFT Business Identifier Code BIC (ISO 9362)

include broker dealers, exchanges, central depositories and clearing institutions. The first version of ISO 9362 was published in 1994.

The SWIFT network does not require a specific format for the transaction, so the identification of accounts and transaction types is left to agreements of the transaction partners. In the **Single Euro Payments Area**, the European central banks have agreed on a common format based on IBAN and BIC, including an XML-based transmission format for standardized transactions. The **TARGET2** is a joint gross clearing system in the European Union that does not require the SWIFT network for transmission (see **EBICS**). The TARGET directory lists all the BICs of the banks that are attached to the TARGET2-network being a subset of the SWIFT-directory of BICs.

Structure

There are two types of BIC: the eight character BIC (BIC8) and the 11 character BIC (BIC11). A BIC8 identifies a financial or non-financial institution in a country or a location. A BIC11 identifies the institution's branch. The BIC is written and printed as a string without spaces.

BIC8

Example: BNPAFRPP

The first four characters are alphabetic and represent the institution; in this case, BNPA represents BNP-Paribas. The fifth and sixth characters are also alphabetic and represent the ISO country code (ISO 3166-1 alpha-2) of the country in which the institution is located; for instance, FR for France. The final two characters can be alphabetic or numeric and represent the location of the institution within a country, such as a city, state, province or time zone; for example, PP represents Paris

BIC11

Optionally, an eight character BIC can be extended to an 11 character BIC by adding a branch code.

Example: BNPAFRPP MAR

The branch code identifies the physical branch of an institution – for example, MAR for Marseille – or its department or type of business. The branch code consists of three alphanumeric characters.

Whenever an eight character BIC code needs to be interpreted in the 11-character format, the branch code XXX is added.

Connected and unconnected BICs

BICs identify both financial and non-financial institutions connected and unconnected to the SWIFT network. However, a BIC of an institution not connected to the SWIFT network has the location code ending with the digit "1" (for example, KESADEF1). Such BIC is also called a non-SWIFT BIC or a BIC1.

A BIC for an institution connected to the SWIFT network has a location code ending with a character other than "1" (for example, BNPAFRPP). Such BIC is also called a connected BIC or a SWIFT BIC. Consequently, only a SWIFT BIC can appear in the header of a SWIFT message.

For more information

http://www.swift.com/index.page?lang=en
https://www.swiftrefdata.com/

Global Industry Classification Standard (GICS)

In brief

The Global Industry Classification Standard (GICS) was developed in 1999 by **MSCI** and **Standard & Poor's** (S&P) for use by the global financial community. It provides the basis for S&P and MSCI financial market indexes in which each company is assigned to a sub-industry, and to a corresponding industry, industry group and sector, according to the definition of its principal business activity.

GICS contact
Standard & Poor's
55 Water Street
New York, NY 10041
United States of America
Tel: +1 212 438 1000
http://www.standardandpoors.com

Morgan Stanley Capital International (MSCI) and Standard & Poor's (S&P) developed the GICS in 1999 to establish a global standard for classifying companies into sectors and industries. The GICS structure today consists of 11 sectors, 24 industry groups, 68 industries and 157 sub-industries. (In September 2016, GICS created its first new sector, for REITs.) The system is similar to the Industry Classification Benchmark (ICB), a classification structure maintained by Dow Jones Indexes and FTSE International. The GICS methodology assigns each company to a sub-industry, and to a corresponding industry, industry group and sector, according to the definition of its principal business activity. Since the classification is strictly hierarchical, at each of the four levels a company can only belong to one grouping.

The GICS structure applies to companies globally and provides analysts and the investment community with four levels of analysis, ranging from the most general sector to the most specialized. Regular GICS reviews

━━━━━

occur annually, although classification of a company will change if a major corporate action redefines its primary line of business.

The GICS methodology has been widely accepted as an industry standard for investment research, portfolio management and asset allocation. Investors use GICS and related industry indices and data for asset management, sector research, portfolio strategy, peer analysis and client account reporting. The use of GICS enables market participants to compare and analyses companies using a common global standard regardless of a company's country of incorporation. All companies in the Standard & Poor's global family of indices have been classified according to the GICS structure. Standard & Poor's indices and sub-indices are designed to reflect the sectoral composition of the broad markets they represent. Many of the broad S&P indices are broken down into sector – and/or industry-level indices to provide performance measurements across these markets.

Companies are classified using information taken from annual reports and financial statements although investment research reports and other industry information can also be used. Generally a company is classified in the sub-industry that most closely reflects the business activity (or activities) that generates the majority of the company's revenues. A company engaged in two or more substantially different business activities, none of which contributes 60% or more of revenues, is classified in the sub-industry that provides the majority of both the company's revenues and earnings. Where no sub-industry accounts for the majority of both the company's revenues and earnings, further analysis will determine the classification.

A company significantly diversified across three or more sectors, none of which contributes the majority of revenues or earnings, is classified either in the industrial conglomerates sub-industry (industrials sector) or the multi-sector holdings sub-industry (financials sector). In the case of a new company issue, classification is determined based on the description of the company's activities and pro-forma results as given in the prospectus. A company's industry classification will be reviewed either when a significant corporate restructuring occurs or when a new financial report is published. Temporary fluctuations in the results of a company's different business activities are usually ignored to maintain the stability of the system.

Global Industry Classification Standard (GICS)

Structure

GICS is a four-tiered, hierarchical industry classification system. GICS classifications can be presented in text or numeric format. The full GICS classification for each company is an 8-digit code with text description. The hierarchical design of the 8-digit coding system allows for easy transition between GICS tiers.

GICS code list

Sector	Industry Group	Industry	Sub-Industry
10 Energy	**1010 Energy**	**101010 Energy, equipment & services**	**10101010 Oil & gas drilling**
			Drilling contractors or owners of drilling rigs that contract their services for drilling wells
			10101020 Oil & gas equipment & services
			Manufacturers of equipment, including drilling rigs and equipment, and providers of supplies and services to companies involved in the drilling, evaluation and completion of oil and gas wells
		101020 Oil, gas & consumable fuels	**10102010 Integrated oil & gas**
			Integrated oil companies engaged in the exploration & production of oil and gas, as well as at least one other significant activity in either refining, marketing and transportation, or chemicals.
			10102020 Oil & gas exploration & Production
			Companies engaged in the exploration and production of oil and gas not classified elsewhere.
			10102030 Oil & gas refining & marketing
			Companies engaged in the refining and marketing of oil, gas and/or refined products not classified in the Integrated Oil & Gas or Independent Power Producers & Energy Traders Sub-Industries.
			10102040 Oil & gas storage & transportation

Global Industry Classification Standard (GICS)

Sector	Industry Group	Industry	Sub-Industry
			Companies engaged in the storage and/or transportation of oil, gas and/or refined products. Includes diversified midstream natural gas companies facing competitive markets, oil and refined product pipelines, coal slurry pipelines and oil & gas shipping companies
			10102050 Coal & consumable fuels
			Companies primarily involved in the production and mining of coal, related products and other consumable fuels related to the generation of energy. Excludes companies primarily producing gases classified in the Industrial Gases sub-industry and companies primarily mining for metallurgical (coking) coal used for steel production.
15 Materials	**1510 Materials**	**151010 Chemicals**	**15101010 Commodity chemicals**
			Companies that primarily produce industrial chemicals and basic chemicals. Including but not limited to plastics, synthetic fibers, films, commodity-based paints & pigments, explosives and petrochemicals. Excludes chemical companies classified in the Diversified Chemicals, Fertilizers & Agricultural Chemicals, Industrial Gases, or Specialty Chemicals Sub-Industries.
			15101020 Diversified chemicals
			Manufacturers of a diversified range of chemical products not classified in the Industrial Gases, Commodity Chemicals, Specialty Chemicals or Fertilizers & Agricultural Chemicals Sub-Industries
			15101030 Fertilizers & agricultural chemicals
			Producers of fertilizers, pesticides, potash or other agriculture-related chemicals not classified elsewhere.
			15101040 Industrial gases
			Manufacturers of industrial gases
			15101050 Specialty chemicals

Global Industry Classification Standard (GICS)

Sector	Industry Group	Industry	Sub-Industry
			Companies that primarily produce high value-added chemicals used in the manufacture of a wide variety of products, including but not limited to fine chemicals, additives, advanced polymers, adhesives, sealants and specialty paints, pigments and coatings.
		151020 Construction materials	**15102010 Construction Materials.**
			Manufacturers of construction materials including sand, clay, gypsum, lime, aggregates, cement, concrete and bricks. Other finished or semi-finished building materials are classified in the Building Products Sub-Industry
		151030 Containers & packaging	**15103010 Metal & glass containers**
			Manufacturers of metal, glass or plastic containers. Includes corks and caps.
			15103020 Paper packaging
			Manufacturers of paper and cardboard containers and packaging.
		151040 Metals & mining	**15104010 Aluminum**
			Producers of aluminum and related products, including companies that mine or process bauxite and companies that recycle aluminum to produce finished or semi-finished products. Excludes companies that primarily produce aluminum building materials classified in the Building Products Sub-Industry.
			15104020 Diversified metals & mining

Global Industry Classification Standard (GICS)

Sector	Industry Group	Industry	Sub-Industry
			Companies engaged in the diversified production or extraction of metals and minerals not classified elsewhere. Including, but not limited to, nonferrous metal mining (except bauxite), salt and borate mining, phosphate rock mining, and diversified mining operations. Excludes iron ore mining, classified in the Steel Sub-Industry, bauxite mining, classified in the Aluminum Sub-Industry, and coal mining, classified in either the Steel or Coal & Consumable Fuels Sub-Industries.
			15104030 Gold
			Producers of gold and related products, including companies that mine or process gold and the South African finance houses which primarily invest in, but do not operate, gold mines.
			15104040 Precious metals & minerals
			Companies mining precious metals and minerals not classified in the Gold Sub-Industry. Includes companies primarily mining platinum.
			15104045 Silver
			Companies primarily mining silver. Excludes companies classified in the Gold or Precious Metals & Minerals Sub-Industries
			15104050 Steel
			Producers of iron and steel and related products, including metallurgical (coking) coal mining used for steel production.
		151050 Paper & forest products	**15105010 Forest products**
			Manufacturers of timber and related wood products. Includes lumber for the building industry.
			15105020 Paper products
			Manufacturers of all grades of paper. Excludes companies specializing in paper packaging classified in the Paper Packaging Sub-Industry.

Global Industry Classification Standard (GICS)

Sector	Industry Group	Industry	Sub-Industry
20 Industrials	2010 Capital goods	201010 Aerospace & defence	20101010 Aerospace & defence
			Manufacturers of civil or military aerospace and defence equipment, parts or products. Includes defence electronics and space equipment.
		201020 Building products	20102010 Building products
			Manufacturers of building components and home improvement products and equipment. Excludes lumber and plywood classified under Forest Products and cement and other materials classified in the Construction Materials Sub-Industry.
		201030 Construction & engineering	20103010 Construction & engineering
			Companies engaged in primarily non-residential construction. Includes civil engineering companies and large-scale contractors. Excludes companies classified in the Homebuilding Sub-Industry.
		201040 Electrical equipment	20104010 Electrical components & equipment
			Companies that produce electric cables and wires, electrical components or equipment not classified in the Heavy Electrical Equipment Sub-Industry.
			20104020 Heavy electrical equipment
			Manufacturers of power-generating equipment and other heavy electrical equipment, including power turbines, heavy electrical machinery intended for fixed-use and large electrical systems. Excludes cables and wires, classified in the Electrical Components & Equipment Sub-Industry.
		201050 Industrial conglomerates	20105010 Industrial conglomerates

Global Industry Classification Standard (GICS)

Sector	Industry Group	Industry	Sub-Industry
			Diversified industrial companies with business activities in three or more sectors, none of which contributes a majority of revenues. Stakes held are predominantly of a controlling nature and stake holders maintain an operational interest in the running of the subsidiaries.
		201060 Machinery	**20106010 Construction & farm machinery & heavy trucks**
			Manufacturers of heavy duty trucks, rolling machinery, earth-moving and construction equipment, and manufacturers of related parts. Includes non-military shipbuilding.
			20106015 Agricultural & Farm Machinery
			Companies manufacturing agricultural machinery, farm machinery, and their related parts. Includes machinery used for the production of crops and agricultural livestock, agricultural tractors, planting and fertilizing machinery, fertilizer and chemical application equipment, and grain dryers and blowers.
			20106020 Industrial machinery
			Manufacturers of industrial machinery and industrial components. Includes companies that manufacture presses, machine tools, compressors, pollution control equipment, elevators, escalators, insulators, pumps, roller bearings and other metal fabrications.
		201070 Trading companies & distributors	**20107010 Trading companies & distributors**
			Trading companies and other distributors of industrial equipment and products.
	2020 Commercial & professional services	**202010 Commercial services & supplies**	**20201010 Commercial printing**
			Companies providing commercial printing services. Includes printers primarily serving the media industry.

Global Industry Classification Standard (GICS)

Sector	Industry Group	Industry	Sub-Industry
			20201020 Data processing services – discontinued effective 04/30/2003 Providers of commercial electronic data processing services.
			20201030 Diversified commercial & professional services – discontinued effective 08/31/2008 Companies primarily providing commercial, industrial and professional services to businesses and governments not classified elsewhere. Includes commercial cleaning services, consulting services, correctional facilities, dining & catering services, document & communication services, equipment repair services, security & alarm services, storage & warehousing, and uniform rental services.
			20201040 Human resource & employment services Companies providing business support services relating to human capital management. Includes employment agencies, employee training, payroll & benefit support services, retirement support services and temporary agencies.
			20201050 Environmental & facilities services Companies providing environmental and facilities maintenance services. Includes waste management, facilities management and pollution control services. Excludes large-scale water treatment systems classified in the Water Utilities Sub-Industry.
			20201060 Office services & supplies Providers of office services and manufacturers of office supplies and equipment not classified elsewhere.
			20201070 Diversified support services

Global Industry Classification Standard (GICS)

Sector	Industry Group	Industry	Sub-Industry
			Companies primarily providing labour oriented support services to businesses and governments. Includes commercial cleaning services, dining & catering services, equipment repair services, industrial maintenance services, industrial auctioneers, storage & warehousing, transaction services, uniform rental services, and other business support services.
			20201080 Security & alarm services
			Companies providing security and protection services to business and governments. Includes companies providing services such as correctional facilities, security & alarm services, armored transportation & guarding. Excludes companies providing security software classified under the Systems Software Sub-Industry and home security services classified under the Specialized Consumer Services Sub-Industry. Also excludes companies manufacturing security system equipment classified under the Electronic Equipment & Instruments Sub-Industry.
		202020 Professional services	**20202010 Human resource & employment services**
			Companies providing business support services relating to human capital management. Includes employment agencies, employee training, payroll & benefit support services, retirement support services and temporary agencies
			20202020 Research & consulting services
			Companies primarily providing research and consulting services to businesses and governments not classified elsewhere. Includes companies involved in management consulting services, architectural design, business information or scientific research, marketing, and testing & certification services. Excludes companies providing information technology consulting services classified in the IT Consulting & Other Services Sub-Industry.

Global Industry Classification Standard (GICS)

Sector	Industry Group	Industry	Sub-Industry
	2030 Transportation	**203010 Air freight & logistics**	**20301010 Air freight & logistics**
			Companies providing air freight transportation, courier, and logistics services, including package and mail delivery and customs agents. Excludes those companies classified in the Airlines, Marine or Trucking Sub-Industries.
		203020 Airlines	**20302010 Airlines**
			Companies providing primarily passenger air transportation.
		203030 Marine	**20303010 Marine**
			Companies providing goods or passenger maritime transportation. Excludes cruise-ships classified in the Hotels, Resorts & Cruise Lines Sub-Industry.
		203040 Road & rail	**20304010 Railroads**
			Companies providing primarily goods and passenger rail transportation.
			20304020 Trucking
			Companies providing primarily goods and passenger land transportation. Includes vehicle rental and taxi companies.
		203050 Transportation infrastructure	**20305010 Airport services**
			Operators of airports and companies providing related services.
			20305020 Highways & rail tracks
			Owners and operators of roads, tunnels and rail tracks.
			20305030 Marine ports & services
			Owners and operators of marine ports and related services.
25 Consumer Discretionary	**2510 Automobiles & components**	**251010 Auto components**	**25101010 Auto parts & equipment**
			Manufacturers of parts and accessories for automobiles and motorcycles. Excludes companies classified in the Tires & Rubber Sub-Industry
			25101020 Tires & rubber

Global Industry Classification Standard (GICS)

Sector	Industry Group	Industry	Sub-Industry
			Manufacturers of tires and rubber.
		251020 Automobiles	**25102010 Automobile manufacturers**
			Companies that produce mainly passenger automobiles and light trucks. Excludes companies producing mainly motorcycles and three-wheelers classified in the Motorcycle Manufacturers Sub-Industry and heavy duty trucks classified in the Construction Machinery & Heavy Trucks Sub-Industry.
			25102020 Motorcycle manufacturers
			Companies that produce motorcycles, scooters or three-wheelers. Excludes bicycles classified in the Leisure Products Sub-Industry.
2520 Consumer durables & apparel	**252010 Household durables**		**25201010 Consumer electronics**
			Manufacturers of consumer electronics products including TVs, home audio equipment, game consoles, digital cameras, and related products. Excludes personal home computer manufacturers classified in the Technology Hardware, Storage & Peripherals Sub-Industry, and electric household appliances classified in the Household Appliances Sub-Industry.
			25201020 Home furnishings
			Manufacturers of soft home furnishings or furniture, including upholstery, carpets and wall-coverings.
			25201030 Homebuilding
			Residential construction companies. Includes manufacturers of prefabricated houses and semi-fixed manufactured homes.
			25201040 Household appliance.

Global Industry Classification Standard (GICS)

Sector	Industry Group	Industry	Sub-Industry
			Manufacturers of electric household appliances and related products. Includes manufacturers of power and hand tools, including garden improvement tools. Excludes TVs and other audio and video products classified in the Consumer Electronics Sub-Industry and personal computers classified in the Technology Hardware, Storage & Peripherals Sub-Industry.
			25201050 Housewares & specialties
			Manufacturers of durable household products, including cutlery, cookware, glassware, crystal, silverware, utensils, kitchenware and consumer specialties not classified elsewhere.
		252020 Leisure products	**25202010 Leisure products**
			Manufacturers of leisure products and equipment including sports equipment, bicycles and toys
			25202020 Photographic products
			Manufacturers of photographic equipment and related products.
		252030 Textiles, apparel & luxury goods	**25203010 Apparel, accessories & luxury goods**
			Manufacturers of apparel, accessories & luxury goods. Includes companies primarily producing designer handbags, wallets, luggage, jewelry and watches. Excludes shoes classified in the Footwear Sub-Industry.
			25203020 Footwear
			Manufacturers of footwear. Includes sport and leather shoes.
			25203030 Textiles
			Manufacturers of textile and related products not classified in the Apparel, Accessories & Luxury Goods, Footwear or Home Furnishings Sub-Industries.
	2530 Consumer services	**253010 Hotels, restaurants & leisure**	**25301010 Casinos & gaming**

Global Industry Classification Standard (GICS)

Sector	Industry Group	Industry	Sub-Industry
			Owners and operators of casinos and gaming facilities. Includes companies providing lottery and betting services.
			25301020 Hotels, resorts & cruise lines
			Owners and operators of hotels, resorts and cruise-ships. Includes travel agencies, tour operators and related services not classified elsewhere. Excludes casino-hotels classified in the Casinos & Gaming Sub-Industry
			25301030 Leisure facilities
			Owners and operators of leisure facilities, including sport and fitness centers, stadiums, golf courses and amusement parks not classified in the Movies & Entertainment Sub-Industry.
			25301040 Restaurants
			Owners and operators of restaurants, bars, pubs, fast-food, or take-out facilities. Includes companies that provide food catering services.
		253020 Diversified consumer cervices	**25302010 Education services**
			Companies providing educational services, either on-line or through conventional teaching methods. Includes, private universities, correspondence teaching, providers of educational seminars, educational materials and technical education. Excludes companies providing employee education programs classified in the Human Resources & Employment Services Sub-Industry
			25302020 Specialised consumer services
			Companies providing consumer services not classified elsewhere. Includes residential services, home security, legal services, personal services, renovation & interior design services, consumer auctions and wedding & funeral services.
	2540 Media	**254010 Media**	**25401010 Advertising**

Global Industry Classification Standard (GICS)

Sector	Industry Group	Industry	Sub-Industry
			Companies providing advertising, marketing or public relations services.
			25401020 Broadcasting
			Owners and operators of television or radio broadcasting systems, including programming. Includes, radio and television broadcasting, radio networks, and radio stations.
			25401025 Cable & satellite
			Providers of cable or satellite television services. Includes cable networks and program distribution.
			25401030 Movies & entertainment
			Companies that engage in producing and selling entertainment products and services, including companies engaged in the production, distribution and screening of movies and television shows, producers and distributors of music, entertainment theaters and sports teams.
			25401040 Publishing
			Publishers of newspapers, magazines and books, and providers of information in print or electronic formats.
	2550 Retailing	**255010 Distributors**	**25501010 Distributors**
			Distributors and wholesalers of general merchandise not classified elsewhere. Includes vehicle distributors.
		255020 Internet & catalogue Retail	**25502010 Catalogue retail**
			Mail order and TV home shopping retailers. Includes companies that provide door-to-door retail.
			25502020 Internet retail
			Companies providing retail services primarily on the internet, not classified elsewhere.
		255030 Multi-line retail	**25503010 Department stores**

Sector	Industry Group	Industry	Sub-Industry
			Owners and operators of department stores.
			25503020 General merchandise stores
			Owners and operators of stores offering diversified general merchandise. Excludes hypermarkets and large-scale super centers classified in the Hypermarkets & Super Centers Sub-Industry.
		255040 Specialty retail	**25504010 Apparel retail**
			Retailers specialized mainly in apparel and accessories.
			25504020 Computer & electronics retail
			Owners and operators of consumer electronics, computers, video and related products retail stores.
			25504030 Home improvement retail
			Owners and operators of home and garden improvement retail stores. Includes stores offering building materials and supplies.
			25504040 Specialty stores
			Owners and operators of specialty retail stores not classified elsewhere. Includes jewelry stores, toy stores, office supply stores, health & vision care stores, and book & entertainment stores.
			25504050 Automotive retail
			Owners and operators of stores specializing in automotive retail. Includes auto dealers, gas stations, and retailers of auto accessories, motorcycles & parts, automotive glass, and automotive equipment & parts.
			25504060 Home furnishing retail
			Owners and operators of furniture and home furnishings retail stores. Includes residential furniture, home furnishings, housewares, and interior design. Excludes home and garden improvement stores, classified in the Home Improvement Retail Sub-Industry.

Global Industry Classification Standard (GICS)

Sector	Industry Group	Industry	Sub-Industry
30 Consumer Staples	**3010 Food & staples retailing**	**301010 Food & staples retailing**	**30101010 Drug retail**
			Owners and operators of primarily drug retail stores and pharmacies.
			30101020 Food distributors
			Distributors of food products to other companies and not directly to the consumer.
			30101030 Food retail
			Owners and operators of primarily food retail stores.
			30101040 Hypermarkets & super centres
			Owners and operators of hypermarkets and super centers selling food and a wide-range of consumer staple products. Excludes Food and Drug Retailers classified in the Food Retail and Drug Retail Sub-Industries, respectively.
	3020 Food, beverage & tobacco	**302010 Beverages**	**30201010 Breweries**
			Producers of beer and malt liquors. Includes breweries not classified in the Restaurants Sub-Industry.
			30201020 Distillers & vintners
			Distillers, vintners and producers of alcoholic beverages not classified in the Brewers Sub-Industry.
			30201030 Soft drinks
			Producers of non-alcoholic beverages including mineral waters. Excludes producers of milk classified in the Packaged Foods Sub-Industry.
		302020 Food products	**30202010 Agricultural products**
			Producers of agricultural products. Includes crop growers, owners of plantations and companies that produce and process foods but do not package and market them. Excludes companies classified in the Forest Products Sub-Industry and those that package and market the food products classified in the Packaged Foods Sub-Industry.

Global Industry Classification Standard (GICS)

Sector	Industry Group	Industry	Sub-Industry
			30202020 Meat, poultry & fish (discountined, effective March 28 2002)
			Companies that raise livestock or poultry, fishing companies and other producers of meat, poultry, or fish products.
			30202030 Packaged foods & meats
			Producers of packaged foods including dairy products, fruit juices, meats, poultry, fish, and pet foods.
		302030 Tobacco	**30203010 Tobacco**
			Manufacturers of cigarettes and other tobacco products.
	3030 Household & personal products	**303010 Household products**	**30301010 Household products**
			Producers of non-durable household products, including detergents, soaps, diapers and other tissue and household paper products not classified in the Paper Products Sub-Industry.
		303020 Personal products	**30302010 Personal products**
			Manufacturers of personal and beauty care products, including cosmetics and perfumes.
35 Health Care	**3510 Health care equipment & services**	**351010 Health care equipment & supplies**	**35101010 Health care equipment**
			Manufacturers of health care equipment and devices. Includes medical instruments, drug delivery systems, cardiovascular & orthopedic devices, and diagnostic equipment.
			35101020 Health care supplies
			Manufacturers of health care supplies and medical products not classified elsewhere. Includes eye care products, hospital supplies, and safety needle & syringe devices.
		351020 Health care providers & services	**35102010 Health care distributors**

Global Industry Classification Standard (GICS)

Sector	Industry Group	Industry	Sub-Industry
			Distributors and wholesalers of health care products not classified elsewhere.
			35102015 Health care services
			Providers of patient health care services not classified elsewhere. Includes dialysis centers, lab testing services, and pharmacy management services. Also, includes companies providing business support services to health care providers, such as clerical support services, collection agency services, staffing services and outsourced sales & marketing service
			35102020 Health care facilities
			Owners and operators of health care facilities, including hospitals, nursing homes, rehabilitation centers and animal hospitals.
			35102030 Managed health care
			Owners and operators of Health Maintenance Organizations (HMOs) and other managed plans.
		351030 Health care technology	**35103010 Health care technology**
			Companies providing information technology services primarily to health care providers. Includes companies providing application, systems and/or data processing software, internet-based tools, and IT consulting services to doctors, hospitals or businesses operating primarily in the Health Care Sector
	3520 Pharmaceuticals, biotechnology & life sciences	**352010 Biotechnology**	**35201010 Biotechnology**
			Companies primarily engaged in the research, development, manufacturing and/or marketing of products based on genetic analysis and genetic engineering. Includes companies specializing in protein-based therapeutics to treat human diseases. Excludes companies manufacturing products using biotechnology but without a health care application.

Global Industry Classification Standard (GICS)

Sector	Industry Group	Industry	Sub-Industry
		352020 Pharmaceuticals	**35202010 Pharmaceuticals**
			Companies engaged in the research, development or production of pharmaceuticals. Includes veterinary drugs.
		352030 Life sciences tools & services	**35203010 Life sciences tools & services**
			Companies enabling the drug discovery, development and production continuum by providing analytical tools, instruments, consumables & supplies, clinical trial services and contract research services. Includes firms primarily servicing the pharmaceutical and biotechnology industries.
40 Financials	**4010 Banks**	**401010 Commercial banks**	**40101010 Diversified banks**
			Large, geographically diverse banks with a national footprint whose revenues are derived primarily from conventional banking operations, have significant business activity in retail banking and small and medium corporate lending, and provide a diverse range of financial services. Excludes banks classified in the Regional Banks and Thrifts & Mortgage Finance Sub-Industries. Also excludes investment banks classified in the Investment Banking & Brokerage Sub-Industry.
			40101015 Regional banks
			Commercial banks whose businesses are derived primarily from conventional banking operations and have significant business activity in retail banking and small and medium corporate lending. Regional banks tend to operate in limited geographic regions. Excludes companies classified in the Diversified Banks and Thrifts & Mortgage Banks sub-industries. Also excludes investment banks classified in the Investment Banking & Brokerage Sub-Industry.

Global Industry Classification Standard (GICS)

Sector	Industry Group	Industry	Sub-Industry
		401020 Thrifts & mortgage finance	**40102010 Thrifts & mortgage finance**
			Financial institutions providing mortgage and mortgage related services. These include financial institutions whose assets are primarily mortgage related, savings & loans, mortgage lending institutions, building societies and companies providing insurance to mortgage banks.
	4020 Diversified financials	**402010 Diversified financial services**	**40101010 Consumer Finance – Discountinued effective 04/30/2003**
			Providers of consumer finance services, including personal credit, credit cards, lease financing, mortgage lenders, travel-related money services and pawn shops.
			40201020 Other diversified financial services
			Providers of a diverse range of financial services and/or with some interest in a wide range of financial services including banking, insurance and capital markets, but with no dominant business line. Excludes companies classified in the Regional Banks and Diversified Banks Sub-Industries.
			40201030 Multi-sector holdings
			A company with significantly diversified holdings across three or more sectors, none of which contributes a majority of profit and/or sales. Stakes held are predominantly of a non-controlling nature. Includes diversified financial companies where stakes held are of a controlling nature. Excludes other diversified companies classified in the Industrials Conglomerates Sub-Industry.
			40201040 Specialised finance
			Providers of specialized financial services. Includes credit agencies, stock exchanges and specialty boutiques. Companies in this Sub-Industry derive a majority of revenue from one, specialized line of business.

Global Industry Classification Standard (GICS)

Sector	Industry Group	Industry	Sub-Industry
		402020 Consumer finance	**40202010 Consumer finance**
			Providers of consumer finance services, including personal credit, credit cards, lease financing, travel-related money services and pawn shops. Excludes mortgage lenders classified in the Thrifts & Mortgage Finance Sub-Industry.
		402030 Capital markets	**40203010 Asset management & custody banks**
			Financial institutions primarily engaged in investment management and/or related custody and securities fee-based services. Includes companies operating mutual funds, closed-end funds and unit investment trusts. Excludes banks and other financial institutions primarily involved in commercial lending, investment banking, brokerage and other specialized financial activities.
			40203020 Investment banking & brokerage
			Financial institutions primarily engaged in investment banking & brokerage services, including equity and debt underwriting, mergers and acquisitions, securities lending and advisery services. Excludes banks and other financial institutions primarily involved in commercial lending, asset management and specialized financial activities.
			40203030 Diversified capital markets
			Financial institutions primarily engaged in diversified capital markets activities, including a significant presence in at least two of the following area: large/major corporate lending, investment banking, brokerage and asset management. Excludes less diversified companies classified in the Asset Management & Custody Banks or Investment Banking & Brokerage sub-industries. Also excludes companies classified in the Banks or Insurance industry groups or the Consumer Finance Sub-Industry.

Global Industry Classification Standard (GICS)

Sector	Industry Group	Industry	Sub-Industry
	4030 Insurance	403010 Insurance	40301010 Insurance brokers
			Insurance and reinsurance brokerage firms.
			40301020 Life & health insurance
			Companies providing primarily life, disability, indemnity or supplemental health insurance. Excludes managed care companies classified in the Managed Health Care Sub-Industry.
			40301030 Multi-line insurance
			Insurance companies with diversified interests in life, health and property and casualty insurance.
			40301040 Property & casualty insurance
			Companies providing primarily property and casualty insurance.
			40301050 Reinsurance
			Companies providing primarily reinsurance.
		404010 Real estate – discountinued effective 04/28/2006	40401010 Real estate investment trust – discountinued effective 04/28/2006
			Real estate investment trusts (REITs). Includes Property Trusts.
			40401020 Real estate management & development – discontinued effective 04/28/2006
			Companies engaged in real estate ownership, development or management.
	4040 Real estate	404020 Real estate investment trusts (REITs)	40402010 Diversified REITs
			A company or Trust with significantly diversified operations across two or more property types.

Global Industry Classification Standard (GICS)

Sector	Industry Group	Industry	Sub-Industry
			40402020 Industrial REITs
			Companies or Trusts engaged in the acquisition, development, ownership, leasing, management and operation of industrial properties. Includes companies operating industrial warehouses and distribution properties.
			40402030 Mortgage REITs
			Companies or Trusts that service, originate, purchase and/or securitize residential and/or commercial mortgage loans. Includes trusts that invest in mortgage-backed securities and other mortgage related assets.
			40402035 Hotel & Resort REITs
			Companies or Trusts engaged in the acquisition, development, ownership, leasing, management and operation of hotel and resort properties.
			40402040 Office REITs
			Companies or Trusts engaged in the acquisition, development, ownership, leasing, management and operation of office properties.
			40402045 Health Care REITs
			Companies or Trusts engaged in the acquisition, development, ownership, leasing, management and operation of properties serving the health care industry, including hospitals, nursing homes, and assisted living properties.
			40402050 Residential REITS
			Companies or Trusts engaged in the acquisition, development, ownership, leasing, management and operation of residential properties including multifamily homes, apartments, manufactured homes and student housing properties
			40402060 Retail REITs
			Companies or Trusts engaged in the acquisition, development, ownership, leasing, management and operation of shopping malls, outlet malls, neighborhood and community shopping centers.

Global Industry Classification Standard (GICS)

Sector	Industry Group	Industry	Sub-Industry
			40402070 Specialised REITs
			Companies or Trusts engaged in the acquisition, development, ownership, leasing, management and operation of properties not classified elsewhere. Includes trusts that operate and invest in storage properties. It also includes REITs that do not generate a majority of their revenues and income from real estate rental and leasing operations.
		404030 Real estate management & development	**40403010 Diversified real estate activities**
			Companies engaged in a diverse spectrum of real estate activities including real estate development & sales, real estate management, or real estate services, but with no dominant business line.
			40403020 Real estate operating companies
			Companies engaged in operating real estate properties for the purpose of leasing & management.
			40403030 Real estate development
			Companies that develop real estate and sell the properties after development. Excludes companies classified in the Homebuilding Sub-Industry.
			40403040 Real estate services
			Real estate service providers such as real estate agents, brokers & real estate appraisers.
45 Information Technology	**4510 Software & services**	**451010 Internet software & services**	**45101010 Internet software & services**
			Companies developing and marketing internet software and/or providing internet services including online databases and interactive services, as well as companies deriving a majority of their revenues from online advertising. Excludes companies classified in the Internet Retail Sub-Industry.

Global Industry Classification Standard (GICS)

Sector	Industry Group	Industry	Sub-Industry
	4520 Technology hardware & equipment	**451020 IT services**	**45102010 IT consulting & other Services**
			Providers of information technology and systems integration services not classified in the Data Processing & Outsourced Services or Internet Software & Services Sub-Industries. Includes information technology consulting and information management services.
			45102020 Data processing & outsourced services
			Providers of commercial electronic data processing and/or business process outsourcing services. Includes companies that provide services for back-office automation.
		451030 Software	**45103010 Application software**
			Companies engaged in developing and producing software designed for specialized applications for the business or consumer market. Includes enterprise and technical software. Excludes companies classified in the Home Entertainment Software Sub-Industry. Also excludes companies producing systems or database management software classified in the Systems Software Sub-Industry.
			45103020 Systems software
			Companies engaged in developing and producing systems and database management software.
			45103030 Home entertainment software
			Manufacturers of home entertainment software and educational software used primarily in the home.
		452010 Communications equipment	**45201020 Communications equipment**

Global Industry Classification Standard (GICS)

Sector	Industry Group	Industry	Sub-Industry
			Manufacturers of communication equipment and products, including LANs, WANs, routers, telephones, switchboards and exchanges. Excludes cellular phone manufacturers classified in the Technology Hardware, Storage & Peripherals Sub-Industry.
			45201010 Networking equipment – discontinued effective 4/30/2003
			Manufacturers of computer networking equipment and products, including LANs, WANs and routers.
			45201020 Telecommunications equipment – discontinued effective 4/30/2003
			Manufacturers of telecommunication equipment, including telephones, switchboards and exchanges. Excludes companies classified in the Networking Equipment Sub-Industry.
		452020 Computers & peripherals	**45202010 Computer hardware**
			Manufacturers of personal computers, servers, mainframes and workstations. Includes manufacturers of Automatic Teller Machines (ATMs). Excludes manufacturers of copiers, faxes and related products classified in the Office Electronics Sub-Industry.
			45202020 Computer storage & peripherals
			Manufacturers of electronic computer components and peripherals. Includes data storage components, motherboards, audio and video cards, monitors, keyboards, printers and other peripherals. Excludes semiconductors classified in the Semiconductors Sub-Industry.
			45202030 Technology Hardware, Storage & Peripherals

Global Industry Classification Standard (GICS)

Sector	Industry Group	Industry	Sub-Industry
			Manufacturers of cellular phones, personal computers, servers, electronic computer components and peripherals. Includes data storage components, motherboards, audio and video cards, monitors, keyboards, printers, and other peripherals. Excludes semiconductors classified in the Semiconductors Sub-Industry.
		452030 Electronic equipment & components	**45203010 Electronic equipment & instruments**
			Manufacturers of electronic equipment and instruments including analytical, electronic test and measurement instruments, scanner/barcode products, lasers, display screens, point-of-sales machines, and security system equipment.
			45203015 Electronic components
			Manufacturers of electronic components. Includes electronic components, connection devices, electron tubes, electronic capacitors and resistors, electronic coil, printed circuit board, transformer and other inductors, signal processing technology/components.
			45203020 Electronic manufacturing services
			Producers of electronic equipment mainly for the OEM (Original Equipment Manufacturers) markets.
			45203030 Technology distributors
			Distributors of technology hardware and equipment. Includes distributors of communications equipment, computers & peripherals, semiconductors, and electronic equipment and components.
		452040 Office electronics	**45204010 Office electronics**
			Manufacturers of office electronic equipment including copiers and faxes.

Global Industry Classification Standard (GICS)

Sector	Industry Group	Industry	Sub-Industry
	4530 Semiconductors & semiconductor equipment	**453010 Semiconductors & semiconductor equipment**	**45301010 Semiconductor equipment**
			Manufacturers of semiconductor equipment.
			45301020 Semiconductors
			Manufacturers of semiconductors and related products.
50 Telecommunications Services	**5010 Telecommunications services**	**501010 Diversified telecommunications services**	**50101010 Alternative carriers**
			Providers of communications and high-density data transmission services primarily through a high bandwidth/fiber-optic cable network.
			50101020 Integrated telecommunication services
			Operators of primarily fixed-line telecommunications networks and companies providing both wireless and fixed-line telecommunications services not classified elsewhere.
		501020 Wireless telecommunication services	**50102010 Wireless telecommunication services**
			Providers of primarily cellular or wireless telecommunication services, including paging services.
55 Utilities	**5510 Utilities**	**551010 Electric utilities**	**55101010 Electric utilities**
			Companies that produce or distribute electricity. Includes both nuclear and non-nuclear facilities.
		551020 Gas utilities	**55102010 Gas utilities**
			Companies whose main charter is to distribute and transmit natural and manufactured gas. Excludes companies primarily involved in gas exploration or production classified in the Oil & Gas Exploration & Production Sub-Industry. Also excludes diversified midstream natural gas companies classified in the Oil & Gas Storage & Transportation Sub-Industry.

Global Industry Classification Standard (GICS)

Sector	Industry Group	Industry	Sub-Industry
		551030 Multi-utilities	**55103010 Multi-utilities**
			Utility companies with significantly diversified activities in addition to core Electric Utility, Gas Utility and/or Water Utility operations.
		551040 Water utilities	**55104010 Water utilities**
			Companies that purchase and redistribute water to the end-consumer. Includes large-scale water treatment systems.
		551050 Independent power producers & energy traders	**55105010 Independent power producers & energy traders**
			Companies that operate as Independent Power Producers (IPPs), Gas & Power Marketing & Trading Specialists and/or Integrated Energy Merchants. Excludes producers of electricity using renewable sources, such as solar power, hydropower, and wind power. Also excludes electric transmission companies and utility distribution companies classified in the Electric Utilities Sub-Industry.
			55105020 Renewable Electricity
			Companies that engage in the generation and distribution of electricity using renewable sources, including, but not limited to, companies that produce electricity using biomass, geothermal energy, solar energy, hydropower, and wind power. Excludes companies manufacturing capital equipment used to generate electricity using renewable sources, such as manufacturers of solar power systems, installers of photovoltaic cells, and companies involved in the provision of technology, components, and services mainly to this market.

GICS codes are reviewed annually to ensure that they accurately represent the global equity markets, enabling asset owners, asset managers and investment research specialists to make consistent global comparisons by industry. The GICS revision is the result of a consultation with members of the global investment community. Changes are being made at the industry and sub-industry levels, and are detailed below.

Global Industry Classification Standard (GICS)

Discontinued codes include:

20201020	Data processing services (30/4/2003)
20201030	Diversified commercial & professional services (31/8/2008)
20201040	Human resource & employment services (31/8/2008)
40201010	Consumer finance (30/4/2003)
404010	Real estate (30/4/2006)
40401010	Real estate investment trusts (30/4/2006)
40401020	Real estate management & development (30/4/2006)
45201010	Networking equipment (30/4/2003)
45201020	Telecommunications equipment (30/4/2003)
452050	Semiconductor equipment & products (30/4/2003)
45205010	Semiconductor equipment (30/4/2003
45205020	Semiconductors (30/4/2003)

For more information

http://www.standardandpoors.com/en_US/web/guest/home
https://www.msci.com/market-cap-weighted-indexes

Industry Classification Benchmark (ICB)

The Industry Classification Benchmark (ICB) is an **industry classification taxonomy** launched by **Dow Jones** and **FTSE** in 2005 and now owned solely by FTSE International. It is used to segregate markets into industry **sectors**. The ICB uses a system of 10 industries, partitioned into 19 super-sectors, which are further divided into 41 sectors, which then contain 114 sub-sectors.

The ICB classifies over 70,000 companies and 75,000 securities worldwide, enabling the comparison of companies across four levels of classification and national boundaries. The ICB system is supported by the ICB database, which is maintained by FTSE International Limited. The system is similar to the GICS industry classification system developed by Morgan Stanley Capital International (MSCI) and Standard & Poor's (S&P) (see GICS entry above).

ICB contacts
FTSE International
1270 6th Ave
New York, NY 10020
United States of America
Tel: +1 866 551 0617
Email: ftse-birr@ftse.com
www.ftserussell.com
http://www.icbenchmark.com/

History

The ICB system evolved from the agreement to merge the Dow Jones Indexes and FTSE Group industry classification systems in 2004 to create a single structure covering equities and corporate bonds worldwide. The new system was introduced at the end of 2004.

The ICB methodology assigns each company to the sub-sector that most closely represents the nature of its business, which is determined by its

Industry Classification Benchmark (ICB)

source of revenue. Companies are classified using information taken from audited annual accounts and directors' reports.

Where a company has businesses in two or more sub-sectors it is allocated to that sub-sector which provides the largest part of the revenue as indicated by the latest available report. A company engaged in businesses in three or more sub-sectors, but within a specific industry, will normally be classified as general mining, diversified industrials, multi-utilities or specialty finance. A company engaged in businesses in three or more sub-sectors that are in two or more industries, will normally be classified as a diversified industrial. A company engaged in three or more classes of business within the Industrials industry that differ substantially from each other, no one of which contributes 50% or more of revenue or less than 10%, will normally be classified as diversified industrial.

If there is a contribution of over 50% from any other single industry group, the sub-sector of that industry group with the highest revenue will be assigned to the company. Classifications may be changed where a significant change takes place in a company's structure as a result of a corporate event, such as a merger or demerger.

Structure

ICB is a four-tiered, hierarchical industry classification system. There are currently 10 industries, 19 super-sectors, 41 sectors and 114 sub-sectors. GICS classifications can be presented in text or numeric format. The full ICB classification for each company is a 4-digit code with text description. The hierarchical design of the 4-digit coding system allows for easy transition between ICB tiers.

ICB code list

Industry	Super-sector	Sector	Sub-sector
0001 Oil & Gas	0500 Oil & gas	0530 Oil & gas producers	0533 Exploration & production
		0570 Oil Equipment, services & distribution	0537 Integrated oil & gas
			0573 Oil equipment & services
		0580 Alternative energy	0577 Pipelines
			0583 Renewable energy equipment
			0587 Alternative fuels
1000 Basic Materials	1300 Chemicals	1350 Chemicals	1353 Commodity chemicals
			1357 Specialty chemicals
	1700 Basic resources	1730 Forestry & paper	1733 Forestry
			1737 Paper
		1750 Industrial metals & mining	1753 Aluminum
			1755 Non-ferrous metals
			1757 Iron & steel
			1771 Coal
		1770 Mining	1773 Diamonds & gemstones
			1775 General mining
			1777 Gold mining
			1779 Platinum & precious metals
2000 Industrials	2300 Construction & materials	2350 Construction & materials	2353 Building materials & fixtures
			2357 Heavy construction
	2700 Industrial goods & services	2710 Aerospace & defence	2713 Aerospace
			2717 Defence
		2720 General industrials	2723 Containers & packaging
			2727 Diversified industrials
		2730 Electronic & electrical equipment	2733 Electrical components & equipment
			2737 Electronic equipment

Industry Classification Benchmark (ICB)

Industry	Super-sector	Sector	Sub-sector
		2750 Industrial engineering	**2753** Commercial vehicles & trucks
			2757 Industrial machinery
		2770 Industrial transportation	**2771** Delivery services
			2773 Marine transportation
			2775 Railroads
			2777 Transportation services
			2779 Trucking
2000 Industrials	**2700** Industrial goods & services	**2790** Support services	**2791** Business support services
			2793 Business training & employment services
			2795 Financial administration
			2797 Industrial suppliers
			2799 Waste & disposal services
3000 Consumer Goods	**3300** Automobiles & parts	**3350** Automobiles & parts	**3353** Automobiles
			3355 Auto parts
			3357 Tires
	3500 Food & beverage	**3530** Beverages	**3533** Brewers
			3535 Distillers & vintners
			3537 Soft drinks
		3570 Food producers	**3573** Farming, fishing & plantations
			3577 Food products
	3700 Personal & household goods	**3720** Household goods & home construction	**3722** Durable household goods
			3724 Non-durable household goods
			3726 Furnishings
			3728 Home construction
		3740 Leisure goods	**3743** Consumer electronics
			3745 Recreational products
			3747 Toys
		3760 Personal goods	**3763** Clothing & accessories

Industry	Super-sector	Sector	Sub-sector
			3765 Footwear
			3767 Personal goods
		3780 Tobacco	**3785** Tobacco
4000 Health Care	**4500** Health care	**4530** Health care equipment & services	**4533** Health care providers
			4535 Medical equipment
			4537 Medical supplies
		4570 Pharmaceuticals & biotechnology	**4573** Biotechnology
			4577 Pharmaceuticals
5000 Consumer Services	**5300** Retail	**5330** Food & drug retailers	**5333** Drug retailers
			5337 Food retailers & wholesalers
		5370 General retailers	**5371** Apparel retailers
			5373 Broadline retailers
			5375 Home improvement retailers
			5377 Specialised consumer services
			5379 Specialty retailers
5000 Consumer Services	**5500** Media	**5550** Media	**5553** Broadcasting & entertainment
			5555 Media agencies
			5557 Publishing
	5750 Travel & leisure		**5751** Airlines
			5752 Gambling
			5753 Hotels
			5755 Recreational services
			5757 Restaurants & bars
			5759 Travel & tourism
6000 Telecommunications	**6500** Telecommunications	**6530** Fixed line telecommunications	**6535** Fixed line telecommunications
		6570 Mobile telecommunications	**6575** Mobile telecommunications
7000 Utilities	**7500** Utilities	**7530** Electricity	**7535** Conventional electricity
			7537 Alternative electricity

Industry Classification Benchmark (ICB)

Industry	Super-sector	Sector	Sub-sector
		7570 Gas, water & multi-utilities	**7573** Gas distribution
			7575 Multi-utilities
			7577 Water
8000 Financials	**8300** Banks	**8350** Banks	**8355** Banks
	8500 Insurance	**8530** Non-life insurance	**8532** Full line insurance
			8534 Insurance brokers
			8536 Property & casualty Insurance
			8538 Reinsurance
		8570 Life insurance	**8575** Life insurance
	8600 Real estate	**8630** Real estate investment & services	**8633** Real estate holding & development
			8637 Real estate services
		8670 Real estate investment trusts	**8671** Industrial & office REITs
			8672 Retail REITs
			8673 Residential REITs
			8674 Diversified REITs
			8675 Specialty REITs
			8676 Mortgage REITs
			8677 Hotel & lodging REITs
8000 Financials	**8700** Financial services	**8770** Financial services	**8771** Asset managers
			8773 Consumer finance
			8775 Specialty finance
			8777 Investment services
			8779 Mortgage finance
	8900 Equity/ non-equity investment instruments	**8980** Equity investment instruments	**8985** Equity investment instruments
		8990 Non-equity investment instruments	**8995** Non-equity investment instruments
9000 Technology	**9500** Technology	**9530** Software & computer services	**9533** Computer services
			9535 Internet
			9537 Software

Industry Classification Benchmark (ICB)

Industry	Super-sector	Sector	Sub-sector
		9570 Technology hardware & equipment	**9572** Computer hardware
			9574 Electronic office equipment
			9576 Semiconductors
			9578 Telecommunications equipment

International Standard Industrial Classification System (ISIC)

International Standard Industrial Classification System (ISIC)

Introduction

The **International Standard Industrial Classification of All Economic Activities** is a **United Nations industry classification** system. ISIC provides a comprehensive framework within which economic data can be collected and reported in a format that is designed for economic analysis and decision – and policy-making. It offers a crucial standard format for detailed information about the state of an economy according to economic principles, and is thus a basic tool in studying economies, fostering international comparability of data, and promoting national statistical systems.

ISIC contacts

statistics@un.org

Classifications	*chl@un.org*
Demographic and social statistics	*demostat@un.org*
Energy statistics	*energy_stat@un.org*
Environment statistics	*envstats@un.org*
General statistics inquiries	*statistics@un.org*
Industry statistics	*industry@un.org*
International merchandise trade statistics	*comtrade@un.org*
Monthly Bulletin of Statistics	*mbs@un.org*
Publications (print and electronic)	*statistics@un.org*
Statistics of international trade in services	*tradeserv@un.org*
System of National Accounts (SNA) and economic statistics	*sna@un.org*

United Nations Statistics Division
1st Ave Tunnel
New York, NY 10017
United States of America
Fax: +1 212 963 9851
Email: statistics@un.org
unstats.un.org/unsd/default.htm

International Standard Industrial Classification System (ISIC)

History

Adopted in 1948, the International Standard Industrial Classification of All Economic Activities (ISIC) has been revised repeatedly – in 1958, 1968, 1990, 2004 and, most recently, with the publication of its fourth edition, in 2006. The economic structure of many countries changed at a phenomenal rate as the emergence of new technologies, new types of activities and new forms of industries developed. It was in response to these changes and the need to improve and strengthen its relevance and comparability with other classifications that the ISIC has been revised.

Most countries use the ISIC as their national activity classification, or have developed national classifications derived from the ISIC. It is therefore an important tool for comparing statistical data on economic activities internationally. The ISIC is widely used, both nationally and internationally, in classifying data according to kind of economic activity in the fields of economic and social statistics, such as for statistics on national accounts, demography of enterprises, employment and others. In addition, the ISIC is increasingly used for non-statistical purposes. The development and maintenance of the ISIC is the responsibility of the United Nations Statistics Division.

Structure

The ISIC covers productive activities, i.e. economic activities within the production boundary of the System of National Accounts (SNA). These economic activities are sub-divided in a hierarchical, four-level structure of mutually exclusive categories, allowing data collection, presentation and analysis of economies in an internationally comparable, standardised way. The categories at the highest level ("sections") are alphabetically coded categories intended to facilitate economic analysis. The sections subdivide the entire spectrum of productive activities into broad groupings, such as "Agriculture, Forestry and Fishing" (Section A), "Manufacturing" (Section C) and "Information and Communication" (Section J). The classification is then organisentered into successively more detailed categories, which are numerically coded – two-digit divisions; three-digit groups; and, at the greatest level of detail, four-digit classes.

The classification is used to classify statistical units, such as establishments or enterprises, according to the economic activity in which they mainly engage.

International Standard Industrial Classification System (ISIC)

At each level of ISIC, each statistical unit is assigned to one and only one ISIC code, as set out below. The set of statistical units that are classified into the same ISIC category is then often referred to as an industry, such as "the furniture industry", which would refer to all units classified in ISIC division 31 (Manufacture of Furniture), or the "construction industry", which would refer to all units classified in ISIC section F (Construction).

What makes ISIC different

Because ISIC classifies by productive activity, it is distinctively different in nature and purpose from the classifications of goods and services, ownership, institutional units or other types of classifications. The standardised categorisation or sub-division of the complete set of producing units in an economy makes ISIC an important tool for the collection, presentation and analysis of socio-economic statistics. All categories at each level of the classification are mutually exclusive.

The principles and criteria that have been used to define and delineate these categories are based on the inputs of goods, services and factors of production; the process and technology of production; the characteristics of outputs; and the use to which the outputs are put. Economic activities that are similar in respect of these criteria have been grouped together in the categories of ISIC. At the most detailed level of the classification, preference has been given to the process and technology of production to define individual ISIC classes, particularly in the classes related to services. At higher levels, characteristics of outputs and the use to which outputs are put become more important to create analytically useful aggregation categories.

ISIC code list

Section A – Agriculture, Forestry & Fishing

Division	Group	Class
01 Crop & Animal Production, Hunting & Related Service Activities	**011** Growing of non-perennial crops	**0111** Growing of cereals ex-rice, leguminous crops & oil seeds
		0112 Growing of rice

International Standard Industrial Classification System (ISIC)

Division	Group	Class
		0113 Growing of vegetables & melons, roots & tubers
		0114 Growing of sugar cane
		0115 Growing of tobacco
		0116 Growing of fibre crops
		0119 Growing of other non-perennial crops
	012 Growing of perennial crops	0121 Growing of grapes
		0122 Growing of tropical & sub-tropical fruits
		0123 Growing of citrus fruits
		0124 Growing of pome fruits & stone fruits
		0125 Growing of other tree & bush fruits & nuts
		0126 Growing of oleaginous fruits
		0127 Growing of beverage crops
		0128 Growing of spices, aromatic, drug & pharmaceutical crops
		0129 Growing of other perennial crops
	013 Plant propagation	0130 Plant propagation
	014 Animal production	0141 Raising of cattle & buffaloes
		0142 Raising of horses & other equines
		0143 Raising of camels & camelids
		0144 Raising of sheep & goats
		0145 Raising of swine & pigs
		0146 Raising of poultry
		0149 Raising of other animals
	015 Mixed farming	0150 Mixed farming
	016 Support activities to agriculture & post-harvest crop activities	0161 Support activities for crop production
		0162 Support activities for animal production
		0163 Post-harvest crop activities
		0164 Seed processing for propagation
	017 Hunting, trapping & related service activities	0170 Hunting, trapping & related service activities

International Standard Industrial Classification System (ISIC)

Division	Group	Class
02 Forestry & Logging	021 Silviculture & other forestry activities	0210 Silviculture & other forestry activities
	022 Logging	0220 Logging
	023 Gathering of non-wood forest products	0230 Gathering of non-wood forest products
	024 Support services to forestry	0240 Support services to forestry
03 Fishing & Aquaculture	031 Fishing	0311 Marine fishing
		0312 Freshwater fishing
	032 Aquaculture	0321 Marine aquaculture
		0322 Freshwater aquaculture

Section B – Mining & Quarrying

Division	Group	Class
05 Mining of Coal & Lignite	051 Mining of hard coal	0510 Mining of hard coal
	052 Mining of lignite	0520 Mining of lignite
06 Extraction of Crude Petroleum & Natural Gas	061 Extraction of crude petroleum	0610 Extraction of crude petroleum
	062 Extraction of natural gas	0620 Extraction of natural gas
07 Mining of Metal Ores	071 Mining of iron ores	0710 Mining of iron ores
	072 Mining of non-ferrous metal ores	0721 Mining of uranium & thorium ores
		0729 Mining of other non-ferrous metal ores
08 Other Mining & Quarrying	081 Quarrying of stone, sand & Clay	0810 Quarrying of stone, sand & clay
	089 Mining & quarrying n.e.c. (not elsewhere covered)	0891 Mining of chemical & fertilizer minerals
		0892 Extraction of peat
		0893 Extraction of salt
		0899 Other mining & quarrying n.e.c.
09 Mining Support Service Activities	091 Support activities for petroleum & natural gas extraction	0910 Support activities for petroleum & natural gas extraction
	099 Support activities for other mining & quarrying	0990 Support activities for other mining & quarrying

International Standard Industrial Classification System (ISIC)

Section C – Manufacturing

Division	Group	Class
10 Manufacture of Food Products	**101** Processing & preserving of meat	**1010** Processing & preserving of meat
	102 Processing & preserving of fish, crustaceans & molluscs	**1020** Processing & preserving of fish, crustaceans & molluscs
	103 Processing & preserving of fruit & vegetables	**1030** Processing & preserving of fruit & vegetables
	104 Manufacture of vegetable & animal oils & fats	**1040** Manufacture of vegetable & animal oils & fats
	105 Manufacture of dairy products	**1050** Manufacture of dairy products
	106 Manufacture of grain mill products, starches & starch products	**1061** Manufacture of grain mill products
		1062 Manufacture of starches & starch products
	107 Manufacture of other food products	**1071** Manufacture of bakery products
		1072 Manufacture of sugar
		1073 Manufacture of cocoa, chocolate & sugar confectionery
		1074 Manufacture of macaroni, noodles, couscous & similar farinaceous products
		1075 Manufacture of prepared meals & dishes
		1079 Manufacture of other food products n.e.c.
	108 Manufacture of prepared animal feeds	**1080** Manufacture of prepared animal feeds
11 Manufacture of Beverages		**1101** Distilling, rectifying & blending of spirits
		1102 Manufacture of wines
		1103 Manufacture of malt liquors & malt
		1104 Manufacture of soft drinks, production of mineral waters & other bottled waters
12 Manufacture of Tobacco Products	**120** Manufacture of tobacco products	**1200** Manufacture of tobacco products
13 Manufacture of Textiles	**131** Spinning, weaving & finishing of textiles	**1311** Preparation & spinning of textile fibres
		1312 Weaving of textiles

International Standard Industrial Classification System (ISIC)

Division	Group	Class
		1313 Finishing of textiles
	139 Manufacture of other textiles	**1391** Manufacture of knitted & crocheted fabrics
		1392 Manufacture of made-up textile articles, ex-apparel
		1393 Manufacture of carpets & rugs
		1394 Manufacture of cordage, rope, twine & netting
		1399 Manufacture of other textiles n.e.c.
14 Manufacture of Wearing Apparel	**141** Manufacturing of wearing apparel, ex-apparel	**1410** Manufacturing of wearing apparel, except fur apparel
	142 Manufacture of articles of fur	**1420** Manufacture of articles of fur
	143 Manufacture of knitted & crocheted apparel	**1430** Manufacture of knitted & crocheted apparel
15 Manufacture of Leather & Related Goods	**151** Tanning & dressing of leather, manufacture of luggage, handbags, saddler & harness, dressing & dyeing of fur	**1511** Tanning & dressing of leather, dressing & dyeing of fur
		1512 Manufacture of luggage, handbags, saddler & harness
	152 Manufacture of footwear	**1520** Manufacture of footwear
16 Manufacture of Wood & products Wood & Cork, Ex-Furniture; Manufacture of Articles of Straw & Plaiting Materials	**161** Sawmilling & planning of wood	**1610** Sawmilling & planning of wood
	162 Manufacture of products of wood, cork, straw & plaiting materials	**1621** Manufacture of veneer sheets & wood-based panels
		1622 Manufacture of builders' carpentry & joinery
		1623 Manufacture of wooden containers
		1629 Manufacture of other wood products, manufacture of articles of cork, straw & plaiting materials
17 Manufacture of Paper & Paper Products		**1701** Manufacture of pulp, paper & paperboard
		1702 Manufacture of corrugated paper & paperboard & containers of paper & paperboard
		1709 Manufacture of other articles of paper & paperboard

International Standard Industrial Classification System (ISIC)

Division	Group	Class
18 Printing & Reproduction of Recorded Material	**181** Printing & service activities related to printing	**1811** Printing
		1812 Service activities related to printing
	182 Reproduction of recorded media	**1820** Reproduction of recorded media
19 Manufacture of Coke & Refined Petroleum Products	**191** Manufacture of coke oven products	**1910** Manufacture of coke oven products
	192 Manufacture of refined petroleum products	**1920** Manufacture of refined petroleum products
20 Manufacture of Chemicals & Chemical Products	**201** Manufacture of basic chemicals, fertilizers & nitrogen compounds, plastics & synthetic rubber in primary forms	**2011** Manufacture of basic chemicals
		2012 Manufacture of fertilizers & nitrogen compounds
		2013 Manufacture of plastics & synthetic rubber in primary forms
	202 Manufacture of other chemical products	**2021** Manufacture of pesticides & other agrochemical products
		2022 Manufacture of paints, varnishes & similar coatings, printing ink & mastics
		2023 Manufacture of soap & detergents, cleaning & polishing preparations, perfumes & toiletry preparations
		2029 Manufacture of other chemical products n.e.c.
21 Manufacture of Pharmaceuticals, Medicinal Chemical & Botanical Products	**210** Manufacture of pharmaceuticals, medicinal chemical & botanical products	**2100** Manufacture of pharmaceuticals, medicinal chemical & botanical products
22 Manufacture of Rubber & Plastics Products	**221** Manufacture of rubber products	**2211** Manufacture of rubber tires & tubes, retreading & rebuilding of rubber tires
		2219 Manufacture of other rubber products
	222 Manufacture of plastics products	**2220** Manufacture of plastics products
23 Manufacture of Other Non-Metallic Mineral Products	**231** Manufacture of glass & glass products	**2310** Manufacture of glass & glass products
	239 Manufacture of non-metallic mineral products n.e.c.	**2391** Manufacture of refractory products
		2392 Manufacture of clay building materials

International Standard Industrial Classification System (ISIC)

Division	Group	Class
		2393 Manufacture of other porcelain & ceramic products
		2394 Manufacture of cement, lime & plaster
		2395 Manufacture of articles of concrete, cement & plaster
		2396 Cutting, shaping & finishing of stone
		2399 Manufacture of other non-metallic mineral products n.e.c.
24 Manufacture of Basic Metals	**241** Manufacture of basic iron & steel	**2410** Manufacture of basic iron & steel
	242 Manufacture of basic precious & other non-ferrous metals	**2420** Manufacture of basic precious & other non-ferrous metals
	243 Casting of metals	**2431** Casting of iron & steel
		2432 Casting of non-ferrous metals
25 Manufacture of Fabricated Metal Products, Ex-Machinery & Equipment	**251** Manufacture of structural metal products, tanks, reservoirs & steam generators	**2511** Manufacture of structural metal products
		2512 Manufacture of tanks, reservoirs & containers of metal
		2513 Manufacture of steam generators, ex-central heating hot water boilers
	252 Manufacture of weapons & ammunition	**2520** Manufacture of weapons & ammunition
	259 Manufacture of other fabricated metal products; metalworking service activities	**2591** Forging, pressing, stamping & roll-forming of metal; powder metallurgy
		2592 Treatment & coating of metals; machining
		2593 Manufacture of cutlery, hand tools & general hardware
		2599 Manufacture of other fabricated metal products n.e.c.
26 Manufacture of Computer, Electronic & Optical Products	**261** Manufacture of electronic components & boards	**261** Manufacture of electronic components & boards
	262 Manufacture of computers & peripheral equipment	**262** Manufacture of computers & peripheral equipment
	263 Manufacture of communication equipment	**263** Manufacture of communication equipment

International Standard Industrial Classification System (ISIC)

Division	Group	Class
	264 Manufacture of consumer electronics	264 Manufacture of consumer electronics
	265 Manufacture of measuring, testing, navigating & control equipment; watches & clocks	2651 Manufacture of measuring, testing, navigating and control equipment
		2652 Manufacture of watches and clocks
	266 Manufacture of irradiation, electro-medical & electrotherapeutic equipment	2660 Manufacture of irradiation, electro-medical & electrotherapeutic equipment
	267 Manufacture of optical instruments & photographic equipment	2670 Manufacture of optical instruments & photographic equipment
	268 Manufacture of magnetic & optical media	2680 Manufacture of magnetic & optical media
27 Manufacture of Electrical Equipment	271 Manufacture of electric motors, generators, transformers & electricity distribution & control apparatus	2710 Manufacture of electric motors, generators, transformers & electricity distribution & control apparatus
	272 Manufacture of batteries & accumulators	2720 Manufacture of batteries & accumulators
	273 Manufacture of wiring & wiring devices	2731 Manufacture of fibre optic cables
		2732 Manufacture of other electronic & electric wires & cables
		2733 Manufacture of wiring devices
	274 Manufacture of electric lighting equipment	2740 Manufacture of electric lighting equipment
	275 Manufacture of domestic appliances	2750 Manufacture of domestic appliances
	279 Manufacture of other electrical equipment	2790 Manufacture of other electrical equipment
28 Manufacture of Machinery & Equipment n.e.c.	281 Manufacture of general-purpose machinery	2811 Manufacture of engines & turbines, ex-aircraft, vehicle & cycle engines
		2812 Manufacture of fluid power equipment
		2813 Manufacture of other pumps, compressors, taps & valves
		2814 Manufacture of bearings, gears, gearing & driving elements
		2815 Manufacture of ovens, furnaces & furnace burners

International Standard Industrial Classification System (ISIC)

Division	Group	Class
		2816 Manufacture of lifting & handling equipment
		2817 Manufacture of office machinery & equipment ex-computers & peripheral equipment
		2818 Manufacture of power-driven hand tools
		2819 Manufacture of other general-purpose machinery
	282 Manufacture of special-purpose machinery	**2821** Manufacture of agricultural & forestry machinery
		2822 Manufacture of metal-forming machinery & machine tools
		2823 Manufacture of machinery for metallurgy
		2824 Manufacture of machinery for mining, quarrying & construction
		2825 Manufacture of machinery for food, beverage & tobacco processing
		2826 Manufacture of machinery for textile, apparel & leather production
		2829 Manufacture of other special-purpose machinery
29 Manufacture of Motor Vehicles, Trailers & Semi-Trailers	**291** Manufacture of motor vehicles	**2910** Manufacture of motor vehicles
	292 Manufacture of bodies (coachwork) for motor vehicles; manufacture of trailers & semi-trailers	**2920** Manufacture of bodies (coachwork) for motor vehicles; manufacture of trailers & semi-trailers
	293 Manufacture of parts & accessories for motor vehicles	**2930** Manufacture of parts & accessories for motor vehicles
30 Manufacture of Other Transport Equipment	**301** Building of ships & boats	**3011** Building of ships & floating structures
		3012 Building of pleasure & sporting boats
	302 Manufacture of railway locomotives & rolling stock	**3020** Manufacture of railway locomotives & rolling stock
	303 Manufacture of air & spacecraft & related machinery	**3030** Manufacture of air & spacecraft & related machinery
	304 Manufacture of military fighting vehicles	**3040** Manufacture of military fighting vehicles

International Standard Industrial Classification System (ISIC)

Division	Group	Class
	309 Manufacture of transport equipment n.e.c.	3091 Manufacture of motorcycles
		3092 Manufacture of bicycles & invalid carriages
		3099 Manufacture of other transport equipment n.e.c.
31 Manufacture of Furniture	310 Manufacture of furniture	3100 Manufacture of furniture
32 Other Manufacturing	321 Manufacture of jewellery, bijouterie & related articles	3211 Manufacture of jewellery & related articles
		3212 Manufacture of imitation jewellery & related articles
	322 Manufacture of musical instruments	3220 Manufacture of musical instruments
	323 Manufacture of sports goods	3230 Manufacture of sports goods
	324 Manufacture of games and toys	3240 Manufacture of games and toys
	325 Manufacture of medical & dental instruments & supplies	3250 Manufacture of medical & dental instruments & supplies
	329 Other manufacturing n.e.c.	3290 Other manufacturing n.e.c.
33 Repair & Installation of Machinery & Equipment	331 Repair of fabricated metal products, machinery & equipment	3311 Repair of fabricated metal products
		3312 Repair of machinery
		3313 Repair of electronic and optical equipment
		3314 Repair of electrical equipment
		3315 Repair of transport equipment, ex-motor vehicles
		3319 Repair of other equipment
	332 Installation of industrial machinery & equipment	332 Installation of industrial machinery & equipment

Section D – Electricity, Gas, Steam & Air Conditioning Supply

Division	Group	Class
35 Electricity, Gas, Steam & Air Conditioning Supply	351 Electric power generation, transmission & distribution	3510 Electric power generation, transmission & distribution

International Standard Industrial Classification System (ISIC)

Division	Group	Class
	352 Manufacture of gas; distribution of gaseous fuels through mains	**3520** Manufacture of gas; distribution of gaseous fuels through mains
	353 Steam & air conditioning supply	**3530** Steam & air conditioning supply

Section E – Water Supply, Sewerage, Waste Management & Remediation Activities

Division	Group	Class
36 Water Collection, Treatment & Supply	**360** Water collection, treatment & supply	**3600** Water collection, treatment & supply
37 Sewerage	**370** Sewerage	**3700** Sewerage
38 Waste Collection, Treatment & Disposal Activities; Materials Recovery	**381** Waste collection	**3811** Collection of non-hazardous waste
		3812 Collection of hazardous waste
	382 Waste treatment & disposal	**3821** Treatment and disposal of non-hazardous waste
		3822 Treatment and disposal of hazardous waste
	383 Materials recovery	**3830** Materials recovery
39 Remediation Activities & Other Waste Management Services	**390** Remediation activities & other waste management services	**3900** Remediation activities & other waste management services

Section F – Construction

Division	Group	Class
41 Construction of Buildings	**410** Construction of buildings	**4100** Construction of buildings
42 Civil Engineering	**421** Construction of roads & railways	**4210** Construction of roads & railways
	422 Construction of utility projects	**4220** Construction of utility projects
	429 Construction of other civil engineering projects	**4290** Construction of other civil engineering projects
43 Specialised Construction Activities	**431** Demolition & site preparation	**4311** Demolition
		4312 Site preparation
	432 Electrical, plumbing & other construction installation activities	**4321** Electrical installation

International Standard Industrial Classification System (ISIC)

Division	Group	Class
		4322 Plumbing, heat & air-conditioning installation
		4329 Other construction installation
	433 Building completion & finishing	**4330** Building completion & finishing
	439 Other specialised construction activities	**4390** Other specialised construction activities

Section G – Wholesale & Retail Trade, Repair of Motor Vehicles & Motorcycles

Division	Group	Class
45 Wholesale & Retail Trade & Repair of Motor Vehicles Motorcycles	**451** Sale of motor vehicles	**4510** Sale of motor vehicles
	452 Maintenance & repair of motor vehicles	**4520** Maintenance & repair of motor vehicles
	453 Sale of motor vehicle parts & accessories	**4530** Sale of motor vehicle parts & accessories
	454 Sale, maintenance & repair of motorcycles & related parts & accessories	**4540** Sale, maintenance & repair of motorcycles & related parts & accessories
46 Wholesale Trade, Ex-Motor Vehicles & Motorcycles	**461** Wholesale on a fee or contract basis	**4610** Wholesale on a fee or contract basis
	462 Wholesale of agricultural raw materials & live animals	**4620** Wholesale of agricultural raw materials & live animals
	463 Wholesale of food, beverages & tobacco	**4630** Wholesale of food, beverages & tobacco
	464 Wholesale of household goods	**4641** Wholesale of textiles, clothing & footwear
		4649 Wholesale of other household goods
	465 Wholesale of machinery, equipment & supplies	**4651** Wholesale of computers, computer peripheral equipment & software
		4652 Wholesale of electronic & telecommunications equipment & parts
		4653 Wholesale of agricultural machinery, equipment & supplies
		4659 Wholesale of other machinery & equipment
	466 Other specialised wholesale	**4661** Wholesale of solid, liquid & gaseous fuels & related products
		4662 Wholesale of metals and metal ores

International Standard Industrial Classification System (ISIC)

Division	Group	Class
		4663 Wholesale of construction materials, hardware, plumbing & heating equipment & supplies
		4669 Wholesale of waste and scrap & other products n.e.c.
	469 Non-specialised wholesale trade	**4690** Non-specialised wholesale trade
47 Retail Trade Ex-Motor Vehicles & Motorcycles	**471** Retail sale in non-specialised stores	**4711** Retail sale in non-specialised stores with food, beverages or tobacco predominating
		4719 Other retail sale in non-specialised stores
	472 Retail sale of food, beverages & tobacco in specialised stores	**4721** Retail sale of food in specialised stores
		4722 Retail sale of beverages in specialised stores
		4723 Retail sale of tobacco products in specialised stores
	473 Retail sale of automotive fuel in specialised stores	**4730** Retail sale of automotive fuel in specialised stores
	474 Retail sale of information & communications equipment in specialised stores	**4741** Retail sale of computers, peripheral units, software & telecommunications equipment in specialised stores
		4742 Retail sale of audio and video equipment in specialised stores
	475 Retail sale of other household equipment in specialised stores	**4751** Retail sale of textiles in specialised stores
		4752 Retail sale of hardware, paints & glass in specialised stores
		4753 Retail sale of carpets, rugs, wall & floor coverings in specialised stores
		4759 Retail sale of electrical household appliances, furniture, lighting equipment & other household articles in specialised stores
	476 Retail sale of cultural & recreation goods in specialised stores	**4761** Retail sale of books, newspapers & stationary in specialised stores
		4762 Retail sale of music & video recordings in specialised stores
		4763 Retail sale of sporting equipment in specialised stores

International Standard Industrial Classification System (ISIC)

Division	Group	Class
		4764 Retail sale of games & toys in specialised stores
	477 Retail sale of other goods in specialised stores	**4771** Retail sale of clothing, footwear & leather articles in specialised stores
		4772 Retail sale of pharmaceutical & medical goods, cosmetic & toilet articles in specialised stores
		4773 Other retail sale of new goods in specialised stores
		4774 Retail sale of second-hand goods
	478 Retail sale via stalls & markets	**4781** Retail sale via stalls & markets of food, beverages & tobacco products
		4782 Retail sale via stalls & markets of textiles, clothing & footwear
		4789 Retail sale via stalls & markets of other goods
	479 Retail trade not in stores, stalls or markets	**4791** Retail sale via mail order houses or via Internet
		4799 Other retail sale not in stores, stalls or markets

Section H – Transportation & Storage

Division	Group	Class
49 Land Transport & Transport via Pipelines	**491** Transport via railways	**4911** Passenger rail transport, interurban
		4912 Freight rail transport
	492 Other land transport	**4921** Urban & suburban passenger land transport
		4922 Other passenger land transport
		4923 Freight transport by road
	493 Transport via pipeline	**4930** Transport via pipeline
50 Water Transport	**501** Sea & coastal water transport	**5011** Sea & coastal passenger water transport
		5012 Sea & coastal freight water transport
	502 Inland water transport	**5021** Inland passenger water transport
		5022 Inland freight water transport
51 Air Transport	**511** Passenger air transport	**5110** Passenger air transport
	512 Freight air transport	**5120** Freight air transport
52 Warehousing & Support Activities for Transportation	**521** Warehousing & storage	**5210** Warehousing & storage

International Standard Industrial Classification System (ISIC)

Division	Group	Class
	522 Support activities for transportation	**5221** Service activities incidental to land transportation
		5222 Service activities incidental to water transportation
		5223 Service activities incidental to air transportation
		5224 Cargo handling
		5229 Other transportation support activities
53 Postal & Courier Activities	**531** Postal activities	**5310** Postal activities
	532 Courier activities	**5320** Courier activities

Section I – Accommodation & Food Service Activities

Division	Group	Class
55 Accommodation	**551** Short-term accommodation activities	**5510** Short-term accommodation activities
	552 Camping grounds, recreational vehicle parks and trailer parks	**5520** Camping grounds, recreational vehicle parks & trailer parks
	559 Other accommodation	**5590** Other accommodation
56 Food & Beverage Service Activities	**561** Restaurants and mobile food service activities	**5610** Restaurants and mobile food service activities
	562 Event catering & other food service activities	**5621** Event catering
		5629 Other food service activities
	563 Beverage serving activities	**5630** Beverage serving activities

Section J – Information & Communication

Division	Group	Class
58 Publishing Activities	**581** Publishing of books, periodicals & other publishing activities	**5811** Book publishing
		5812 Publishing of directories and mailing lists
		5813 Publishing of newspapers, journals & periodicals
		5819 Other publishing activities
	582 Software publishing	**5820** Software publishing

International Standard Industrial Classification System (ISIC)

Division	Group	Class
59 Motion Picture, Video and Television Programme Production, Sound Recording and Music Publishing Activities	**591** Motion picture, video and television programme activities	**5911** Motion picture, video and television programme production activities
		5912 Motion picture, video and television programme post-production activities
		5913 Motion picture, video and television programme distribution activities
		5914 Motion picture projection activities
	592 Sound recording and music publishing activities	**5920** Sound recording and music publishing activities
60 Programming & Broadcasting Activities	**601** Radio broadcasting	**6010** Radio broadcasting
	602 Television programming & broadcasting activities	**6020** Television programming & broadcasting activities
61 Telecommunications	**611** Wired telecommunications activities	**6110** Wired telecommunications activities
	612 Wireless telecommunications activities	**6120** Wireless telecommunications activities
	613 Satellite telecommunications activities	**6130** Satellite telecommunications activities
	619 Other telecommunications activities	**6190** Other telecommunications activities
62 Computer Programming, Consultancy & Related Activities		**6201** Computer programming activities
		6202 Computer consultancy & computer facilities management activities
		6209 Other information technology & computer service activities
63 Information Service Activities	**631** Data processing, hosting & related activities; web portals	**6311** Data processing, hosting & related activities
		6312 Web reference portals
	639 Other information service activities	**6391** News agency activities
		6399 Other information service activities n.e.c.

International Standard Industrial Classification System (ISIC)

Section K – Financial & Insurance Activities

Division	Group	Class
64 Financial Service Activities Ex-Insurance & Pension Funding	**641** Monetary intermediation	**6411** Central banking
		6419 Other monetary intermediation
	642 Activities of holding companies	**6420** Activities of holding companies
	643 Trusts, funds & similar financial entities	**6430** Trusts, funds & similar financial entities
	649 Other financial service activities ex-insurance & pension funding activities	**6491** Financial leasing
		6492 Other credit granting
		6499 Other financial service activities, ex-insurance & pension funding activities n.e.c.
65 Insurance, Reinsurance & Pension Funding Ex-Compulsory Social Security	**651** Insurance	**6511** Life insurance
		6512 Non-life insurance
	652 Reinsurance	**6520** Reinsurance
	653 Pension funding	**6530** Pension funding
66 Activities Auxiliary to Financial Service & Insurance Activities	**661** Activities auxiliary to financial service activities ex-insurance & pension funding	**6611** Administration of financial markets
		6612 Security and commodity contracts brokerage
		6619 Other activities auxiliary to financial service activities
	662 Activities auxiliary to insurance & pension funding	**6621** Risk and damage evaluation
		6622 Activities of insurance agents & brokers
		6629 Other activities auxiliary to insurance & pension funding
	663 Fund management activities	**6630** Fund management activities

International Standard Industrial Classification System (ISIC)

Section L – Real Estate Activities

Division	Group	Class
68 Real Estate Activities	681 Real estate activities with own or leased property	6810 Real estate activities with own or leased property
	682 Real estate activities on a fee or contract basis	6820 Real estate activities on a fee or contract basis

Section M – Professional, Scientific & Technical Activities

Division	Group	Class
69 Legal & Accounting Activities	691 Legal activities	6910 Legal activities
	692 Accounting, bookkeeping & auditing activities; tax consultancy	6920 Accounting, bookkeeping and auditing activities; tax consultancy
70 Activities of Head Offices, Management Consultancy Activities	701 Activities of head offices	7010 Activities of head offices
71 Architectural & Engineering Activities, Technical Testing & Analysis	702 Management consultancy activities	7020 Management consultancy activities
	711 Architectural and engineering activities & related technical consultancy	7110 Architectural and engineering activities & related technical consultancy
	712 Technical testing & analysis	7120 Technical testing & analysis
72 Scientific Research & Development	721 Research & experimental development on natural sciences & engineering	7210 Research & experimental development on natural sciences & engineering
	722 Research & experimental development on social sciences & humanities	7220 Research & experimental development on social sciences & humanities
73 Advertising & Market Research	731 Advertising	7310 Advertising
	732 Market research & public opinion polling	7320 Market research & public opinion polling
74 Other Professional, Scientific & Technical Activities	741 Specialised design activities	7410 Specialised design activities
	742 Photographic activities	7420 Photographic activities
	749 Other professional, scientific & technical activities n.e.c.	7490 Other professional, scientific & technical activities n.e.c.

International Standard Industrial Classification System (ISIC)

Division	Group	Class
75 Veterinary Activities	**750** Veterinary activities	**7500** Veterinary activities

Section N – Administrative & Support Service Activities

Division	Group	Class
77 Rental & Leasing Activities	**771** Renting & leasing of motor vehicles	**7710** Renting & leasing of motor vehicles
	772 Renting & leasing of personal & household goods	**7721** Renting & leasing of recreational & sports goods
		7722 Renting of video tapes & disks
		7729 Renting & leasing of other personal & household goods
	773 Renting & leasing of other machinery, equipment & tangible goods	**7730** Renting & leasing of other machinery, equipment & tangible goods
	774 Leasing of intellectual property & similar products, ex-copyrighted works	**7740** Leasing of intellectual property & similar
78 Employment Activities	**781** Activities of employment placement agencies	**7810** Activities of employment placement agencies
	782 Temporary employment agency activities	**7820** Temporary employment agency activities
	783 Other human resources provision	**7830** Other human resources provision
79 Travel Agency, Tour Operator, Reservation Service & Related Activities	**791** Travel agency & tour operator activities	**7911** Travel agency activities
		7912 Tour operator activities
	799 Other reservation service & related activities	**7990** Other reservation service & related activities
80 Security & Investigation Activities	**801** Private security activities	**8010** Private security activities
	802 Security systems service activities	**8020** Security systems service activities
	803 Investigation activities	**8030** Investigation activities
81 Services to Buildings & Landscape Activities	**811** Combined facilities support activities	**8110** Combined facilities support activities
	812 Cleaning activities	**8121** General cleaning of buildings
		8129 Other building & industrial cleaning activities
	813 Landscape care & maintenance service activities	**8130** Landscape care & maintenance service activities

International Standard Industrial Classification System (ISIC)

Division	Group	Class
82 Office Administrative, Office Support & Other Business Support Activities	821 Office administrative and support activities	8211 Combined office administrative service activities
		8219 Photocopying, document preparation & other specialised office support activities
	822 Activities of call centres	8220 Activities of call centres
	823 Organisation of conventions & trade shows	8230 Organisation of conventions & trade shows
	829 Business support service activities n.e.c.	8291 Activities of collection agencies & credit bureaus
		8292 Packaging activities
		8299 Other business support service activities n.e.c.

Section O – Public Administration & Defence, Compulsory Social Security

Division	Group	Class
84 Public Administration & Defence, Compulsory Social Security	841 Administration of the state & the economic & social policy of the community	8411 General public administration activities
		8412 Regulation of the activities of providing health care, education, cultural services & other social services, ex-social security
		8413 Regulation of & contribution to more efficient operation of businesses
	842 Provision of services to the community as a whole	8421 Foreign affairs
		8422 Defence activities
		8423 Public order and safety activities
	843 Compulsory social security activities	8430 Compulsory social security activities

Section P – Education

Division	Group	Class
85 Education	851 Pre-primary & primary education	8510 Pre-primary & primary education

International Standard Industrial Classification System (ISIC)

Division	Group	Class
	852 Secondary education	**8521** General secondary education
		8522 Technical & vocational secondary education
	853 Higher education	**8530** Higher education
	854 Other education	**8541** Sports and recreation education
		8542 Cultural education
		8549 Other education n.e.c.
	855 Educational support activities	**8550** Educational support activities

Section Q – Human Health & Social Work Activities

Division	Group	Class
86 Human Health Activities	**861** Hospital activities	**8610** Hospital activities
	862 Medical & dental practice activities	**8620** Medical & dental practice activities
	869 Other human health activities	**8690** Other human health activities
87 Residential Care Activities	**871** Residential nursing care facilities	**8710** Residential nursing care facilities
	872 Residential care activities for mental retardation, mental health & substance abuse	**8720** Residential care activities for mental retardation, mental health & substance abuse
	873 Residential care activities for the elderly & disabled	**8730** Residential care activities for the elderly & disabled
	879 Other residential care activities	**8790** Other residential care activities
88 Social Work Activities Without Accommodation	**881** Social work activities without accommodation for the elderly & disabled	**8810** Social work activities without accommodation for the elderly & disabled
	889 Other social work activities without accommodation	**8890** Other social work activities without accommodation

Section R – Arts, Entertainment & Recreation

Division	Group	Class
90 Creative, Arts & Entertainment Activities	**900** Creative, arts & entertainment activities	**9000** Creative, arts & entertainment activities

International Standard Industrial Classification System (ISIC)

Division	Group	Class
91 Libraries, Archives, Museums & Other Cultural Activities		9101 Library & archives activities
		9102 Museums activities & operation of historical sites & buildings
		9103 Botanical & zoological gardens & nature reserves activities
92 Gambling & Betting Activities	920 Gambling & betting activities	9200 Gambling & betting activities
93 Sports Activities & Amusement & Recreation Activities	931 Sports activities	9311 Operation of sports facilities
		9312 Activities of sports clubs
		9319 Other sports activities
	932 Other amusement & recreation activities	9321 Activities of amusement parks & theme parks
		9329 Other amusement & recreation activities n.e.c.

Section S – Other Service Activities

Division	Group	Class
94 Activities of Membership Organisations	941 Activities of business, employers & professional membership organisations	9411 Activities of business & employers membership organisations
		9412 Activities of professional membership organisations
	942 Activities of trade unions	9420 Activities of trade unions
	949 Activities of other membership organisations	9491 Activities of religious organisations
		9492 Activities of political organisations
		9499 Activities of other membership organisations n.e.c.
95 Repair of Computers & Personal & Household Goods	951 Repair of computers & communication equipment	9511 Repair of computers & peripheral equipment
		9512 Repair of communication equipment
	952 Repair of personal & household goods	9521 Repair of consumer electronics
		9522 Repair of household appliances & home & garden equipment
		9523 Repair of footwear & leather goods

International Standard Industrial Classification System (ISIC)

Division	Group	Class
		9524 Repair of furniture & home furnishings
		9529 Repair of other personal & household goods
96 Other Personal Service Activities		**9601** Washing & dry cleaning of textile & fur products
		9602 Hairdressing & other beauty treatment
		9603 Funeral & related activities
		9609 Other personal service activities n.e.c.

Section T – Activities of Households as Employers, Undifferentiated Goods & Services Producing Activities of Households for Own Use

Division	Group	Class
97 Activities of Households as Employers of Domestic Personnel	**970** Activities of households as employers of domestic personnel	**9700** Activities of households as employers of domestic personnel
98 Undifferentiated Goods & Services Producing Activities of Private Households for Own Use	**981** Undifferentiated goods-producing activities of private households for own use	**9810** Undifferentiated goods producing activities of private households for own use
	982 Undifferentiated service-producing activities of private households for own use	**9820** Undifferentiated service producing activities of private households for own use

Section U – Activities of Extraterritorial Organisations & Bodies

Division	Group	Class
99 Activities of Extraterritorial Organisations & Bodies	**990** Activities of extraterritorial organisations & bodies	**9900** Activities of extraterritorial organisations & bodies

National Codes

NACE Codes

In brief

The Nomenclature Statistique des Activitées Economiques dans la Communautée Européenne, or NACE, is a pan-European industry standard classification system which groups organisations according to their business activities. NACE is similar in function to the International Standard Industrial Classification system (ISIC), the Standard Industrial Classification (SIC) and North American Industry Classification System (NAICS).

NACE contact
Statistical Office of the European Communities
5, Rue Alphonse Weicker
Luxembourg City, L-2721
Luxembourg
Mts. Ana Franco Lopes (Unit DDG/02)
Tel: +352 4301 33209
Email: Ana.Franco@ec.europa.eu
ec.europa.eu

History

Between 1961 and 1963, the Nomenclature des Industries Etablies dans les Communautées Européennes (NICE), or Classification of Industries in the European Communities, was established. In 1965, a separate classification system (Commerce sans la CEE) for trade and commerce in the European Community was established. This was followed by two further classifications for services and agriculture in 1967. In 1970, all the established classification systems were brought together as the Nomenclature Générale des Activitées Economiques dans les Communautées Européennes (NACE), a general industrial classification of economic activities within the European Communities. NACE was first revised in 1990 (NACE Rev.1) when details were added to reflect European activities that were inadequately represented in the third revision of the International Standard Industrial Classification (ISIC) system. Two further revisions occurred in 2002 (NACE Rev.1.1) and 2006 (NACE Rev.2).

Structure

NACE is a classification by productive activity; in this respect, it is different in nature and purpose from the classifications of goods and services, ownership, institutional units or other types of classifications. The standardised categorisation or sub-division of the complete set of producing units in an economy makes NACE an important tool for the collection, presentation and analysis of socio-economic statistics. All categories at each level of the classification are mutually exclusive. The principles and criteria that have been used to define and delineate these categories are based on the inputs of goods, services and factors of production; the process and technology of production; the characteristics of outputs; and the use to which the outputs are put. At the most detailed level of classification, NACE gives preference to the process and technology of production, particularly in relationship to services. At higher levels of categorisation, NACE creates analytically useful categories based on outputs and their application. ISIC and NACE have exactly the same items at the highest levels, although NACE is more detailed at lower levels.

Like other codes, NACE consists of a hierarchical structure:

— A first level consisting of headings identified by an alphabetical code (that is, the broadest category into which a company fits is its Section. An oil company, for instance, is in Section B, Mining & Quarrying).
— A second level ('Division') consisting of headings identified by a two-digit numerical code.
— A third level ('Group') consisting of headings identified by a three-digit numerical code.
— A fourth level ('Class') consisting of headings identified by a four-digit numerical code.
The divisions are coded consecutively. However, some "gaps" have been provided to allow the introduction of additional divisions without a complete change of the NACE coding. These gaps have been introduced in sections that are most likely to prompt the need for additional divisions. For this purpose, the following division code numbers have been left unused in the 2006 NACE Rev.2 – 04, 34, 40, 44, 48, 54, 57, 67, 76, 83 and 89.

NACE Codes

Code list

Section A – Agriculture, Forestry & Fishing

Division	Group	Class
A01 Crop & Animal Production, Hunting & Related Service Activities	**A01.1** Growing of non-perennial crops	**A01.11** Growing of cereals ex-rice, leguminous crops & oil seeds
		A01.12 Growing of rice
		A01.13 Growing of vegetables & melons, roots & tubers
		A01.14 Growing of sugar cane
		A01.15 Growing of tobacco
		A01.16 Growing of fibre crops
		A01.19 Growing of other non-perennial crops
	A01.2 Growing of perennial crops	**A01.21** Growing of grapes
		A01.22 Growing of tropical & sub-tropical fruits
		A01.23 Growing of citrus fruits
		A01.24 Growing of pome fruits & stone fruits
		A01.25 Growing of other tree & bush fruits & nuts
		A01.26 Growing of oleaginous fruits
		A01.27 Growing of beverage crops
		A01.28 Growing of spices, aromatic, drug & pharmaceutical crops
		A01.29 Growing of other perennial crops
	A01.3 Plant propagation	**A01.30** Plant propagation
	A01.4 Animal production	**A01.41** Raising of dairy cattle
		A01.42 Raising of other cattle & buffaloes
		A01.43 Raising of horses & other equines
		A01.44 Raising of camels & camelids
		A01.45 Raising of sheep & goats
		A01.46 Raising of swine & pigs
		A01.47 Raising of poultry
		A01.49 Raising of other animals
	A01.5 Mixed farming	**A01.50** Mixed farming

Division	Group	Class
	A01.6 Support activities to agriculture & post-harvest crop activities	**A01.61** Support activities for crop production
		A01.62 Support activities for animal production
		A01.63 Post-harvest crop activities
		A01.64 Seed processing for propagation
	A01.7 Hunting, trapping & related service activities	**A01.70** Hunting, trapping & related service activities
A02 Forestry & Logging	**A02.1** Silviculture & other forestry activities	**A02.10** Silviculture & other forestry activities
	A02.2 Logging	**A02.20** Logging
	A02.3 Gathering of non-wood forest products	**A02.30** Gathering of non-wood forest products
	A02.4 Support services to forestry	**A02.40** Support services to forestry
A03 Fishing & Aquaculture	**A03.1** Fishing	**A03.11** Marine fishing
		A03.12 Freshwater fishing
	A03.2 Aquaculture	**A03.21** Marine aquaculture
		A03.22 Freshwater aquaculture

Section B – Mining & Quarrying

Division	Group	Class
B05 Mining of Coal & Lignite	**B05.1** Mining of hard coal	**B05.10** Mining of hard coal
	B05.2 Mining of lignite	**B05.20** Mining of lignite
B06 Extraction of Crude Petroleum & Natural Gas	**B06.1** Extraction of crude petroleum	**B06.10** Extraction of crude petroleum
	B06.2 Extraction of natural gas	**B06.20** Extraction of natural gas
B07 Mining of Metal Ores	**B07.1** Mining of iron ores	**B07.10** Mining of iron ores
	B07.2 Mining of non-ferrous metal ores	**B07.21** Mining of uranium & thorium ores
		B07.29 Mining of other non-ferrous metal ores
B08 Other Mining & Quarrying	**B08.1** Quarrying of stone, sand & clay	**B08.11** Quarrying of ornamental & building stone, limestone, gypsum, chalk & slate
		B08.12 Operation of gravel & sandpits, mining of clays & kaolin

NACE Codes

Division	Group	Class
	B08.9 Mining & quarrying n.e.c.	**B08.91** Mining of chemical & fertilizer minerals
		B08.92 Extraction of peat
		B08.93 Extraction of salt
		B08.99 Other mining & quarrying n.e.c.
B09 Mining Support Service Activities	**B09.1** Support activities for petroleum & natural gas extraction	**B09.10** Support activities for petroleum & natural gas extraction
	B09.9 Support activities for other mining & quarrying	**B09.90** Support activities for other mining & quarrying

Section C – Manufacturing

Division	Group	Class
C10 Manufacture of Food Products	**C10.1** Processing & preserving of meat & production of meat products	**C10.11** Processing & preserving of meat
		C10.12 Processing & production of poultry meat
		C10.13 Production of meat & poultry meat products
	C10.2 Processing & preserving of fish, crustaceans & molluscs	**C10.20** Processing & preserving of fish, crustaceans & molluscs
	C10.3 Processing & preserving of fruit & vegetables	**C10.31** Processing & preserving of potatoes
		C10.32 Manufacture of fruit & vegetable juice
		C10.39 Other processing & preserving of fruit & vegetables
	C10.4 Manufacture of vegetable & animal oils & fats	**C10.41** Manufacture of oils & fats
		C10.42 Manufacture of margarine & similar edible fats
	C10.5 Manufacture of dairy products	**C10.51** Operation of dairies & cheese making
		C10.52 Manufacture of ice cream
	C10.6 Manufacture of grain mill products, starches & starch products	**C10.61** Manufacture of grain mill products

Division	Group	Class
		C10.62 Manufacture of starches & starch products
	C10.7 Manufacture of bakery & farinaceous products	**C10.71** Manufacture of bread, fresh pastry goods & cakes
		C10.72 Manufacture of rusks & biscuits, preserved pastry goods & cakes
		C10.73 Manufacture of macaroni, noodles, couscous & similar farinaceous products
	C10.8 Manufacture of other food products	**C10.81** Manufacture of sugar
		C10.82 Manufacture of cocoa, chocolate & sugar confectionery
		C10.83 Processing of tea & coffee
		C10.84 Manufacture of condiments & seasonings
		C10.85 Manufacture of prepared meals & dishes
		C10.86 manufacture of homogenized food preparations & dietetic food
		C10.89 Manufacture of other food products n.e.c.
	C10.9 Manufacture of prepared animal feeds	**C10.91** Manufacture of prepared feeds for farm animals
		C10.92 Manufacture of prepared pet foods
C11 Manufacture of Beverages		**C11.01** Distilling, rectifying & blending of spirits
		C11.02 Manufacture of wine from grape
		C11.03 Manufacture of cider & other fruit wines
		C11.04 Manufacture of other non-distilled fermented beverages
		C11.05 Manufacture of beer
		C11.06 Manufacture of malt
		C11.07 Manufacture of soft drinks, production of mineral waters & other bottled waters
C12 Manufacture of Tobacco Products	**C12.0** Manufacture of tobacco products	**C12.00** Manufacture of tobacco products
C13 Manufacture of Textiles	**C13.1** Preparation & spinning of textile fibres	**C13.10** Preparation & spinning of textile fibres
	C13.2 Weaving of textiles	**C13.20** Weaving of textiles

NACE Codes

Division	Group	Class
	C13.3 Finishing of textiles	C13.30 Finishing of textiles
	C13.9 Manufacture of other textiles	C13.91 Manufacture of knitted & crocheted fabrics
		C13.92 Manufacture of made-up textile articles, ex-apparel
		C13.93 Manufacture of carpets & rugs
		C13.94 Manufacture of cordage, rope, twine & netting
		C13.95 Manufacture of non-woven & articles made from non-woven ex-apparel
		C13.96 Manufacture of other technical & industrial textiles
		C13.99 Manufacture of other textiles n.e.c.
C14 Manufacture of Wearing Apparel	C14.1 Manufacturing of wearing apparel, ex-fur apparel	C14.11 Manufacture of leather clothes
		C14.12 Manufacture of work wear
		C14.13 Manufacture of other outerwear
		C14.14 Manufacture of underwear
		C14.19 Manufacture of other wearing apparel & accessories
	C14.2 Manufacture of articles of fur	C14.20 Manufacture of articles of fur
	C14.3 Manufacture of knitted & crocheted apparel	C14.31 Manufacture of knitted & crocheted hosiery
		C14.39 Manufacture of other knitted & crocheted apparel
C15 Manufacture of Leather & Related Goods	C15.1 Tanning & dressing of leather, manufacture of luggage, handbags, saddler & harness, dressing & dyeing of fur	C15.11 Tanning & dressing of leather, dressing & dyeing of fur
		C15.12 Manufacture of luggage, handbags, saddler & harness
	C15.2 Manufacture of footwear	C15.20 Manufacture of footwear
C16 Manufacture of Wood Products Wood & Cork, Ex-Furniture; Manufacture of Articles of Straw & Plaiting Materials	C16.1 Sawmilling & planning of wood	C16.10 Sawmilling & planning of wood
	C16.2 Manufacture of products of wood, cork, straw & plaiting materials	C16.21 Manufacture of veneer sheets & wood-based panels

Division	Group	Class
		C16.22 Manufacture of assembled parquet floors
		C16.23 Manufacture of other builders' carpentry & joinery
		C16.24 Manufacture of wooden containers
		C16.29 Manufacture of other wood products, manufacture of articles of cork, straw & plaiting materials
C17 Manufacture of Paper & Paper Products	C17.1 Manufacture of pulp, paper & paperboard	C17.11 Manufacture of pulp
		C17.12 Manufacture of paper & paperboard
	C17.2 Manufacture of articles of paper & paperboard	C17.21 Manufacture of corrugated paper & paperboard & containers of paper & paperboard
		C17.22 Manufacture of household & sanitary goods & toilet requisites
		C17.24 Manufacture of wallpaper
		C17.29 Manufacture of other articles of paper & paperboard
	C17.3 Manufacture of paper stationery	
C18 Printing & Reproduction of Recorded Material	C18.1 Printing & service activities related to printing	C18.11 Printing of newspapers
		C18.12 Other printing
		C18.13 Pre-press & pre-media services
		C18.14 Binding & related services
	C18.2 Reproduction of recorded media	C18.20 Reproduction of recorded media
C19 Manufacture of Coke & Refined Petroleum Products	C19.1 Manufacture of coke oven products	C19.10 Manufacture of coke oven products
	C19.2 Manufacture of refined petroleum products	C19.20 Manufacture of refined petroleum products
C20 Manufacture of Chemicals & Chemical Products	C20.1 Manufacture of basic chemicals, fertilizers & nitrogen compounds, plastics & synthetic rubber in primary forms	C20.11 Manufacture of industrial gases
		C20.12 Manufacture of dyes & pigments
		C20.13 Manufacture of other inorganic basic chemicals

NACE Codes

Division	Group	Class
		C20.14 Manufacture of other organic basic chemicals
		C20.15 Manufacture of fertilizers & nitrogen compounds
		C20.16 Manufacture of plastics in primary forms
		C20.17 Manufacture of synthetic rubber in primary form
	C20.2 Manufacture of pesticides & other agrochemical products	C20.20 Manufacture of pesticides & other agrochemical products
	C20.3 Manufacture of paints, varnishes & similar coatings, printing ink & mastics	C20.30 Manufacture of paints, varnishes & similar coatings, printing ink & mastics
	C20.4 Manufacture of soaps & detergents, cleaning & polishing preparations, perfumes & toilet preparations	C20.41 Manufacture of soap & detergents, cleaning & polishing preparations
		C20.42 Manufacture of perfumes & toilet preparations
	C20.5 Manufacture of other chemical products	C20.51 Manufacture of explosives
		C20.52 Manufacture of glues
		C20.53 Manufacture of essential oils
		C20.59 Manufacture of other chemical products n.e.c.
	C20.6 Manufacture of man-made fibres	C20.60 Manufacture of man-made fibres
C21 Manufacture of pharmaceuticals, medicinal chemical & botanical products	C21.1 Manufacture of basic pharmaceutical products	C21.10 Manufacture of basic pharmaceutical products
	C21.2 Manufacture of pharmaceutical preparations	C21.20 Manufacture of pharmaceutical preparations
C22 Manufacture of Rubber & Plastics Products	C22.1 Manufacture of rubber products	C22.11 Manufacture of rubber tIres & tubes, retreading & rebuilding of rubber tIres
		C22.19 Manufacture of other rubber products
	C22.2 Manufacture of plastics products	C22.21 Manufacture of plastic plates, sheets, tubes & profiles
		C22.22 Manufacture of plastic packing goods

Division	Group	Class
		C22.23 Manufacture of builders' ware of plastic
		C22.29 Manufacture of other plastic products
C23 Manufacture of Other Non-Metallic Mineral Products	**C23.1** Manufacture of glass & glass products	**C23.11** Manufacture of flat glass
		C23.12 Shaping & processing of flat glass
		C23.13 Manufacture of hollow glass
		C23.14 Manufacture of glass fibres
		C23.19 Manufacture & processing of other glass, including technical glassware
	C23.2 Manufacture of refractory products	**C23.20** Manufacture of refractory products
	C23.3 Manufacture of clay building materials	**C23.31** Manufacture of ceramic tiles & flags
		C23.32 Manufacture of bricks, tiles & construction products in baked clay
	C23.4 Manufacture of other porcelain & ceramic products	**C23.41** Manufacture of ceramic household & ornamental articles
		C23.42 Manufacture of ceramic sanitary fixtures
		C23.43 Manufacture of ceramic insulations & insulating fittings
		C23.44 Manufacture of other technical ceramic products
		C23.49 Manufacture of other ceramic products
	C23.5 Manufacture of cement, lime & plaster	**C23.51** Manufacture of cement
		C23.52 Manufacture of lime & plaster
	C23.6 Manufacture of articles of concrete, cement & plaster	**C23.61** Manufacture of concrete products for construction purposes
		C23.62 Manufacture of plaster products for construction purposes
		C23.63 manufacture of ready mixed concrete
		C23.64 Manufacture of mortars
		C23.65 Manufacture of fibre cement
		C23.69 Manufacture of other articles of concrete, plaster & cement

NACE Codes

Division	Group	Class
	C23.7 Cutting, shaping & finishing of stone	C23.70 Cutting, shaping & finishing of stone
	C23.9 Manufacture of abrasive & non-metallic mineral products n.e.c.	C23.91 Production of abrasive products
		C23.99 Manufacture of other non-metallic mineral products n.e.c.
C24 Manufacture of Basic Metals	C24.1 Manufacture of basic iron & steel & ferro-alloys	C24.10 Manufacture of basic iron & steel & ferro-alloys
	C24.2 Manufacture of tubes, pipes, hollow profiles & related fittings of steel	C24.20 Manufacture of tubes, pipes, hollow profiles & related fittings of steel
	C24.3 Manufacture of other products of first processing of steel	C24.31 Cold drawing of bars
		C24.32 Cold rolling of narrow strip
		C24.33 Cold forming or folding
		C24.34 Cold drawing of wire
	C24.4 Manufacture of basic precious & other non-ferrous metals	C24.41 Precious metals production
		C24.42 Aluminium production
		C24.43 Lead, zinc & tin production
		C23.44 Copper production
		C24.45 Other non-ferrous metal production
		C24.46 Processing of nuclear fuel
	C24.5 Casting of metals	C24.51 Casting of iron
		C24.52 Casting of steel
		C24.53 Casting of light metals
		C24.54 Casting of other non-ferrous metals
C25 Manufacture of Fabricated Metal Products, Ex-Machinery & Equipment	C25.1 Manufacture of structural metal products	C25.11 Manufacture of metal structures & parts of structures
		C25.12 Manufacture of doors & windows of metal
	C25.2 Manufacture of tanks, reservoirs & containers of metal	C25.21 Manufacture of central heating radiators & boilers

Division	Group	Class
		C25.29 Manufacture of other tanks, reservoirs & containers of metal
	C25.3 Manufacture of steam generators, ex-central heating hot water boilers	C25.30 Manufacture of steam generators, ex-central heating hot water boilers
	C25.4 Manufacture of weapons & ammunition	C25.40 Manufacture of weapons & ammunition
	C25.5 Forging, pressing, stamping & roll-forming of metal; powder metallurgy	C25.50 Forging, pressing, stamping & roll-forming of metal; powder metallurgy
	C25.6 Treatment & coating of metals; machining	C25.61 Treatment & coating of metals
		C25.62 Machining
	C25.7 Manufacture of cutlery, tools & general hardware	C25.71 Manufacture of cutlery
		C25.72 Manufacture of locks & hinges
		C25.73 Manufacture of tools
	C25.9 Manufacture of other fabricated metal productse	C25.91 Manufacture of steel drums & similar containers
		C25.92 Manufacture of light metal packaging
		C25.93 Manufacture of wire products, chain & springs
		C25.94 Manufacture of fasteners & screw machine products.
		C25.99 Manufacture of other fabricated metal products n.e.c
C26 Manufacture of Computer, Electronic & Optical Products	C26.1 Manufacture of electronic components & boards	C26.11 Manufacture of electronic components
		C26.12 Manufacture of loaded electronic boards
	C26.2 Manufacture of computers & peripheral equipment	C26.20 Manufacture of computers & peripheral equipment
	C26.3 Manufacture of communication equipment	C26.30 Manufacture of communication equipment
	C26.4 Manufacture of consumer electronics	C26.40 Manufacture of consumer electronics

NACE Codes

Division	Group	Class
	C26.5 Manufacture of instruments & appliances for measuring, testing & navigation, watches & clocks	C26.51 Manufacture of instruments & appliances for measuring, testing & navigation
		C26.52 Manufacture of watches and clocks
	C26.6 Manufacture of irradiation, electromedical & electrotherapeutic equipment	C26.60 Manufacture of irradiation, electromedical & electrotherapeutic equipment
	C26.7 Manufacture of optical instruments & photographic equipment	C26.70 Manufacture of optical instruments & photographic equipment
	C26.8 Manufacture of magnetic & optical media	C26.80 Manufacture of magnetic & optical media
C27 Manufacture of Electrical Equipment	C27.1 Manufacture of electric motors, generators, transformers & electricity distribution & control apparatus	C27.11 Manufacture of electric motors, generators & transformers
		C27.12 Manufacture of electricity distribution & control apparatus
	C27.2 Manufacture of batteries & accumulators	C27.20 Manufacture of batteries & accumulators
	C27.3 Manufacture of wiring & wiring devices	C27.31 Manufacture of fibre optic cables
		C27.32 Manufacture of other electronic & electric wires & cables
		C27.33 Manufacture of wiring devices
	C27.4 Manufacture of electric lighting equipment	C27.40 Manufacture of electric lighting equipment
	C27.5 Manufacture of domestic appliances	C27.51 Manufacture of electric domestic appliances
		C27.52 Manufacture of non-electric domestic appliances
	C27.9 Manufacture of other electrical equipment	C27.90 Manufacture of other electrical equipment
C28 Manufacture of Machinery & Equipment n.e.c.	C28.1 Manufacture of general-purpose machinery	C28.11 Manufacture of engines & turbines, ex-aircraft, vehicle & cycle engines
		C28.12 Manufacture of fluid power equipment
		C28.13 Manufacture of other pumps, compressors
		C28.14 Manufacture of other taps & valves

Division	Group	Class
		C28.15 Manufacture of bearings, gears, gearing & driving elements
	C28.2 Manufacture of other general purpose machinery	**C28.21** Manufacture of ovens, furnaces & furnace burners
		C28.22 Manufacture of lifting & handling equipment
		C28.23 Manufacture of office machinery & equipment ex-computers & peripheral equipment
		C28.24 Manufacture of power-driven hand tools
		C28.25 Manufacture of non-domestic cooling & ventilation equipment
		C28.29 Manufacture of other general-purpose machinery n.e.c.
	C28.3 Manufacture of agricultural & forestry machinery	**C28.30** Manufacture of agricultural & forestry machinery
	C28.4 Manufacture of metal-forming machinery & machine tools	**C28.41** Manufacture of metal-forming machinery
		C28.49 Manufacture of other machine tools
	C28.9 Manufacture of other special-purpose machinery	**C28.91** Manufacture of machinery for metallurgy
		C28.92 Manufacture of machinery for mining, quarrying & construction
		C28.93 Manufacture of machinery for food, beverage & tobacco processing
		C28.94 Manufacture of machinery for textile, apparel & leather production
		C28.95 Manufacture of machinery for paper & paperboard production
		C28.96 Manufacture of plastics & rubber machinery
		C28.99 Manufacture of other special-purpose machinery n.e.c.
C29 Manufacture of Motor Vehicles, Trailers & Semi-Trailers	**C29.1** Manufacture of motor vehicles	**C29.10** Manufacture of motor vehicles

NACE Codes

Division	Group	Class
	C29.2 Manufacture of bodies (coachwork) for motor vehicles; manufacture of trailers & semi-trailers	C29.20 Manufacture of bodies (coachwork) for motor vehicles; manufacture of trailers & semi-trailers
	C29.3 Manufacture of parts & accessories for motor vehicles	C29.31 Manufacture of electrical & electronic equipment for motor vehicles
		C29.32 Manufacture of other parts & accessories for motor vehicles
C30 Manufacture of Other Transport Equipment	C30.1 Building of ships & boats	C30.11 Building of ships & floating structures
		C30.12 Building of pleasure & sporting boats
	C30.2 Manufacture of railway locomotives & rolling stock	C30.20 Manufacture of railway locomotives & rolling stock
	C30.3 Manufacture of air & spacecraft & related machinery	C30.30 Manufacture of air & spacecraft & related machinery
	C30.4 Manufacture of military fighting vehicles	C30.40 Manufacture of military fighting vehicles
	C30.9 Manufacture of transport equipment n.e.c.	C30.91 Manufacture of motorcycles
		C30.92 Manufacture of bicycles & invalid carriages
		C30.99 Manufacture of other transport equipment n.e.c.
C31 Manufacture of Furniture	C31.0 Manufacture of furniture	C31.01 Manufacture of office & shop furniture
		C31.02 Manufacture of kitchen furniture
		C31.03 Manufacture of mattresses
		C31.09 Manufacture of other furniture
C32 Other Manufacturing	C32.1 Manufacture of jewellery, bijouterie & related articles	C32.11 Striking of coins
		C32.12 Manufacture of jewellery & related articles
		C32.13 Manufacture of imitation jewellery & related articles
	C32.2 Manufacture of musical instruments	C32.20 Manufacture of musical instruments
	C32.3 Manufacture of sports goods	C32.30 Manufacture of sports goods

Division	Group	Class
	C32.4 Manufacture of games and toys	C32.40 Manufacture of games and toys
	C32.5 Manufacture of medical & dental instruments & supplies	C32.50 Manufacture of medical & dental instruments & supplies
	C32.9 Other manufacturing n.e.c.	C32.91 Manufacture of brooms & brushes
		C32.92 Other manufacturing n.e.c.
C33 Repair & Installation of Machinery & Equipment	C33.1 Repair of fabricated metal products, machinery & equipment	C33.11 Repair of fabricated metal products
		C33.12 Repair of machinery
		C33.13 Repair of electronic and optical equipment
		C33.14 Repair of electrical equipment
		C33.15 Repair & maintenance of ships & boats
		C33.16 Repair & maintenance of aircraft & spacecraft
		C33.17 Repair & maintenance of other transport equipment
		C33.19 Repair of other equipment
	C33.2 Installation of industrial machinery & equipment	C33.20 Installation of industrial machinery & equipment

Section D – Electricity, Gas, Steam & Air Conditioning Supply

Division	Group	Class
D35 Electricity, Gas, Steam & Air Conditioning Supply	D35.1 Electric power generation, transmission & distribution	D35.11 Production of electricity
		D35.12 Transmission of electricity
		D35.13 Distribution of electricity
		D35.14 Trade of electricity
	D35.2 Manufacture of gas; distribution of gaseous fuels through mains	D35.21 Manufacture of gas
		D35.22 Distribution of gaseous fuels through mains
		D35.23 Trade of gas through mains

NACE Codes

Division	Group	Class
	D35.3 Steam & air conditioning supply	**D35.30** Steam & air conditioning supply

Section E – Water Supply, Sewerage, Waste Management & Remediation Activities

Division	Group	Class
E36 Water Collection, Treatment & Supply	**E36.0** Water collection, treatment & supply	**E36.00** Water collection, treatment & supply
E37 Sewerage	**E37.0** Sewerage	**E37.00** Sewerage
E38 Waste Collection, Treatment & Disposal Activities; Materials Recovery	**E38.1** Waste collection	**E38.11** Collection of non-hazardous waste
		E38.12 Collection of hazardous waste
	E38.2 Waste treatment & disposal	**E38.21** Treatment and disposal of non-hazardous waste
		E38.22 Treatment and disposal of hazardous waste
	E38.3 Materials recovery	**E38.31** Dismantling of wrecks
		E38.32 Recovery of sorted materials
E39 Remediation Activities & Other Waste Management Services	**E39.0** Remediation activities & other waste management services	**E39.00** Remediation activities & other waste management services

Section F – Construction

Division	Group	Class
F41 Construction of Buildings	**F41.1** Development of building projects	**F41.10** Development of building projects
	F41.2 Construction of residential & non-residential buildings	**F41.20** Construction of residential & non-residential buildings
F42 Civil Engineering	**F42.1** Construction of roads & railways	**F42.11** Construction of roads & motorways
		F42.12 Construction of railways & underground railways
	F42.2 Construction of utility projects	**F42.13** Construction of bridges & tunnels
		F42.21 Construction of utility projects for fluids
		F42.22 Construction of utility projects for electricity & telecommunications

Division	Group	Class
	F42.9 Construction of other civil engineering projects	**F42.91** Construction of water projects
		F42.99 Construction of other civil engineering projects n.e.c.
F43 Specialised Construction Activities	**F43.1** Demolition & site preparation	**F43.11** Demolition
		F43.12 Site preparation
		F43.13 Test drilling & boring
	F43.2 Electrical, plumbing & other construction installation activities	**F43.21** Electrical installation
		F43.22 Plumbing, heat & air-conditioning installation
		F43.29 Other construction installation
	F43.3 Building completion & finishing	**F43.31** Plastering
		F43.32 Joinery installation
		F43.33 Floor & wall covering
		F43.34 Painting & glazing
		F43.39 Other building completion & finishing
	F43.9 Other specialised construction activities	**F43.91** Roofing activities
		F43.99 Other specialised construction activities n.e.c.

Section G – Wholesale & Retail Trade, Repair of Motor Vehicles & Motorcycles

Division	Group	Class
G45 Wholesale & Retail Trade & Repair of Motor Vehicles & Motorcycles	**G45.1** Sale of motor vehicles	**G45.11** Sale of cars & light motor vehicles
		G45.19 Sale of other motor vehicles
	G45.2 Maintenance & repair of motor vehicles	**G45.20** Maintenance & repair of motor vehicles
	G45.3 Sale of motor vehicle parts & accessories	**G45.31** Wholesale trade of motor vehicle parts & accessories
		G45.32 Retail trade of motor vehicle parts & accessories

NACE Codes

Division	Group	Class
	G45.4 Sale, maintenance & repair of motorcycles & related parts & accessories	G45.40 Sale, maintenance & repair of motorcycles & related parts & accessories
G46 Wholesale Trade, Ex-Motor Vehicles & Motorcycles	G46.1 Wholesale on a fee or contract basis	G46.11 Agents involved in the sale of agricultural raw materials, live animals, textile raw materials & semi-finished goods
		G46.12 Agents involved in the sale of fuels, ores, metals & industrial chemicals
		G46.13 Agents involved in the sale of timber & building materials
		G46.14 Agents involved in the sale of machinery, industrial equipment, ships & aircraft
		G46.15 Agents involved in the sale of furniture, household goods, hardware & ironmongery
		G46.16 Agents involved in the sale of textiles, clothing, fur, footwear & leather goods
		G46.17 Agents involved in the sale of food, beverages & tobacco
		G46.18 Agents specialised in the sale of other particular products
		G46.19 Agents involved in the sale of a variety of goods
	G46.2 Wholesale of agricultural raw materials & live animals	G46.21 Wholesale of grain, un-manufactured tobacco, seeds & animal feeds
		G46.22 Wholesale of flowers & plants
		G46.23 Wholesale of live animals
		G46.24 Wholesale of hides, skins & leather
	G46.3 Wholesale of food, beverages and tobacco	G46.31 Wholesale of fruit & vegetables
		G46.32 Wholesale of meat & meat products
		G46.33 Wholesale of dairy products, eggs & edible oils & fats
		G46.34 Wholesale of beverages
		G46.35 Wholesale of tobacco products
		G46.36 Wholesale of sugar & chocolate & sugar confectionery
		G46.37 Wholesale of coffee, tea, cocoa & spices

Division	Group	Class
		G46.38 Wholesale of other food, including fish, crustaceans & molluscs
		G46.39 Non-specialised wholesale of food, beverages & tobacco
	G46.4 Wholesale of household goods	**G46.41** Wholesale of textiles
		G46.42 Wholesale of clothing & footwear
		G46.43 Wholesale of electrical household appliances
		G46.44 Wholesale of china and glassware & cleaning materials
		G46.45 Wholesale of perfume & cosmetics
		G46.46 Wholesale of pharmaceutical goods
		G46.47 Wholesale of furniture, carpets & lighting equipment
		G46.48 Wholesale of watches and jewellery
		G46.49 Wholesale of other household goods
	G46.5 Wholesale of information & communication equipment	**G46.51** Wholesale of computers, computer peripheral equipment & software
		G46.52 Wholesale of electronic & telecommunications equipment & parts
	G46.6 Wholesale of other machinery, equipment & supplies	**G46.61** Wholesale of agricultural machinery, equipment & supplies
		G46.62 Wholesale of machine tools
		G46.63 Wholesale of mining, construction & civil engineering machinery
		G46.64 Wholesale of machinery for the textile industry & of sewing & knitting machines
		G46.65 Wholesale of office furniture
		G46.66 Wholesale of other office machinery & equipment
		G46.69 Wholesale of other machinery & equipment
G46 Wholesale Trade, Ex-Motor Vehicles & Motorcycles	**G46.7** Other specialised wholesale	**G46.71** Wholesale of solid, liquid & gaseous fuels & related products
		G46.72 Wholesale of metals & metal ores

NACE Codes

Division	Group	Class
		G46.73 Wholesale of wood, construction materials & sanitary equipment
		G46.74 Wholesale of hardware, plumbing & heating equipment & supplies
		G46.75 Wholesale of chemical products
		G46.76 Wholesale of other intermediate products
		G46.77 Wholesale of waste & scrap
	G46.9 Non-specialised wholesale trade	G46.90 Non-specialised wholesale trade
G47 Retail Trade Ex-Motor Vehicles & Motorcycles	G47.1 Retail sale in non-specialised stores	G47.11 Retail sale in non-specialised stores with food, beverages or tobacco predominating
		G47.19 Other retail sale in non-specialised stores
	G47.2 Retail sale of food, beverages & tobacco in specialised stores	G47.21 Retail sale of fruit & vegetables in specialised stores
		G.47.22 Retail sale of meat & meat products in specialised stores
		G.47.23 Retail sale of fish, crustaceans & molluscs in specialised stores
		G47.24 Retail sale of bread, cakes, flour confectionery & sugar confectionery in specialised stores
		G47.25 Retail sale of beverages in specialised stores
		G47.26 Retail sale of tobacco products in specialised stores
		G47.29 Other retail sale of food in specialised stores
	G47.3 Retail sale of automotive fuel in specialised stores	G47.30 Retail sale of automotive fuel in specialised stores
	G47.4 Retail sale of information & communications equipment in specialised stores	G47.41 Retail sale of computers, peripheral units, software in specialised stores
		G47.42 Retail sale of telecommunications equipment in specialised stores
		G47.43 Retail sale of audio & video equipment in specialised stores
	G47.5 Retail sale of other household equipment in specialised stores	G47.51 Retail sale of textiles in specialised stores

Division	Group	Class
		G47.52 Retail sale of hardware, paints & glass in specialised stores
		G47.53 Retail sale of carpets, rugs, wall & floor coverings in specialised stores
		G47.54 Retail sale of electrical household appliances in specialised stores
		G47.59 Retail sale of furniture, lighting equipment & other household articles in specialised stores
	G47.6 Retail sale of cultural & recreation goods in specialised stores	**G47.61** Retail sale of books in specialised stores
		G47.62 Retail sale of newspapers & stationary in specialised stores
		G47.63 Retail sale of music & video recordings in specialised stores
		G47.64 Retail sale of sporting equipment in specialised stores
		G47.65 Retail sale of games & toys in specialised stores
	G47.7 Retail sale of other goods in specialised stores	**G47.71** Retail sale of clothing in specialised stores
		G47.72 Retail sale of footwear & leather articles in specialised stores
		G47.73 Dispensing chemist in specialised stores
		G47.74 Retail sale of medical & orthopaedic goods in specialised stores
		G47.75 Retail sale of cosmetic & toilet articles in specialised stores
		G47.76 Retail sale of flowers, plants, seeds, fertilizers, pet animals & pet food in specialised stores
		G47.77 Retail sale of watches & jewellery in specialised stores
		G47.78 Other retail sale of new goods in specialised stores
		G47.79 Retail sale of second-hand goods in specialised stores
G47 Retail Trade Ex-Motor Vehicles & Motorcycles	**G47.8** Retail sale via stalls & markets	**G47.81** Retail sale via stalls & markets of food, beverages & tobacco products
		G47.82 Retail sale via stalls & markets of textiles, clothing & footwear

NACE Codes

Division	Group	Class
		G47.89 Retail sale via stalls & markets of other goods
	G47.9 Retail trade not in stores, stalls or markets	**G47.91** Retail sale via mail order houses or via Internet
		G47.99 Other retail sale not in stores, stalls or markets

Section H – Transportation & Storage

Division	Group	Class
H49 Land Transport & Transport via Pipelines	**H49.1** Passenger rail transport, interurban	**H49.10** Passenger rail transport, inter-urban
	H49.2 Freight rail transport	**H49.20** Freight rail transport
	H49.3 Other passenger land transport	**H49.31** Urban & suburban passenger land transport
		H49.32 Taxi operation
		H49.39 Other passenger land transport n.e.c.
	H49.4 Freight transport by road & removal services	**H49.41** Freight transport by road
		H49.42 Removal services
	H49.5 Transport via pipeline	**H49.50** Transport via pipeline
H50 Water Transport	**H50.1** Sea & coastal passenger water transport	**H50.10** Sea & coastal passenger water transport
	H50.2 Sea & coastal freight water transport	**H50.20** Sea & coastal freight water transport
	H50.3 Inland passenger water transport	**H50.30** Inland passenger water transport
	H50.4 Inland freight water transport	**H50.40** Inland freight water transport
H51 Air Transport	**H51.1** Passenger air transport	**H51.10** Passenger air transport
	H51.2 Freight air transport & space transport	**H51.21** Freight air transport
		H51.22 Space transport
H52 Warehousing & Support Activities for Transportation	**H52.1** Warehousing & storage	**H52.10** Warehousing & storage
	H52.2 Support activities for transportation	**H52.21** Service activities incidental to land transportation
		H52.22 Service activities incidental to water transportation

Division	Group	Class
		H52.23 Service activities incidental to air transportation
		H52.24 Cargo handling
		H52.29 Other transportation support activities
H53 Postal & Courier Activities	**H53.1** Postal activities under universal service obligation	**H53.10** Postal activities under universal service obligation
	H53.2 Other postal & courier activities	**H53.20** Other postal & courier activities

Section I – Accommodation & Food Service Activities

Division	Group	Class
I55 Accommodation	**I55.1** Hotels & similar accommodation	**I55.10** Hotels & similar accommodation
	I55.2 Holiday & other short stay accommodation	**I55.20** Holiday & other short stay accommodation
	I55.3 Camping grounds, recreational vehicle parks & trailer parks	**I55.30** Camping grounds, recreational vehicle parks & trailer parks
	I55.9 Other accommodation	**I55.90** Other accommodation
I56 Food & Beverage Service Activities	**I56.1** Restaurants & mobile food service activities	**I56.10** Restaurants & mobile food service activities
	I56.2 Event catering & other food service activities	**I56.21** Event catering
		I56.29 Other food service activities
	I56.3 Beverage serving activities	**I56.30** Beverage serving activities

Section J – Information & Communication

Division	Group	Class
J58 Publishing Activities	**J58.1** Publishing of books, periodicals & other publishing activities	**J58.11** Book publishing
		J58.12 Publishing of directories & mailing lists
		J58.13 Publishing of newspapers
		J59.14 Publishing of journals & periodicals
		J58.19 Other publishing activities

NACE Codes

Division	Group	Class
	J58.2 Software publishing	J58.21 Publishing of computer games
		J58.29 Other software publishing
J59 Motion Picture, Video & Television Programme Production, Sound Recording & Music Publishing Activities	J59.1 Motion picture, video & television programme activities	J59.11 Motion picture, video & television programme production activities
		J59.12 Motion picture, video & television programme post-production activities
		J59.13 Motion picture, video & television programme distribution activities
		J59.14 Motion picture projection activities
	J59.2 Sound recording & music publishing activities	J59.20 Sound recording & music publishing activities
J60 Programming & Broadcasting Activities	J60.1 Radio broadcasting	J60.10 Radio broadcasting
	J60.2 Television programming & broadcasting activities	J60.20 Television programming & broadcasting activities
J61 Telecommunications	J61.1 Wired telecommunications activities	J61.10 Wired telecommunications activities
	J61.2 Wireless telecommunications activities	J61.20 Wireless telecommunications activities
	J61.3 Satellite telecommunications activities	J61.30 Satellite telecommunications activities
	J61.9 Other telecommunications activities	J61.90 Other telecommunications activities
J62 Computer Programming, Consultancy & Related Activities	J62.0 Computer programming, consultancy & related activities	J62.01 Computer programming activities
		J62.02 Computer consultancy activities
		J62.03 Computer facilities management activities
		J62.09 Other information technology & computer service activities
J63 Information Service Activities	J63.1 Data processing, hosting & related activities; web portals	J63.11 Data processing, hosting & related activities
		J63.12 Web reference portals
	J63.9 Other information service activities	J63.91 News agency activities
		J63.99 Other information service activities n.e.c.

Section K – Financial & Insurance Activities

Division	Group	Class
K64 Financial Service Activities Ex-Insurance & Pension Funding	K64.1 Monetary intermediation	K64.11 Central banking
		K64.19 Other monetary intermediation
	K64.2 Activities of holding companies	K64.20 Activities of holding companies
	K64.3 Trusts, funds & similar financial entities	K64.30 Trusts, funds & similar financial entities
	K64.9 Other financial service activities ex-insurance & pension funding activities	K64.91 Financial leasing
		K64.92 Other credit granting
		K64.99 Other financial service activities, ex-insurance & pension funding activities n.e.c.
K65 Insurance, Reinsurance & Pension Funding Ex-Compulsory Social Security	K65.1 Insurance	K65.11 Life insurance
		K65.12 Non-life insurance
	K65.2 Reinsurance	K65.20 Reinsurance
	K65.3 Pension funding	K65.30 Pension funding
K66 Activities Auxiliary to Financial Service & Insurance Activities	K66.1 Activities auxiliary to financial service activities ex-insurance & pension funding	K66.11 Administration of financial markets
		K66.12 Security and commodity contracts brokerage
		K66.19 Other activities auxiliary to financial service activities ex-insurance & pension funding
	K66.2 Activities auxiliary to insurance & pension funding	K66.21 Risk and damage evaluation
		K66.22 Activities of insurance agents & brokers
		K66.29 Other activities auxiliary to insurance & pension funding
	K66.3 Fund management activities	K66.30 Fund management activities

NACE Codes

Section L – Real Estate Activities

Division	Group	Class
L68 Real Estate Activities	**L68.1** Buying & selling of own real estate	**L68.10** Buying & selling of own real estate
	L68.2 Renting & operating of own or leased real estate	**L68.20** Renting & operating of own or leased real estate
	L68.3 Real estate activities on a fee or contract basis	**L68.31** Real estate agencies
		L68.32 Management of real estate on a fee or contract basis

Section M – Professional, Scientific & Technical Activities

Division	Group	Class
M69 Legal & Accounting Activities	**M69.1** Legal activities	**M69.10** Legal activities
	M69.2 Accounting, bookkeeping & auditing activities; tax consultancy	**M69.20** Accounting, bookkeeping and auditing activities; tax consultancy
M70 Activities of Head Offices, Management Consultancy Activities	**M70.1** Activities of head offices	**M70.10** Activities of head offices
	M70.2 Management consultancy activities	**M70.21** Public relations & communication activities
		M70.22 Business & other management consultancy activities
M71 Architectural & Engineering Activities, Technical Testing & Analysis	**M71.1** Architectural and engineering activities & related technical consultancy	**M71.11** Architectural activities
		M71.12 Engineering activities & related technical consultancy
	M71.2 Technical testing & analysis	**M71.20** Technical testing & analysis
M72 Scientific Research & Development	**M72.1** Research & experimental development on natural sciences & engineering	**M72.11** Research & experimental development on biotechnology
		M72.19 Other research & experimental development on natural sciences & engineering
	M72.2 Research & experimental development on social sciences & humanities	**M72.20** Research & experimental development on social sciences & humanities

Division	Group	Class
M73 Advertising & Market Research	**M73.1** Advertising	**M73.11** Advertising agencies
		M73.12 Media representation
	M73.2 Market research & public opinion polling	**M73.20** Market research & public opinion polling
M74 Other Professional, Scientific & Technical Activities	**M74.1** Specialised design activities	**M74.10** Specialised design activities
	M74.2 Photographic activities	**M74.20** Photographic activities
	M74.3 Translation & interpretation activities	**M74.30** Translation & interpretation activities
	M74.9 Other professional, scientific & technical activities n.e.c.	**M74.90** Other professional, scientific & technical activities n.e.c.
M75 Veterinary Activities	**M75.0** Veterinary activities	**M75.00** Veterinary activities

Section N – Administrative & Support Service Activities

Division	Group	Class
N77 Rental & Leasing Activities	**N77.1** Renting & leasing of motor vehicles	**N77.11** Renting & leasing of cars & light motor vehicles
		N77.12 Renting & leasing of trucks
	N77.2 Renting & leasing of personal & household goods	**N77.21** Renting & leasing of recreational & sports goods
		N77.22 Renting of video tapes & disks
		N77.29 Renting & leasing of other personal & household goods
	N77.3 Renting & leasing of other machinery, equipment & tangible goods	**N77.31** Renting & leasing of agricultural machinery & equipment
		N77.32 Renting & leasing of construction & civil engineering machinery & equipment
		N77.33 Renting & leasing of office machinery & equipment (including computers)
		N77.34 Renting & leasing of water transport equipment
		N77.35 Renting & leasing of air transport equipment
		N77.39 Renting & leasing of other machinery, equipment & tangible goods n.e.c.

NACE Codes

Division	Group	Class
	N77.4 Leasing of intellectual property & similar products, ex-copyrighted works	**N77.40** Leasing of intellectual property & similar products, ex-copyrighted works
N78 Employment Activities	**N78.1** Activities of employment placement agencies	**N78.10** Activities of employment placement agencies
	N78.2 Temporary employment agency activities	**N78.20** Temporary employment agency activities
	N78.3 Other human resources provision	**N78.30** Other human resources provision
N79 Travel Agency, Tour Operator, Reservation Service & Related Activities	**N79.1** Travel agency & tour operator activities	**N79.11** Travel agency activities
		N79.12 Tour operator activities
	N79.9 Other reservation service & related activities	**N79.90** Other reservation service & related activities
N80 Security & Investigation Activities	**N80.1** Private security activities	**N80.10** Private security activities
	N80.2 Security systems service activities	**N80.20** Security systems service activities
	N80.3 Investigation activities	**N80.30** Investigation activities
N81 Services to Buildings & Landscape Activities	**N81.1** Combined facilities support activities	**N81.10** Combined facilities support activities
	N81.2 Cleaning activities	**N81.21** General cleaning of buildings
		N81.22 Other building & industrial cleaning activities
		N81.29 Other cleaning activities
	N81.3 Landscape care & maintenance service activities	**N81.30** Landscape care & maintenance service activities
N82 Office Administrative, Office Support & Other Business Support Activities	**N82.1** Office administrative and support activities	**N82.11** Combined office administrative service activities
		N82.19 Photocopying, document preparation & other specialised office support activities
	N82.2 Activities of call centres	**N82.20** Activities of call centres
	N82.3 Organisation of conventions & trade shows	**N82.30** Organisation of conventions & trade shows
	N82.9 Business support service activities n.e.c.	**N82.91** Activities of collection agencies & credit bureaus
		N82.92 Packaging activities

Division	Group	Class
		N82.99 Other business support service activities n.e.c.

Section O – Public Administration & Defense, Compulsory Social Security

Division	Group	Class
O84 Public Administration & Defence, Compulsory Social Security	**O84.1** Administration of the state & the economic & social policy of the community	**O84.11** General public administration activities
		O84.12 Regulation of the activities of providing health care, education, cultural services & other social services, ex-social security
		O84.13 Regulation of & contribution to more efficient operation of businesses
	O84.2 Provision of services to the community as a whole	**O84.21** Foreign affairs
		O84.22 Defence activities
		O84.23 Justice & judicial activities
		O84.24 Public order & safety activities
		O84.25 Fire service activities
	O84.3 Compulsory social security activities	**O84.30** Compulsory social security activities

Section P – Education

Division	Group	Class
P85 Education	**P85.1** Pre-primary	**P85.10** Pre-primary
	P85.2 Primary education	**P85.20** Primary education
	P853 Secondary education	**P85.31** General secondary education
		P85.32 Technical & vocational secondary education
	P85.4 Higher education	**P85.41** Post-secondary, non-tertiary education
		P85.42 Tertiary education
	P85.5 Other education	**P85.51** Sports and recreation education
		P85.52 Cultural education
		P85.53 Driving school activities

NACE Codes

Division	Group	Class
		P85.59 Other education n.e.c.
	P85.6 Educational support activities	P85.60 Educational support activities

Section Q – Human Health & Social Work Activities

Division	Group	Class
Q86 Human Health Activities	Q86.1 Hospital activities	Q86.10 Hospital activities
	Q86.2 Medical & dental practice activities	Q86.21 General medical practice activities
		Q86.22 Specialist medical practice activities
		Q86.23 Dental practice activities
	Q86.9 Other human health activities	Q86.90 Other human health activities
Q87 Residential Care Activities	Q87.1 Residential nursing care facilities	Q87.10 Residential nursing care facilities
	Q87.2 Residential care activities for mental retardation, mental health & substance abuse	Q87.20 Residential care activities for mental retardation, mental health & substance abuse
	Q87.3 Residential care activities for the elderly & disabled	Q87.30 Residential care activities for the elderly & disabled
	Q87.9 Other residential care activities	Q87.90 Other residential care activities
Q88 Social Work Activities without Accommodation	Q88.1 Social work activities without accommodation for the elderly & disabled	Q88.10 Social work activities without accommodation for the elderly & disabled
	Q88.9 Other social work activities without accommodation	Q88.91 Child care activities
		Q88.99 Other social work activities without accommodation

Section R – Arts, Entertainment & Recreation

Division	Group	Class
R90 Creative, Arts & Entertainment Activities	R90.0 Creative, arts & entertainment activities	R90.01 Performing arts
		R90.02 Support activities to performing arts
		R90.03 Artistic creation

Division	Group	Class
		R90.04 Operation of arts facilities
R91 Libraries, Archives, Museums & Other Cultural Activities	**R91.0** Libraries, archives, museums & other cultural activities	**R91.01** Library & archives activities
		R91.02 Museums activities
		R91.03 Operation of historical sites & buildings & similar visitor attractions
		R91.04 Botanical & zoological gardens & nature reserves activities
R92 Gambling & Betting Activities	**R92.0** Gambling & betting activities	**R92.00** Gambling & betting activities
R93 Sports Activities & Amusement & Recreation Activities	**R93.1** Sports activities	**R93.11** Operation of sports facilities
		R93.12 Activities of sports clubs
		R91.13 Fitness facilities
		R93.19 Other sports activities
	R93.2 Amusement & recreation activities	**R93.21** Activities of amusement parks & theme parks
		R93.29 Other amusement & recreation activities n.e.c.

Section S – Other Service Activities

Division	Group	Class
S94 Activities of Membership Organisations	**S94.1** Activities of business, employers & professional membership organizations	**S94.11** Activities of business & employers membership organisations
		S94.12 Activities of professional membership organisations
	S94.2 Activities of trade unions	**S94.20** Activities of trade unions
	S94.9 Activities of other membership organisations	**S94.91** Activities of religious organisations
		S94.92 Activities of political organisations
		S94.99 Activities of other membership organisations n.e.c.
S95 Repair of Computers & Personal & Household Goods	**S95.1** Repair of computers & communication equipment	**S95.11** Repair of computers & peripheral equipment

NACE Codes

Division	Group	Class
		S95.12 Repair of communication equipment
	S95.2 Repair of personal & household goods	**S95.21** Repair of consumer electronics
		S95.22 Repair of household appliances & home & garden equipment
		S95.23 Repair of footwear & leather goods
		S95.24 Repair of furniture & home furnishings
		S95.25 Repair of watches & clocks
		S95.29 Repair of other personal & household goods
S96 Other Personal Service Activities	**S96.0** Other personal service activities	**S96.01** Washing & dry cleaning of textile & fur products
		S96.02 Hairdressing & other beauty treatment
		S96.03 Funeral & related activities
		S96.04 Physical well-being activities
		S96.09 Other personal service activities n.e.c.

Section T – Activities of Households as Employers, Undifferentiated Goods & Services Producing Activities of Households for Own Use

Division	Group	Class
T97 Activities of Households as Employers of Domestic Personnel	**T97.0** Activities of households as employers of domestic personnel	**T97.00** Activities of households as employers of domestic personnel
T98 Undifferentiated Goods & Services Producing Activities of Private Households for Own Use	**T98.1** Undifferentiated goods-producing activities of private households for own use	**T98.10** Undifferentiated goods producing activities of private households for own use
	T98.2 Undifferentiated service-producing activities of private households for own use	**T98.20** Undifferentiated service producing activities of private households for own use

Section U – Activities of Extraterritorial Organisations & Bodies

Division	Group	Class
U99 Activities of Extraterritorial Organisations & Bodies	**U99.0** Activities of extraterritorial organisations & bodies	**U99.00** Activities of extraterritorial organisations & bodies

North American Industry Classification System (NAICS)

North American Industry Classification System (NAICS)

In brief

The North American Industry Classification System, or NAICS, is used by businesses and governments to classify business establishments according to type of economic activity (that is, the process of production) in Canada, Mexico and the US. It has largely replaced the older **Standard Industrial Classification** (SIC) system; however, certain government departments and agencies, such as the US Securities and Exchange Commission (SEC), still use the **SIC codes**.

An establishment is typically a single physical location, though administratively distinct operations at a single location may be treated as distinct establishments. Each establishment is classified by industry according to its primary business activity. NAICS does not offer guidance on the classification of companies which are composed of multiple establishments. New versions of NAICS versions are released every five years.

> ## NAICS contact
> US Department of Commerce
> 1401 Constitution Ave NW
> Washington, DC 20230
> United States of America
> Tel: +1 202 482 2000
> *Email: naics@census.gov*
> *www.naics.com*

History
NAICS was developed under the auspices of the US Office of Management and Budget (OMB), and adopted in 1997 to replace the Standard Industrial Classification (SIC) system. It was developed jointly by the US Economic Classification Policy Committee (ECPC), Statistics Canada and Mexico's In-

North American Industry Classification System (NAICS)

stituto Nacional de Estadistica y Geografia to permit comparison of business statistics among the North American countries. With the first version NAICS offered enhanced coverage of the service sector, relative to SIC. The 2002 revision accommodated significant changes in the information sector. The 2012 revision slightly reduced the number of industries and modified six sectors.

Structure

NAICS has a hierarchical structure. At the highest level, it divides the economy into 20 sectors. At lower levels, it further distinguishes the different economic activities in which businesses are engaged. The system employs a six-digit code at the most detailed industry level. The first five digits are generally (although not always) the same in all three countries. The first two digits designate the largest business sector, the third digit designates the sub-sector, the fourth digit designates an industry group, the fifth digit designates NAICS industries, and the sixth digit designates national industries.

NAICS code list

Please note that trilateral agreements between Canada, Mexico and the US are indicated in the code list by an asterisk.

NAICS Code	Sector
11	Agriculture, forestry, fishing & hunting
21	Mining
22	Utilities
23	Construction
31–33	Manufacturing
42	Wholesale Trade
44–45	Retail trade
48–49	Transportation & warehousing
51	Information
52	Finance & insurance
53	Real estate & rental and leasing
54	Professional, scientific & technical services
55	Management of companies & enterprises
56	Administrative & support & waste management & remediation services

North American Industry Classification System (NAICS)

61	Education services
62	Health care & social assistance
71	Arts, entertainment & recreation
72	Accommodation & food services
81	Other services (except public administration)
92	Public administration

Agriculture, Forestry, Fishing & Hunting

Sub-Sector	Industry Group	NAICS Industry	National Industry
111 Crop Production	**1111** Oilseed & grain farming	**11111** Soybean farming	**111110** Soybean farming
		11112 Oilseed (ex-soybean) farming	**111120** Oilseed (ex-soybean) farming
		11113 Dry pea & bean farming	**111130** Dry pea & bean farming
		11114 Wheat farming	**111140** Wheat farming
		11115 Corn farming	**111150** Corn farming
		11116 Rice farming	**111160** Rice farming
		11119 Other grain farming	**111191** Oilseed & grain combination farming
			111199 All other grain farming
	1112 Vegetable & melon farming	**11121** Vegetable & melon farming	**111211** Potato farming
			111219 Other vegetable (ex-potato) & melon farming
	1113 Fruit & tree nut farming	**11131** Orange groves	**111310** Orange groves
		11132 Citrus (ex-orange) groves	**111320** Citrus (ex-orange) groves
		11133 Non-citrus fruit & tree nut farming	**111331** Apple orchards
			111332 Grape vineyards
			111333 Strawberry farming
			111334 Berry (ex-strawberry) farming
			111335 Tree nut farming
			111336 Fruit & tree nut combination farming
			111339 Other non-citrus fruit farming

North American Industry Classification System (NAICS)

Sub-Sector	Industry Group	NAICS Industry	National Industry
	1114 Green-house, nursery, & floriculture production	**11141** Food crops grown under cover	**111411** Mushroom production
			111419 Other food crops grown under cover
		11142 Nursery & floriculture production	**111421** Nursery & tree production
			111422 Floriculture production
	1119 Other crop farming	**11191** Tobacco farming	**111910** Tobacco farming
		11192 Cotton farming	**111920** Cotton farming
		11193 Sugarcane framing	**111930** Sugarcane framing
		11194 Hay farming	**111940** Hay farming
		11199 All other crop farming	**111991** Sugar beet farming
			111992 Peanut farming
			111998 All other miscellaneous crop farming
112 Animal Production & Aquaculture	**1121** Cattle ranching & farming	**11211** Beef cattle ranching & farming, including feedlots	**112111** Beef cattle ranching & farming
			112112 Cattle feedlots
			112120 Dairy cattle & milk production
		11212 Dairy cattle & milk production	**11213** Dual-purpose cattle ranching & farming
		11213 Dual-purpose cattle ranching & farming	**112130** Dual-purpose cattle ranching & farming
	1122 Hog & pig farming	**11221** Hog & pig farming	**112210** Hog & pig farming
112 Animal Production & Aquaculture	**1123** Poultry & egg production	**11231** Chicken egg production	**112310** Chicken egg production
		11232 Broilers & other chicken meat production	**112320** Broilers & other chicken meat production
		11233 Turkey production	**112330** Turkey production
		11234 Poultry hatcheries	**112340** Poultry hatcheries
		11239 Other poultry production	**112390** Other poultry production
	1124 Sheep & goat farming	**11241** Sheep farming	**112410** Sheep farming
		11242 Goat farming	**112420** Goat farming

North American Industry Classification System (NAICS)

Sub-Sector	Industry Group	NAICS Industry	National Industry
	1125 Aquaculture	**11251** Aquaculture	**112511** Finfish farming & fish hatcheries
			112512 Shellfish farming
			112519 Other aquaculture
	1129 Other animal production	**11291** Apiculture	**112910** Apiculture
		11292 Horses & other equine production	**112920** Horses & other equine production
		11293 Fur-bearing animal & rabbit production	**112930** Fur-bearing animal & rabbit production
		11299 All other animal production	**112990** All Other animal production
113 Forestry & Logging	**1131** Timber tract operations	**11311** Timber tract operations	**113110** Timber tract operations
	1132 Forest nurseries & gathering of forest products	**11321** Forest nurseries & gathering of forest products	**113210** Forest nurseries & gathering of forest products
	1133 Logging	**11331** Logging	**113310** Logging
114 Fishing, Hunting & Trapping	**1141** Fishing	**11411** Fishing	**114111** Finfish fishing
			114112 Shellfish fishing
			114119 Other marine fishing
	1142 Hunting & trapping	**11421** Hunting & trapping	**114210** Hunting & trapping
115 Support Activities for Agriculture & Forestry	**1151** Support activities for crop production	**11511** Support activities for crop production	**115111** Cotton ginning
			115112 Soil preparation, planting & cultivating
			115113 Crop harvesting, primarily by machine
			115114 Postharvest crop activities (ex-cotton ginning)
			115115 Farm labour contractors & crew leaders
			115116 Farm management services
	1152 Support activities for animal production	**11521** Support activities for animal production	**115210** Support activities for animal production

North American Industry Classification System (NAICS)

Sub-Sector	Industry Group	NAICS Industry	National Industry
	1153 Support activities for forestry	11531 Support activities for forestry	115310 Support activities for forestry

21 – Mining, Quarrying & Oil & Gas Extraction

Sub-Sector	Industry Group	NAICS Industry	National Industry
211 Oil & Gas Extraction	2111 Oil & gas extraction	21111 Oil & gas extraction	211111 Crude petroleum & natural gas extraction
			211112 Natural gas liquid extraction
212 Mining (ex-Oil & Gas)	2121 Coal mining	21211 Coal mining	212111 Bituminous coal & lignite surface mining
			212112 Bituminous coal underground mining
			212113 Anthracite mining
		21221 Iron ore mining	212210 Iron ore mining
	2122 Metal ore Mining	21222 Gold ore & silver ore mining	212221 Gold ore mining
			212222 Silver ore mining
		21223 Copper, nickel, lead & zinc mining	212231 Lead ore & zinc ore mining
			212234 Copper ore & nickel ore mining
		21229 Other metal ore mining	212291 Uranium-radium-vanadium ore mining
			212299 All other metal ore mining
	2123 Non-metallic mineral mining and quarrying	21231 Stone mining and quarrying	212311 Dimension stone mining & quarrying
			212312 Crushed & broken limestone mining & quarrying
			212313 Crushed & broken granite mining & quarrying
			212319 Other crushed & broken stone mining & quarrying
		21232 Sand & gravel, clay, & ceramic & refractory minerals mining & quarrying	212321 Construction sand & gravel mining
			212322 Industrial sand & mining

North American Industry Classification System (NAICS)

Sub-Sector	Industry Group	NAICS Industry	National Industry
			212324 Kaolin & ball clay mining
			212325 Clay & ceramic & refractory minerals mining
		21239 Other non-metallic mineral mining & quarrying	**212391** Potash, soda, & borate mineral mining
			212392 Phosphate rock mining
			212393 Other chemical & fertilizer mineral mining
			212399 All other non-metallic mineral mining
213 Support Activities for Mining	**2131** Support activities for mining	**21311** Support activities for mining	**213111** Drilling oil & gas wells
			213112 Support activities for oil & gas operations
			213113 Support activities for coal mining
			213114 Support activities for metal mining
			213115 Support activities for non-metallic minerals (ex-fuels) mining

22 – Utilities

Sub-Sector	Industry Group	NAICS Industry	National Industry
221 Utilities	**2211** Electric power generation, transmission & distribution	**22111** Electric power generation	**221111** Hydroelectric power generation
			221112 Fossil fuel electric power generation
			221113 Nuclear electric power generation
			221114 Solar electric power generation
			221115 Wind electric power generation
			221116 Geothermal electric power generation
			221117 Biomass electric power generation

North American Industry Classification System (NAICS)

Sub-Sector	Industry Group	NAICS Industry	National Industry
			221118 Other electric power generation
		22112 Electric power transmission, control & distribution	**221121** Electric bulk power transmission & control
			221122 Electric power distribution
	2212 Natural gas distribution	**22121** Natural gas distribution	**221210** Natural gas distribution
	2213 Water, sewage & other systems	**22131** Water, sewage & other systems	**221310** Water, sewage & other systems
		22132 Sewage treatment facilities	**221320** Sewage treatment facilities
		22133 Steam & air-conditioning supply	**221330** Steam & air-conditioning supply

23 – Construction

Sub-Sector	Industry Group	NAICS Industry	National Industry
236 Construction of Buildings	**2361** Residential building construction	**23611** Residential building construction	**236115** New single-family housing construction (ex-for-sale builders)
			236116 New multifamily housing construction (ex-for-sale builders)
			236117 New housing for-sale builders
			236118 Residential remodelers
	2362 Non-residential building construction	**23621** Industrial building construction	**236210** Industrial building construction
		23622 Commercial & institutional building construction	**236220** Commercial & institutional building construction
237 Heavy & Civil Engineering Construction	**2371** Utility system construction	**23711** Water & sewer line & related structures construction	**237110** Water & sewer line & related structures construction
		23712 Oil & gas pipeline & related structures construction	**237120** Oil & gas pipeline & related structures construction
		23713 Power & communication line & related structures construction	**237130** Power & communication line & related structures construction
	2372 Land subdivision	**23721** Land subdivision	**237210** Land subdivision

North American Industry Classification System (NAICS)

Sub-Sector	Industry Group	NAICS Industry	National Industry
	2373 Highway, street & bridge construction	**23731** Highway, street & bridge construction	**237310** Highway, street & bridge construction
237 Heavy & Civil Engineering Construction	**2379** Other heavy & civil engineering construction	**23799** Other heavy & civil engineering construction	**237990** Other heavy & civil engineering construction
238 Specialty Trade Contractors	**2381** Foundation, structure & building exterior contractors	**23811** Poured concrete foundation & structure contractors	**238110** Poured concrete foundation & structure contractors
		23812 Structural steel & precast concrete contractors	**238120** Structural steel & precast concrete contractors
		23813 Framing contractors	**238130** Framing contractors
		23814 Masonry contractors	**238140** Masonry contractors
		23815 Glass & glazing contractors	**238150** Glass & glazing contractors
		23816 Roofing contractors	**238160** Roofing contractors
		23817 Siding contractors	**238170** Siding contractors
		23819 Other foundation, structure & building exterior contractors	**238190** Other coundation, structure & building exterior contractors
	2382 Building equipment contractors	**23821** Electrical contractors & other wiring installation contractors	**238210** Electrical contractors & other wiring installation contractors
		23822 Plumbing, heating & air-conditioning contractors	**238220** Plumbing, heating & air-conditioning contractors
		23829 Other building equipment contractors	**238290** Other building equipment contractors
	2383 Building finishing contractors	**23831** Drywall & insulation contractors	**238310** Drywall & insulation contractors
		23832 Painting & wall covering contractors	**238320** Painting & wall covering contractors
		23833 Flooring contractors	**238330** Flooring contractors
		23834 Tile & terrazzo contractors	**238340** Tile & terrazzo contractors
		23835 Finish carpentry contractors	**238350** Finish carpentry contractors
		23839 Other building finishing contractors	**238390** Other building finishing contractors
	2389 Other specialty trade contractors	**23891** Site preparation contractors	**238910** Site preparation contractors

North American Industry Classification System (NAICS)

Sub-Sector	Industry Group	NAICS Industry	National Industry
		23899 All other specialty trade contractors	238990 All other specialty trade contractors

31–33 – Manufacturing

Sub-Sector	Industry Group	NAICS Industry	National Industry
311 Food Manufacturing	3111 Animal food manufacturing	31111 Animal food manufacturing	311111 Dog & cat food manufacturing
			311119 Other animal food manufacturing
	3112 Grain & oilseed milling	31121 Flour milling & malt manufacturing	311211 Flour milling
			311212 Rice milling
			311213 Malt manufacturing
		31122 Starch & vegetable fats & oils manufacturing	311221 Wet corn milling
			311224 Soybean & other oilseed processing
			311225 Fats & oils refining & blending
		31123 Breakfast cereal manufacturing	311230 Breakfast cereal manufacturing
	3113 Sugar & confectionery Product manufacturing	31131 Sugar manufacturing	311313 Beet sugar manufacturing
			311314 Cane sugar manufacturing
		31134 Non-chocolate confectionery manufacturing	311340 Non-chocolate confectionery manufacturing
		31135 Chocolate & confectionery manufacturing	311351 Chocolate & confectionery manufacturing from cacao beans
			311352 Confectionery manufacturing from purchased chocolate
	3114 Fruit & vegetable preserving & specialty food manufacturing	31141 Frozen food manufacturing	311411 Frozen fruit, juice & vegetable manufacturing
			311412 Frozen specialty food manufacturing
		31142 Fruit & vegetable canning, pickling & drying	311421 Fruit & vegetable canning

North American Industry Classification System (NAICS)

Sub-Sector	Industry Group	NAICS Industry	National Industry
			311422 Specialty canning
			311423 Dried & dehydrated food manufacturing
	3115 Dairy product manufacturing	**31151** Dairy product (ex-Frozen) manufacturing	**311511** Fluid milk manufacturing
			311512 Creamery butter manufacturing
			311513 Cheese manufacturing
			311514 Dry, condensed & evaporated dairy product manufacturing
		31152 Ice cream & frozen dessert manufacturing	**311520** Ice cream & frozen dessert manufacturing
	3116 Animal slaughtering & processing	**31161** Animal slaughtering & processing	**311611** Animal (ex-poultry) slaughtering
			311612 Meat processed from carcass
			311613 Rendering & meat by-product processing
			311615 Poultry processing
	3117 Seafood product preparation & packaging	**31171** Seafood product preparation & packaging	**311710** Seafood product preparation & packaging
	3118 Bakeries & tortilla manufacturing	**31181** Bread & bakery product manufacturing	**311811** Retail bakeries
			311812 Commercial bakeries
			311813 Frozen cakes, pies & other pastries manufacturing
311 Food Manufacturing	**3118** Bakeries & tortilla manufacturing	**31182** Cookie, cracker & pasta manufacturing	**311821** Cookie & cracker manufacturing
			311824 Dry pasta, dough & flour mixes manufacturing from purchased flour
		31183 Tortilla manufacturing	**311830** Tortilla manufacturing
	3119 Other food manufacturing	**31191** Snack food manufacturing	**311911** Roasted nuts & peanut butter manufacturing
			311919 Other snack food manufacturing

North American Industry Classification System (NAICS)

Sub-Sector	Industry Group	NAICS Industry	National Industry
		31192 Coffee & tea manufacturing	311920 Coffee & tea manufacturing
		31193 Flavoring syrup & concentrate manufacturing	311930 Flavoring syrup & concentrate manufacturing
		31194 Seasoning & dressing manufacturing	311941 Mayonnaise, dressing & other prepared sauce manufacturing
			311942 Spice & extract manufacturing
		31199 All other food manufacturing	311991 Perishable prepared food manufacturing
			311999 All other miscellaneous food manufacturing
312 Beverage & Tobacco Product Manufacturing	3121 Beverage manufacturing	31211 Soft drink & ice manufacturing	312111 Soft drink manufacturing
			312112 Bottled water manufacturing
			312113 Ice manufacturing
		31212 Breweries	312120 Breweries
		31213 Wineries	312130 Wineries
		31214 Distilleries	312140 Distilleries
	3122 Tobacco manufacturing	31223 Tobacco manufacturing	312230 Tobacco manufacturing
313 Textile Mills	3131 Fibre, yarn & thread mills	31311 Fibre, yarn & thread mills	313110 Fibre, yarn & thread mills
	3132 Fabric mills	31321 Broadwoven fabric mills	313210 Broadwoven fabric mills
		31322 Narrow fabric mills & schiffli machine embroidery	313220 Narrow fabric mills & schiffli machine embroidery
		31323 Non-woven fabric mills	313230 Non-woven fabric mills
		31324 Knit fabric mills	313240 Knit fabric mills
	3133 Textile & fabric finishing & fabric coating mills	31331 Textile & fabric finishing mills	313310 Textile & fabric finishing mills
		31332 Fabric coating mills	313320 Fabric coating mills
314 Textile Product Mills	3141 Textile furnishings mills	31411 Carpet & rug mills	314110 Carpet & rug mills
		31412 Curtain & linen mills	314120 Curtain & linen mills
	3149 Other textile product mills	31491 Textile bag & canvas mills	314910 Textile bag & canvas mills

North American Industry Classification System (NAICS)

Sub-Sector	Industry Group	NAICS Industry	National Industry
		31499 All other textile product mills	**314994** Rope, cordage, twine, tire cord & tire fabric mills
			314999 All other miscellaneous textile product mills
315 Apparel Manufacturing	**3151** Apparel knitting mills	**31511** Hosiery & sock mills	**315110** Hosiery & sock mills
		31519 Other apparel knitting mills	**315190** Other apparel knitting mills
	3152 Cut & sew apparel manufacturing	**31521** Cut & sew apparel contractors	**315120** Cut & sew apparel contractors
		31522 Men's & boys' cut & sew apparel manufacturing	**315220** Men's & boys' cut & sew apparel manufacturing
		31524 Women's, girls', & infants' cut & sew apparel manufacturing	**315240** Women's, girls', & infants' cut & sew apparel manufacturing
		31528 Other cut & sew apparel manufacturing	**315280** Other cut & sew apparel manufacturing
	3159 Apparel accessories & other apparel manufacturing	**31599** Apparel accessories & other apparel manufacturing	**315990** Apparel accessories & other apparel manufacturing
316 Leather & Allied Product Manufacturing	**3161** Leather & hide tanning & finishing	**31611** Leather & hide tanning & finishing	**316110** Leather & hide tanning & finishing
	3162 Footwear manufacturing	**31621** Footwear manufacturing	**316210** Footwear manufacturing
	3169 Other leather & allied product manufacturing	**31699** Other leather & allied product manufacturing	**316992** Women's handbag & purse manufacturing
			316998 All Other leather good & allied product manufacturing
321 Wood Product Manufacturing	**3211** Sawmills & wood preservation	**32111** Sawmills & wood preservation	**321113** Sawmills
			321114 Wood preservation
	3212 Veneer, plywood, & engineered wood product manufacturing	**32121** Veneer, plywood, & engineered wood product manufacturing	**321211** Hardwood veneer & plywood manufacturing
			321212 Softwood veneer & plywood manufacturing
			321213 Engineered wood member (ex-truss) manufacturing

North American Industry Classification System (NAICS)

Sub-Sector	Industry Group	NAICS Industry	National Industry
			321214 Truss manufacturing
			321219 Reconstituted wood product manufacturing
	3219 Other wood product manufacturing	**32191** Millwork	**321911** Wood window & door manufacturing
			321912 Cut stock, re-sawing lumber & planning
			321918 Other millwork (including flooring)
		32192 Wood container & pallet manufacturing	**321920** Wood container & pallet manufacturing
		32199 All other wood product manufacturing	**321991** Manufactured home (mobile home) manufacturing
			321992 Prefabricated wood building manufacturing
			321999 All other miscellaneous wood product manufacturing
322 Paper Manufacturing	**3221** Pulp, paper & paperboard mills	**32211** Pulp mills	**322110** Pulp mills
		32212 Paper mills	**322121** Paper (ex-newsprint) mills
			322122 Newsprint mills
		32213 Paperboard mills	**322130** Paperboard mills
322 Paper Manufacturing	**3222** Converted paper product manufacturing	**32221** Paperboard container manufacturing	**322211** Corrugated & solid fibre box manufacturing
			322212 Folding paperboard box manufacturing
			322219 Other paperboard container manufacturing
		32222 Paper bag & coated & treated paper manufacturing	**322220** Paper bag & coated & treated paper manufacturing
		32223 Stationery product manufacturing	**322230** Stationery product manufacturing
		32229 Other converted paper product manufacturing`	**322291** Sanitary paper product manufacturing
			322299 All other converted paper product manufacturing
323 Printing & Related Support Activities	**3231** Printing & related support activities	**32311** Printing	**323111** Commercial printing (ex-screen & books)

North American Industry Classification System (NAICS)

Sub-Sector	Industry Group	NAICS Industry	National Industry
			323113 Commercial screen printing
			323117 Books printing
		32312 Support activities for printing	**323120** Support activities for printing
324 Petroleum & Coal Products Manufacturing	**3241** Petroleum & coal products manufacturing	**32411** Petroleum refineries	**324110** Petroleum refineries
		32412 Asphalt paving, roofing, & saturated materials manufacturing	**324121** Asphalt paving mixture & block manufacturing
			324122 Asphalt shingle & coating materials manufacturing
		32419 Other petroleum & coal products manufacturing	**324191** Petroleum lubricating oil & grease manufacturing
			324199 All other petroleum & coal products manufacturing
325 Chemical Manufacturing	**3251** Basic chemical manufacturing	**32511** Petrochemical manufacturing	**325110** Petrochemical manufacturing
		32512 Industrial gas manufacturing	**325120** Industrial gas manufacturing
		32513 Synthetic dye & pigment manufacturing	**325130** Synthetic dye & pigment manufacturing
		32518 Other basic inorganic chemical manufacturing	**325180** Other basic inorganic chemical manufacturing
		32519 Other basic organic chemical manufacturing	**325193** Ethyl alcohol manufacturing
			325194 Cyclic crude, intermediate & gum & wood chemical manufacturing
			325199 All other basic organic chemical manufacturing
	3252 Resin, synthetic rubber & artificial synthetic fibres & filaments manufacturing	**32521** Resin & synthetic rubber manufacturing	**325211** Plastics material & resin manufacturing
			325212 Synthetic rubber manufacturing
		32522 Artificial & synthetic fibres & filaments manufacturing	**325220** Artificial & synthetic fibres & filaments manufacturing

North American Industry Classification System (NAICS)

Sub-Sector	Industry Group	NAICS Industry	National Industry
	3253 Pesticide, fertiliser & other agricultural chemical manufacturing	**32531** Fertiliser manufacturing	**325311** Nitrogenous fertiliser manufacturing
			325312 Phosphatic fertiliser manufacturing
			325314 Fertiliser (mixing only) manufacturing
		32532 Pesticide & other agricultural chemical manufacturing	**325320** Pesticide & other agricultural chemical manufacturing
325 Chemical Manufacturing	**3254** Pharmaceutical & medicine manufacturing	**32541** Pharmaceutical & medicine manufacturing	**325411** Medicinal & botanical manufacturing
			325412 Pharmaceutical preparation manufacturing
			325413 In-vitro diagnostic substance manufacturing
			325414 Biological product (except diagnostic) manufacturing
	3255 Paint, coating & adhesive manufacturing	**32551** Paint & coating manufacturing	**325510** Paint & coating manufacturing
		32552 Adhesive manufacturing	**325520** Adhesive manufacturing
	3256 Soap, cleaning compound & toilet preparation manufacturing	**32561** Soap & cleaning compound manufacturing	**325611** Soap & other detergent manufacturing
			325612 Polish & other sanitation goods manufacturing
			325613 Surface active agent manufacturing
		32562 Toilet preparation manufacturing	**325620** Toilet preparation manufacturing
	3259 Other chemical product & preparation manufacturing	**32591** Printing ink manufacturing	**325910** Printing ink manufacturing
		32592 Explosives manufacturing	**325920** Explosives manufacturing
		32599 All other chemical product & preparation manufacturing	**325991** Custom compounding of purchased resins

North American Industry Classification System (NAICS)

Sub-Sector	Industry Group	NAICS Industry	National Industry
			325992 Photographic film, paper, plate & chemical manufacturing
			325998 All other miscellaneous chemical product & preparation manufacturing
326 Plastics & Rubber Products Manufacturing	3261 Plastics product manufacturing	32611 Plastics packaging materials & unlaminated film & sheet manufacturing	326111 Plastic bag & pouch manufacturing
			326112 Plastic packaging film & sheet (including laminated) manufacturing
			326113 Unlaminated plastic film & sheet (except packaging) manufacturing
		32612 Plastics pipe, Pipe fitting & unlaminated profile shape manufacturing	326121 Unlaminated plastics profile shape manufacturing
			326122 Plastics pipe & pipe fitting manufacturing
		32613 Laminated plastic plate, sheet (ex-packaging) & shape manufacturing	326130 Laminated plastics plate, sheet (ex-packaging) & shape manufacturing
		32614 Polystyrene foam product manufacturing	326140 Polystyrene foam product manufacturing
		32615 Urethane & other foam product (ex-polystyrene) manufacturing	326150 Urethane & other foam product (ex-polystyrene) manufacturing
		32616 Plastics bottle manufacturing	326160 Plastic bottle manufacturing
		32619 Other plastic product manufacturing	326191 Plastic plumbing fixture manufacturing
			326199 All other plastic product manufacturing
326 Plastics & Rubber Products Manufacturing	3262 Rubber product manufacturing	32621 Tire manufacturing	326211 Tire manufacturing (ex-retreading)
			326212 Tire retreading
		32622 Rubber & plastics hoses & belting manufacturing	326220 Rubber & plastic hoses & belting manufacturing
		32629 Other rubber product manufacturing	326291 Rubber product manufacturing for mechanical use
			326299 All other rubber product manufacturing

North American Industry Classification System (NAICS)

Sub-Sector	Industry Group	NAICS Industry	National Industry
327 Non-metallic Mineral Product Manufacturing	**3271** Clay product & refractory manufacturing	**32711** Pottery, ceramics & plumbing fixture manufacturing	**327110** Pottery, ceramics & plumbing fixture manufacturing
		32712 Clay building material & refractories manufacturing	**327120** Clay building material & refractories manufacturing
	3272 Glass & glass product manufacturing	**32721** Glass & glass product manufacturing	**327211** Flat glass manufacturing
			327212 Other pressed & blown glass & glassware manufacturing
			327213 Glass container manufacturing
			327215 Glass product manufacturing made of purchased glass
	3273 Cement & concrete product manufacturing	**32731** Cement manufacturing	**327310** Cement manufacturing
		32732 Ready-mix concrete manufacturing	**327320** Ready-mix concrete manufacturing
		32733 Concrete pipe, brick & block manufacturing	**327331** Concrete block & brick manufacturing
			327332 Concrete pipe manufacturing
		32739 Other concrete product manufacturing	**327390** Other concrete product manufacturing
	3274 Lime & gypsum product manufacturing	**32741** Lime manufacturing	**327410** Lime manufacturing
		32742 Gypsum product manufacturing	**327420** Gypsum product manufacturing
	3279 Other non-metallic mineral product manufacturing	**32791** Abrasive product manufacturing	**327910** Abrasive product manufacturing
		32799 All other non-metallic mineral product manufacturing	**327991** Cut stone & stone product manufacturing
			327992 Ground or treated mineral & earth manufacturing
			327993 Mineral wool manufacturing
			327999 All other miscellaneous non-metallic mineral product manufacturing

North American Industry Classification System (NAICS)

Sub-Sector	Industry Group	NAICS Industry	National Industry
331 Primary Metal Manufacturing	**3311** Iron & steel mills & ferroalloy manufacturing	**33111** Iron & steel mills & ferroalloy manufacturing	**331110** Iron & steel mills & ferroalloy manufacturing
	3312 Steel product manufacturing from purchased steel	**33121** Iron & steel pipe & tube manufacturing from purchased steel	**331210** Iron & steel pipe & tube manufacturing from purchased steel
		33122 Rolling & drawing of purchased steel	**331221** Rolled steel shape manufacturing
			331222 Steel wire drawing
331 Primary Metal Manufacturing	**3313** Alumina & aluminium production & processing	**33131** Alumina & aluminium production & processing	**331313** Alumina refining & primary aluminium production
			331314 Secondary smelting & alloying of aluminium
			331315 Aluminium sheet, plate & foil manufacturing
			331318 Other aluminium rolling, drawing & extruding
	3314 Non-ferrous metal ex-aluminium production & processing	**33141** Non-ferrous metal ex-aluminium smelting & refining	**331410** Non-ferrous metal ex-aluminium smelting & refining
		33142 Copper rolling, drawing, extruding & alloying	**331420** Copper rolling, drawing, extruding & alloying
		33149 Non-ferrous metal ex-copper & aluminium rolling, drawing, extruding & alloying	**331491** Non-ferrous metal ex-copper & aluminium rolling, drawing & extruding
			331492 Secondary smelting, refining & alloying of non-ferrous metal ex-copper & aluminium
	3315 Foundries	**33151** Ferrous metal foundries	**331511** Iron foundries
			331512 Steel investment foundries
			331513 Steel foundries ex-investment
		33152 Non-ferrous metal foundries	**331523** Non-ferrous metal die-casting foundries
			331524 Aluminium foundries ex-die-casting foundries
			331529 Other non-ferrous metal foundries ex-die-casting

North American Industry Classification System (NAICS)

Sub-Sector	Industry Group	NAICS Industry	National Industry
332 Fabricated Metal Product Manufacturing	**3321** Forging & stamping	**33211** Forging & stamping	**332111** Iron & steel forging
			332112 Non-ferrous forging
			332114 Custom roll forging
			332117 Powder metallurgy part manufacturing
			332119 Metal crown, closure & other metal stamping ex-automotive
	3322 Cutlery & handtool manufacturing	**33221** Cutlery & handtool manufacturing	**332215** Metal kitchen cookware, utensil, cutlery & flatware ex-precious manufacturing
			332216 Saw blade & handtool manufacturing
	3323 Architectural & structural metals manufacturing	**33231** Plate work & fabricated structural products manufacturing	**332311** Prefabricated metal building & component manufacturing
			332312 Fabricated structural metal manufacturing
			332313 Plate work manufacturing
		33232 Ornamental & architectural metal products manufacturing	**332321** Metal window & door manufacturing
			332322 Sheet metal work manufacturing
			332323 Ornamental & architectural metal work manufacturing
332 Fabricated Metal Product Manufacturing	**3324** Boiler, tank & shipping container manufacturing	**33241** Power boiler & heat exchanger manufacturing	**332410** Power boiler & heat exchanger manufacturing
		33242 Metal tank (heavy gauge) manufacturing	**332420** Metal tank (heavy gauge) manufacturing
		33243 Metal can, box & other metal container (light gauge) manufacturing	**332431** Metal can manufacturing
			332439 Other metal container manufacturing
	3325 Hardware manufacturing	**33251** Hardware manufacturing	**332510** Hardware manufacturing
	3326 Spring & wire product manufacturing	**33261** Spring & wire product manufacturing	**332613** Spring manufacturing

North American Industry Classification System (NAICS)

Sub-Sector	Industry Group	NAICS Industry	National Industry
			332618 Other fabricated wire product manufacturing
	3327 Machine shops, turned product, screw, nut & bolt manufacturing	**33271** Machine shops	**332710** Machine shops
		33272 Turned product, screw, nut & bolt manufacturing	**332721** Precision turned product manufacturing
			332722 Bolt, nut, screw, rivet & washer manufacturing
	3328 Coating, engraving, heat treating & allied activities	**33281** Coating, engraving, heat treating & allied activities	**332811** Metal heat turning
			332812 Metal coating, engraving, ex-jewellery & silverware & allied services to manufacturers
			332813 Electroplating, plating, polishing, anodising & colouring
	3329 Other fabricated metal product manufacturing	**33291** Metal valve manufacturing	**332911** Industrial valve manufacturing
			332912 Fluid power valve & hose fitting manufacturing
			332913 Plumbing fixture fitting & trim manufacturing
			332919 Other metal valve & pipe fitting manufacturing
		33299 All other fabricated metal product manufacturing	**332991** Ball & roller bearing manufacturing
			332992 Small arms ammunition manufacturing
			332993 Ammunition ex-small arms manufacturing
			332994 Small arms, ordnance & ordnance accessories manufacturing
			332996 Fabricated pipe & pipe fitting manufacturing
			332999 All other miscellaneous fabricated metal product manufacturing

North American Industry Classification System (NAICS)

Sub-Sector	Industry Group	NAICS Industry	National Industry
333 Machinery Manufacturing	**3331** Agriculture, construction & mining machinery manufacturing	**33311** Agricultural implement manufacturing	**333111** Farm machinery & equipment manufacturing
			333112 Lawn & garden tractor & home lawn & garden equipment manufacturing
		33312 Construction machinery manufacturing	**333120** Construction machinery manufacturing
		33313 Mining & oil & gas field machinery manufacturing	**333131** Mining machinery & equipment manufacturing
			333132 Oil & gas field machinery & equipment manufacturing
333 Machinery Manufacturing	**3332** Industrial machinery manufacturing	**33324** Industrial machinery manufacturing	**333241** Food product machinery manufacturing
			333242 Semiconductor machinery manufacturing
			333243 Sawmill, woodworking & paper machinery manufacturing
			333244 Printing machinery & equipment manufacturing
			333249 Other industrial machinery manufacturing
	3333 Commercial & service industry machinery manufacturing	**33331** Commercial & service industry machinery manufacturing	**333314** Optical instrument & lens manufacturing
			333316 Photographic & photocopying equipment manufacturing
			333318 Other commercial & service industry machinery manufacturing
	3334 Ventilation, heating, air-conditioning & commercial refrigeration equipment manufacturing	**33341** Ventilation, heating, air-conditioning & commercial refrigeration equipment manufacturing	**333413** Industrial & commercial fan & blower & air purification equipment manufacturing
			333414 Heating equipment ex-warm air furnaces manufacturing

North American Industry Classification System (NAICS)

Sub-Sector	Industry Group	NAICS Industry	National Industry
			333415 Air conditioning & warm air heating equipment & commercial & industrial refrigeration equipment manufacturing
	3335 Metalworking machinery manufacturing	**33351** Metalworking machinery manufacturing	**333511** Industrial mold manufacturing
			333514 Special die & tool, die set, jig & fixture manufacturing
			333515 Cutting tool & machine tool accessory manufacturing
			333517 Machine tool manufacturing
			333519 Rolling mill & other metalworking machinery manufacturing
	3336 Engine, turbine & power transmission equipment manufacturing	**33361** Engine, turbine & power transmission equipment manufacturing	**333611** Turbine & turbine generator set units manufacturing
			333612 Speed changer, industrial high-speed drive & gear manufacturing
			333613 Mechanical power transmission equipment manufacturing
			333618 Other engine equipment manufacturing
	3339 Other general purpose machinery manufacturing	**33391** Pump & compressor manufacturing	**333911** Pump & pumping equipment manufacturing
			333912 Air & gas compressor manufacturing
			333913 Measuring & dispensing pump manufacturing
		33392 Material handling equipment manufacturing	**333921** Elevator & moving stairway manufacturing
			333922 Conveyor & conveying equipment manufacturing
333 Machinery Manufacturing	**3339** Other general purpose machinery manufacturing	**33392** Material handling equipment manufacturing	**333923** Overhead traveling crane, hoist & monorail system manufacturing

North American Industry Classification System (NAICS)

Sub-Sector	Industry Group	NAICS Industry	National Industry
			333924 Industrial truck, tractor, trailer & stacker machinery manufacturing
		33399 All other general purpose machinery manufacturing	**333991** Power-driven handtool manufacturing
			333992 Welding & soldering equipment manufacturing
			333993 Packaging machinery manufacturing
			333994 Industrial process furnace & oven manufacturing
			333995 Fluid power cylinder & actuator manufacturing
			333996 Fluid power pump & motor manufacturing
			333999 All other miscellaneous general purpose machinery manufacturing
334 Computer & Electronic Product Manufacturing	**3341** Computer & peripheral equipment manufacturing	**33411** Computer & peripheral equipment manufacturing	**334111** Electronic computer manufacturing
			334112 Computer storage device manufacturing
			334118 Computer terminal & other computer peripheral equipment manufacturing
	3342 Communications equipment manufacturing	**33421** Telephone apparatus manufacturing	**334210** Telephone apparatus manufacturing
		33422 Radio & television broadcasting & wireless communications equipment manufacturing	**334220** Radio & television broadcasting & wireless communications equipment manufacturing
		33429 Other communications equipment manufacturing	**334290** Other communications equipment manufacturing
	3343 Audio & video equipment manufacturing	**33431** Audio & video equipment manufacturing	**334310** Audio & video equipment manufacturing
	3344 Semiconductor & Other electronic component manufacturing	**33441** Semiconductor & other electronic component manufacturing	**334412** Bare printed circuit board manufacturing

North American Industry Classification System (NAICS)

Sub-Sector	Industry Group	NAICS Industry	National Industry
			334413 Semiconductor & related device manufacturing
			334416 Capacitor, resistor, coil, transformer & other inductor manufacturing
			334417 Electronic connector manufacturing
			334418 Printed circuit assembly (electronic assembly) manufacturing
			334419 Other electronic component manufacturing
	3345 Navigational, measuring, electromedical & control instruments manufacturing	**33451** Navigational, measuring, electromedical & control instruments manufacturing	**334510** Electromedical & electrotherapeutic apparatus manufacturing
			334511 Search, detection, navigation, guidance, aeronautical & nautical system & instrument manufacturing
			334512 Automatic environmental control manufacturing for residential, commercial & appliance use
334 Computer & Electronic Product Manufacturing	**3345** Navigational, measuring, electromedical & control instruments manufacturing	**33451** Navigational, measuring, electromedical & control instruments manufacturing	**334513** Instruments & related products manufacturing for measuring, Displaying & controlling industrial process variables
			334514 Totalising fluid meter & counting device manufacturing
			334515 Instrument manufacturing for measuring & testing electricity & electrical signals
			334516 Analytical laboratory instrument manufacturing
			334517 Irradiation apparatus manufacturing
			334519 Other measuring & controlling device manufacturing
	3346 Manufacturing & reproducing magnetic & optical media	**33461** Manufacturing & reproducing magnetic & optical media	**334613** Blank magnetic & optical recording media manufacturing

North American Industry Classification System (NAICS)

Sub-Sector	Industry Group	NAICS Industry	National Industry
			334614 Software & other pre-recorded compact disc, Tape & record reproducing
335 Electrical Equipment, Appliance & Component Manufacturing	**3351** Electric lighting equipment manufacturing	**33511** Electric lamp bulb & part manufacturing	**335110** Electric lamp bulb & part manufacturing
		33512 Lighting fixture manufacturing	**335121** Residential electric lighting fixture manufacturing
			335122 Commercial, industrial & institutional electric lighting fixture manufacturing
			335129 Other lighting equipment manufacturing
	3352 Household appliance manufacturing	**33521** Small electrical appliance manufacturing	**335210** Small electrical appliance manufacturing
		33522 Major appliance manufacturing	**335221** Household cooking appliance manufacturing
			335222 Household refrigerator & home freezer manufacturing
			335224 Household laundry equipment manufacturing
			335228 Other major household appliance manufacturing
	3353 Electrical equipment manufacturing	**33531** Electrical equipment manufacturing	**335311** Power, distribution & specialty transformer manufacturing
			335312 Motor & generator manufacturing
			335313 Switch gear & switchboard apparatus manufacturing
			335314 Relay & industrial control manufacturing
	3359 Other electrical equipment & component manufacturing	**33591** Battery manufacturing	**335911** Storage battery manufacturing
			335912 Primary battery manufacturing
		33592 Communication & energy wire & cable manufacturing	**335921** Fiber optic cable manufacturing
			335929 Other communication & energy wire manufacturing

North American Industry Classification System (NAICS)

Sub-Sector	Industry Group	NAICS Industry	National Industry
335 Electrical Equipment, Appliance & Component Manufacturing	**3359** Other electrical equipment & component manufacturing	**33593** Wiring device manufacturing	**335931** Current-carrying wiring device manufacturing
			335932 Noncurrent-carrying wiring device manufacturing
		33599 All other electrical equipment & component manufacturing	**335991** Carbon & graphite product manufacturing
			335999 All other miscellaneous electrical equipment & component manufacturing
336 Transportation Equipment Manufacturing	**3361** Motor vehicle manufacturing	**33611** Automobile & light duty motor vehicle manufacturing	**336111** Automobile manufacturing
			336112 Light truck & utility vehicle manufacturing
		33612 Heavy duty truck manufacturing	**336120** Heavy duty truck manufacturing
	3362 Motor vehicle body & trailer manufacturing	**33621** Motor vehicle body & trailer manufacturing	**336211** Motor vehicle body manufacturing
			336212 Truck trailer manufacturing
			336213 Motor home manufacturing
			336214 Travel trailer & camper manufacturing
	3363 Motor vehicle parts manufacturing	**33631** Motor vehicle gasoline engine & engine parts manufacturing	**336310** Motor vehicle gasoline engine & engine parts manufacturing
		33632 Motor vehicle electrical & electronic equipment manufacturing	**336320** Motor vehicle electrical & electronic equipment manufacturing
		33633 Motor vehicle steering & suspension components ex-spring manufacturing	**336330** Motor vehicle steering & suspension components excl spring manufacturing
		33634 Motor vehicle brake system manufacturing	**336340** Motor vehicle brake system manufacturing
		33635 Motor vehicle transmission & power train parts manufacturing	**336350** Motor vehicle Transmission & power train parts manufacturing
		33636 Motor vehicle seating & interior trim manufacturing	**336360** Motor vehicle seating & interior trim manufacturing

North American Industry Classification System (NAICS)

Sub-Sector	Industry Group	NAICS Industry	National Industry
		33637 Motor Vehicle Metal Stamping	**336370** Motor vehicle metal stamping
		33639 Other motor vehicle parts manufacturing	**336390** Other motor vehicle parts manufacturing
	3364 Aerospace product & parts Manufacturing	**33641** Aerospace product & parts manufacturing	**336411** Aircraft manufacturing
			336412 Aircraft engine & engine parts manufacturing
			336413 Other aircraft parts & auxiliary equipment manufacturing
			336414 Guided missile & space vehicle manufacturing
			336415 Guided missile & space vehicle propulsion unit & propulsion unit parts manufacturing
			336419 Other guided missile & space vehicle parts & auxiliary equipment manufacturing
	3365 Other guided missile & space vehicle parts & auxiliary equipment manufacturing	**33651** Other guided missile & space vehicle parts & auxiliary equipment manufacturing	**336510** Other guided missile & space vehicle parts & auxiliary equipment manufacturing
336 Transportation Equipment Manufacturing	**3366** Ship & boat building	**33661** Ship & boat building	**336611** Ship building & repairing
			336612 Boat building
	3369 Other transportation equipment manufacturing	**33699** Other transportation equipment manufacturing	**336991** Motorcycle, bicycle & parts manufacturing
			336992 Military armored vehicle, tank & tank component manufacturing
			336999 All other transportation equipment manufacturing
337 Furniture & Related Product Manufacturing	**3371** Household & institutional furniture & kitchen cabinet manufacturing	**33711** Wood kitchen cabinet & countertop manufacturing	**337110** Wood kitchen cabinet & countertop manufacturing
		33712 Household & institutional furniture manufacturing	**337121** Upholstered household furniture manufacturing

North American Industry Classification System (NAICS)

Sub-Sector	Industry Group	NAICS Industry	National Industry
			337122 Non-upholstered wood household furniture manufacturing
			337124 Metal household furniture manufacturing
			337125 Household furniture excl wood & metal manufacturing
			337127 Institutional furniture manufacturing
	3372 Office furniture (including fixtures) manufacturing	**33721** Office furniture (including fixtures) manufacturing	**337211** Wood office furniture
			337212 Custom architectural woodwork & millwork
			337214 Office furniture excl wood manufacturing
			337215 Showcase, partition, shelving & lockers
	3379 Other furniture related product manufacturing	**33791** Mattress manufacturing	**337910** Mattress manufacturing
		33792 Blind & shade manufacturing	**337920** Blind & shade manufacturing
339 Miscellaneous Manufacturing	**3391** Medical equipment & supplies manufacturing	**33911** Medical equipment & supplies manufacturing	**339112** Surgical & medical instrument manufacturing
			339113 Surgical appliance & supplies manufacturing
			339114 Dental equipment & supplies manufacturing
			339115 Ophthalmic goods manufacturing
			339116 Dental laboratories
	3399 Other miscellaneous manufacturing	**33991** Jewelry & silverware manufacturing	**339910** Jewelry & silverware manufacturing
		33992 Sporting & athletic goods manufacturing	**339920** Sporting & athletic goods manufacturing
		33993 Doll, toy & game manufacturing	**339930** Doll, toy & game manufacturing
		33994 Office supplies excl paper manufacturing	**339940** Office supplies excl paper manufacturing

North American Industry Classification System (NAICS)

Sub-Sector	Industry Group	NAICS Industry	National Industry
		33995 Sign manufacturing	339950 Sign manufacturing
		33999 All other miscellaneous manufacturing	339991 Gasket, packing & sealing device manufacturing
			339992 Musical instrument manufacturing
			339993 Fastener, button, needle & pin manufacturing
			339994 Broom, brush & mop manufacturing
			339995 Burial casket manufacturing
			339999 All other miscellaneous manufacturing

42 – Wholesale Trade

Sub-Sector	Industry Group	NAICS Industry	National Industry
423 Merchant Wholesalers, Durable Goods	4231 Motor vehicle & motor vehicle parts & supplies merchant wholesalers	42311 Automobile & other motor vehicle merchant wholesalers	423110 Automobile & other motor vehicle merchant wholesalers
		42312 Motor vehicle supplies & New parts merchant wholesalers	423120 Motor vehicle supplies & New parts merchant wholesalers
		42313 Tire & tube merchant wholesalers	423130 Tire & tube merchant wholesalers
		42314 Motor vehicle parts (used) merchant wholesalers	423140 Motor vehicle parts (used) merchant wholesalers
	4232 Furniture & home furnishing merchant wholesalers	42321 Furniture merchant wholesalers	423210 Furniture merchant wholesalers
		42322 Home furnishing merchant wholesalers	423220 Home furnishing merchant wholesalers
	4233 Lumber & other construction materials merchant wholesalers	42331 Lumber, plywood, millwork & wood panel merchant wholesalers	423310 Lumber, plywood, millwork & wood panel merchant wholesalers
		42332 Brick, stone & related construction material merchant wholesalers	423320 Brick, stone & related construction material merchant wholesalers
		42333 Roofing, siding & insulation material merchant wholesalers	423330 Roofing, siding & insulation material merchant wholesalers

North American Industry Classification System (NAICS)

Sub-Sector	Industry Group	NAICS Industry	National Industry
		42339 Other construction material merchant wholesalers	**423390** Other construction material merchant wholesalers
	4234 Professional & commercial equipment & supplies merchant wholesalers	**42341** Photographic equipment & supplies merchant wholesalers	**423410** Photographic equipment & supplies merchant wholesalers
		42342 Office equipment merchant wholesalers	**423420** Office equipment merchant wholesalers
		42343 Computer & computer peripheral equipment & software merchant wholesalers	**423430** Computer & computer peripheral equipment & Software merchant wholesalers
		42344 Other commercial equipment merchant wholesalers	**423440** Other commercial equipment merchant wholesalers
		42345 Medical, dental & hospital equipment & supplies merchant wholesalers	**423450** Medical, dental & hospital equipment & supplies merchant wholesalers
		42346 Ophthalmic goods merchant wholesalers	**423460** Ophthalmic goods merchant wholesalers
		42349 Other professional equipment & supplies merchant wholesalers	**423490** Other professional equipment & supplies merchant wholesalers
	4235 Metal & mineral excl petroleum merchant wholesalers	**42351** Metal service centres & other metal merchant wholesalers	**423510** Metal service centres & other metal merchant wholesalers
		42352 Coal & other mineral & ore merchant wholesalers	**423520** Coal & other mineral & ore merchant wholesalers
	4236 Household appliances & electrical & electronic goods merchant wholesalers	**42361** Electrical apparatus & equipment, wiring supplies & related equipment merchant wholesalers	**423610** Electrical apparatus & equipment, wiring supplies & related equipment merchant wholesalers
		42362 Household appliances, electric housewares & consumer electronics merchant wholesalers	**423620** Household appliances, electric housewares & consumer electronics merchant wholesalers
		42369 Other electronic parts & equipment merchant wholesalers	**423690** Other electronic parts & equipment merchant wholesalers
	4237 Hardware, & plumbing & heating equipment & supplies merchant wholesalers	**42371** Hardware merchant wholesalers	**423710** Hardware merchant wholesalers

North American Industry Classification System (NAICS)

Sub-Sector	Industry Group	NAICS Industry	National Industry
		42372 Plumbing & heating equipment & supplies (hydronics) merchant wholesalers	**423720** Plumbing & heating equipment & supplies (hydronics) merchant wholesalers
423 Merchant Wholesalers, Durable Goods	**4237** Hardware, & plumbing & heating equipment & supplies merchant wholesalers	**42373** Warm air heating & air conditioning equipment & supplies merchant wholesalers	**423730** Warm air heating & air conditioning equipment & supplies merchant wholesalers
		42374 Refrigeration equipment & supplies merchant wholesalers	**423740** Refrigeration equipment & supplies merchant wholesalers
	4238 Machinery, equipment & supplies merchant wholesalers	**42381** Construction & mining excl oil well machinery & equipment merchant wholesaler	**423810** Construction & mining excl oil well machinery & equipment merchant wholesaler
		42382 Farm & garden machinery & equipment merchant wholesalers	**423820** Farm & garden machinery & equipment merchant wholesalers
		42383 Industrial machinery & equipment merchant wholesalers	**423830** Industrial machinery & equipment merchant wholesalers
		42384 Industrial supplies merchant wholesalers	**423840** Industrial supplies merchant wholesalers
		42385 Service establishment equipment & supplies merchant wholesalers	**423850** Service establishment equipment & supplies merchant wholesalers
		42386 Transportation equipment & supplies excl motor vehicle merchant wholesalers	**423860** Transportation equipment & supplies excl motor vehicle merchant wholesalers
	4239 Miscellaneous durable goods merchant wholesalers	**42391** Sporting & recreational goods & supplies merchant wholesalers	**423910** Sporting & recreational goods & supplies merchant wholesalers
		42392 Toy & hobby goods & supplies merchant wholesalers	**423920** Toy & hobby goods & supplies merchant wholesalers
		42393 Recyclable material merchant wholesalers	**423930** Recyclable material merchant wholesalers
		42394 Jewelry, watch, precious stone & precious metal merchant wholesalers	**423940** Jewelry, watch, precious stone & precious metal merchant wholesalers
		42399 Other miscellaneous durable goods merchant wholesalers	**423990** Other miscellaneous durable goods merchant wholesalers
424 Merchant Wholesalers, Non-durable Goods	**4241** Paper & paper product merchant wholesalers	**42411** Printing & writing paper merchant wholesalers	**424110** Printing & writing paper merchant wholesalers

North American Industry Classification System (NAICS)

Sub-Sector	Industry Group	NAICS Industry	National Industry
		42412 Stationery & office supplies merchant wholesalers	**424120** Stationery & office supplies merchant wholesalers
		42413 Industrial & personal service paper merchant wholesalers	**424130** Industrial & personal service paper merchant wholesalers
	4242 Drugs & druggists Sundries Merchant wholesalers	**42421** Drugs & druggists sundries merchant wholesalers	**424110** Drugs & druggists sundries merchant wholesalers
	4243 Piece goods, notions, & other dry goods merchant wholesalers	**42431** Piece Goods, notions & other dry goods merchant wholesalersc	**424310** Piece Goods, notions & other dry goods merchant wholesalers
		42432 Men's & boys' clothing & furnishings merchant wholesalers	**424320** Men's & boys' clothing & furnishings merchant wholesalers
		42433 Women's, children's, & infants clothing & accessories merchant wholesalers	**424330** Women's, children's, & infants' clothing & accessories merchant wholesalers
		42434 Footwear merchant wholesalers	**424340** Footwear merchant wholesalers
424 Merchant Wholesalers, Non-durable Goods	**4244** Grocery & related product merchant wholesalers	**42441** General line grocery merchant wholesalers	**424410** General line grocery merchant wholesalers
		42442 Packaged frozen food merchant wholesalers	**424420** Packaged frozen food merchant wholesalers
		42443 Dairy product excl dried or canned merchant wholesalers	**424430** Dairy product excl dried or canned merchant wholesalers
		42444 Poultry & poultry product merchant wholesalers	**424440** Poultry & poultry product merchant wholesalers
		42445 Confectionery merchant wholesalers	**424450** Confectionery merchant wholesalers
		42446 Fish & seafood merchant wholesalers	**424460** Fish & seafood merchant wholesalers
		42447 Meat & meat product merchant wholesalers	**424470** Meat & meat product merchant wholesalers
		42448 Fresh fruit & vegetable merchant wholesalers	**424480** Fresh fruit & vegetable merchant wholesalers
		42449 Other grocery & related products merchant wholesalers	**424490** Other grocery & related products merchant wholesalers

North American Industry Classification System (NAICS)

Sub-Sector	Industry Group	NAICS Industry	National Industry
	4245 Farm product raw material merchant wholesalers	**42451** Grain & field bean merchant wholesalers	**424510** Grain & field bean merchant wholesalers
		42452 Livestock merchant wholesalers	**424520** Livestock merchant wholesalers
		42459 Other farm product raw material merchant wholesalers	**424590** Other farm product raw material merchant wholesalers
	4246 Chemical & allied products merchant wholesalers	**42461** Plastics materials & basic forms & shapes merchant wholesalers	**424610** Plastics materials & basic forms & shapes merchant wholesalers
		42469 Other chemical & allied products merchant wholesalers	**424690** Other chemical & allied products merchant wholesalers
	4247 Petroleum & petroleum products merchant wholesalers	**42471** Petroleum bulk stations & terminals	**424710** Petroleum bulk stations & terminals
		42472 Petroleum & petroleum products merchant wholesalers excl bulk stations & terminals	**424720** Petroleum & petroleum products merchant wholesalers excl bulk stations & terminals
	4248 Beer, wine & distilled alcoholic beverage merchant wholesalers	**42481** Beer & ale merchant wholesalers	**424810** Beer & ale merchant wholesalers
		42482 Wine & distilled alcoholic beverage merchant wholesalers	**424820** Wine & distilled alcoholic beverage merchant wholesalers
	4249 Miscellaneous non-durable goods merchant wholesalers	**42491** Farm supplies merchant wholesalers	**424910** Farm supplies merchant wholesalers
		42492 Book, periodical & newspaper merchant wholesalers	**424920** Book, periodical & newspaper merchant wholesalers
		42493 Flower, nursery stock & florists supplies merchant wholesalers	**424930** Flower, nursery stock & florists supplies merchant wholesalers
		42494 Tobacco & tobacco product merchant wholesalers	**424940** Tobacco & tobacco product merchant wholesalers
		42495 Paint, varnish & supplies merchant wholesalers	**424950** Paint, varnish & supplies merchant wholesalers
		42499 Other miscellaneous non-durable goods merchant wholesalers	**424990** Other miscellaneous non-durable goods merchant wholesalers

North American Industry Classification System (NAICS)

Sub-Sector	Industry Group	NAICS Industry	National Industry
425 Wholesale Electronic Markets & Agents & Brokers	**4251** Wholesale electronic markets & agents & brokers	**42511** Business to business electronic markets	**425110** Business to business electronic markets
		42512 Wholesale trade agents & brokers	**425120** Wholesale trade agents & brokers

44–45 – Retail Trade

Sub-Sector	Industry Group	NAICS Industry	National Industry
441 Motor Vehicle & Parts Dealers	**4411** Automobile dealers	**44111** New car dealers	**441110** New car dealers
		44112 Used car dealers	**441120** Used car dealers
	4412 Other motor vehicle dealers	**44121** Recreational vehicle dealers	**441210** Recreational vehicle dealers
		44122 Motorcycle, boat & other motor vehicle dealers	**441222** Boat dealers
			441228 Motorcycle, atv & all other motor vehicle dealers
	4413 Automotive parts, accessories & tire store	**44131** Automotive parts & accessories stores	**441310** Automotive parts & accessories stores
		44132 Tire dealers	**441320** Tire dealers
442 Furniture & Home Furnishings Stores	**4421** Furniture stores	**44211** Furniture stores	**442110** Furniture stores
	4422 Home furnishings stores	**44221** Floor covering stores	**442210** Floor covering stores
		44229 Other home furnishings stores	**442291** Window treatment stores
			442299 All other home furnishings stores
443 Electronics & Appliance Stores	**4431** Electronics & appliance stores	**44314** Electronics & appliance stores	**443141** Household appliance stores
			443142 Electronics stores
444 Building Material & Garden Equipment & Supplies Dealers	**4441** Building Material & supplies dealers	**44411** Home centers	**444110** Home centers
		44412 Paint & wallpaper stores	**444120** Paint & wallpaper stores

North American Industry Classification System (NAICS)

Sub-Sector	Industry Group	NAICS Industry	National Industry
		44413 Hardware stores	**444130** Hardware stores
		44419 Other building material dealers	**444190** Other building material dealers
444 Building Material & Garden Equipment & Supplies Dealers	**4442** Lawn & garden equipment & supplies stores	**44421** Outdoor power equipment stores	**444210** Outdoor power equipment stores
		44422 Nursery, garden center & farm supply stores	**444220** Nursery, garden center & farm supply stores
445 Food & Beverage Stores	**4451** Grocery stores	**44511** Supermarkets & other grocery ex-convenience stores	**445110** Supermarkets & other grocery ex-convenience stores
		44512 Convenience stores	**445120** Convenience stores
	4452 Specialty food stores	**44521** Meat markets	**445210** Meat markets
		44522 Fish & seafood markets	**445220** Fish & seafood markets
		44523 Fruit & vegetable markets	**445230** Fruit & vegetable markets
		44529 Other specialty food stores	**445291** Baked goods stores
			445292 Confectionery & nut stores
			445299 All other specialty food stores
	4453 Beer, wine & liquor stores	**44531** Beer, wine & liquor stores	**445310** Beer, wine & liquor stores
446 Health & Personal Care Stores	**4461** Health & personal care stores	**44611** Pharmacies & Drug Stores	**446110** Pharmacies & drug stores
		44612 Cosmetics, beauty supplies & perfume stores	**446120** Cosmetics, beauty supplies & perfume stores
		44613 Optical goods stores	**446130** Optical goods stores
		44619 Other health & personal care stores	**446191** Food (health) supplement stores
			446199 All other health & personal care stores
447 Gasoline Stations	**4471** Gasoline stations	**44711** Gasoline stations with convenience stores	**447110** Gasoline stations with convenience stores
		44719 Other gasoline stations	**447190** Other gasoline stations
448 Clothing & Clothing Accessories Stores	**4481** Clothing stores	**44811** Men's clothing stores	**448110** Men's clothing stores
		44812 Women's clothing stores	**448120** Women's clothing stores

North American Industry Classification System (NAICS)

Sub-Sector	Industry Group	NAICS Industry	National Industry
		44813 Children's & infants clothing stores	**448130** Children's & infants clothing stores
		44814 Family clothing stores	**448140** Family clothing stores
		44815 Clothing accessories stores	**448150** Clothing accessories stores
		44819 Other clothing stores	**448190** Other clothing stores
	4482 Shoe stores	**44821** Shoe stores	**448210** Shoe stores
	4483 Jewellery, luggage & leather goods stores	**44831** Jewellery stores	**448310** Jewellery stores
		44832 Luggage & leather goods stores	**448320** Luggage & leather goods stores
451 Sporting Goods, Hobby, Musical Instrument & Book Stores	**4511** Sporting goods, hobby & musical instrument stores	**45111** Sporting goods stores	**451110** Sporting goods stores
		45112 Hobby, toy & game stores	**451120** Hobby, toy & game stores
		45113 Sewing, needlework & piece goods stores	**451130** Sewing, needlework & piece goods stores
		45114 Musical instrument & supplies stores	**451140** Musical instrument & supplies stores
	4512 Book stores & news dealers	**45121** Book stores & news dealers	**451211** Book stores
			451212 News dealers & newsstands
452 General Merchandise Stores	**4521** Department stores	**45211** Department stores	**452111** Department stores ex-discount department stores
			452112 Discount department stores
	4529 Other general merchandise stores	**45291** Warehouse clubs & supercenters	**452910** Warehouse clubs & supercenters
		45299 All other general merchandise stores	**452990** All other general merchandise stores
453 Miscellaneous Store Retailers	**4531** Florists	**45311** Florists	**453110** Florists
	4532 Office supplies, stationery & gift stores	**45321** Office supplies & stationery stores	**453210** Office supplies & stationery stores

North American Industry Classification System (NAICS)

Sub-Sector	Industry Group	NAICS Industry	National Industry
		45322 Gift, novelty & souvenir stores	453220 Gift, novelty & souvenir stores
	4533 Used merchandise stores	45331 Used merchandise stores	453310 Used merchandise stores
	4539 Other miscellaneous store retailers	45391 Pet & pet supplies stores	453910 Pet & pet supplies stores
		45392 Art dealers	453920 Art dealers
		45393 Manufactured (mobile) home dealers	453930 Manufactured (mobile) home dealers
		45399 All other miscellaneous Store retailers	453991 Tobacco stores
			453998 All other miscellaneous store retailers excl tobacco stores
454 Non-store Retailers	4541 Electronic shopping & mail order houses	45411 Electronic shopping & mail order houses	454111 Electronic shopping
			454112 Electronic auctions
			454113 Mail Order houses
	4542 Vending machine operators	45421 Vending machine operators	454210 Vending machine operators
	4543 Direct selling establishments	45431 Fuel dealers	454310 Fuel dealers
		45439 Other direct selling establishments	454390 Other direct selling establishments

48–49 – Transportation & Warehousing

Sub-Sector	Industry Group	NAICS Industry	National Industry
481 Air Transportation	4811 Scheduled air transportation	48111 Scheduled air transportation	481111 Scheduled passenger air transportation
			481112 Scheduled freight air transportation
	4812 Non-scheduled air transportation	48121 Non-scheduled Air transportation	481211 Non-scheduled chartered passenger air transportation
			481212 Non-scheduled chartered freight air transportation
			481219 Other non-scheduled air transportation

North American Industry Classification System (NAICS)

Sub-Sector	Industry Group	NAICS Industry	National Industry
482 Rail Transportation	**4821** Rail transportation	**48211** Rail transportation	**482111** Line haul railroads
			482112 Short line railroads
483 Water Transportation	**4831** Deep sea, coastal & great lakes water transportation	**48311** Deep sea, coastal & great lakes water transportation	**483111** Deep sea freight transportation
			483112 Deep sea passenger transportation
			483113 Coastal & great lakes freight transportation
			483114 Coastal & great lakes passenger transportation
	4832 Inland & water transportation	**48321** Inland & water transportation	**483211** Inland & water freight transportation
			483212 Inland & water passenger transportation
484 Truck Transportation	**4841** General freight trucking	**48411** General freight trucking, local	**484110** General freight trucking, local
		48412 General freight trucking, long distance	**484121** General freight trucking, long distance, truckload
			484122 General freight trucking, long distance, less than truckload
	4842 Specialised freight trucking	**48421** Used household & office goods moving	**484210** Used household & office goods moving
		48422 Specialised freight excl used goods trucking, local	**484220** Specialized freight excl used goods trucking, local
		48423 Specialized freight excl used goods trucking, long-distance	**484230** Specialized freight excl used goods trucking, long-distance
485 Transit & Ground Passenger Transportation	**4851** Urban transit systems	**48511** Urban transit systems	**485111** Mixed mode transit systems
			485112 Commuter rail systems
			485113 Bus & other motor vehicle transit systems
			485119 Other urban transit systems
	4852 Inter-urban & rural bus transportation	**48521** Inter-urban & rural bus transportation	**485210** Inter-urban & rural bus transportation

North American Industry Classification System (NAICS)

Sub-Sector	Industry Group	NAICS Industry	National Industry
	4853 Taxi & limousine service	48531 Taxi service	485310 Taxi service
		48532 Limousine service	485320 Limousine service
	4854 School & employee bus transportation	48541 School & employee bus transportation	485410 School & employee bus transportation
	4855 Charter bus industry	48551 Charter bus industry	485510 Charter bus industry
485 Transit & Ground Passenger Transportation	4859 Other transit & ground passenger transportation	48599 Other transit & ground passenger transportation	485991 Special needs transportation
			485999 All other transit & ground passenger transportation
486 Pipeline Transportation	4861 Pipeline transportation of crude oil	48611 Pipeline transportation of crude oil	486110 Pipeline transportation of crude oil
	4862 Pipeline transportation of Natural gas	48621 Pipeline transportation of natural gas	486210 Pipeline transportation of natural gas
	4869 Other pipeline transportation	48691 Pipeline transportation of refined petroleum products	486910 Pipeline transportation of refined petroleum products
		48699 All other pipeline transportation	486990 All other pipeline transportation
487 Scenic & Sightseeing Transportation	4871 Scenic & sightseeing transportation, land	48711 Scenic & sightseeing transportation, land	487110 Scenic & sightseeing transportation, land
	4872 Scenic & sightseeing transportation, water	48721 Scenic & sightseeing transportation, water	487210 Scenic & sightseeing transportation, water
	4879 Scenic & sightseeing transportation, other	48791 Scenic & sightseeing transportation, other	487910 Scenic & sightseeing transportation, other
488 Support Activities for Transportation	4881 Support activities for air transportation	48811 Airport operations	488111 Air traffic control
		48819 Other support activities for Air transportation	488119 Other airport operations
			488190 Other support activities for Air transportation

North American Industry Classification System (NAICS)

Sub-Sector	Industry Group	NAICS Industry	National Industry
	4882 Support activities for rail transportation	**48821** Support activities for Rail transportation	**488210** Support activities for Rail transportation
	4883 Support activities for water transportation	**48831** Port & harbor operations	**488310** Port & harbor operations
		48832 Marine cargo handling	**488320** Marine cargo handling
		48833 Navigational services to shipping	**488330** Navigational services to shipping
		48839 Other support activities for Water transportation	**488390** Other support activities for water transportation
	4884 Support activities for road transportation	**48841** Motor vehicle towing	**488410** Motor vehicle towing
		48849 Other support activities for road transportation	**488490** Other support activities for road transportation
	4885 Freight transportation arrangement	**48851** Freight transportation arrangement	**488510** Freight transportation arrangement
	4889 Other support activities for transportation	**48899** Other support activities for transportation	**488991** Packing & crating
			488999 All other support activities for transportation
491 Postal Service	**4911** Postal service	**49111** Postal service	**491110** Postal service
492 Couriers & Messengers	**4921** Couriers & express delivery services	**49211** Couriers & express delivery services	**492110** Couriers & express delivery services
	4922 Local messengers & local delivery	**49221** Local messengers & local delivery	**492210** Local messengers & local delivery
493 Warehousing & Storage	**4931** Warehousing & storage	**49311** General warehousing & storage	**493110** General warehousing & storage
		49312 Refrigerated warehousing & storage	**493120** Refrigerated warehousing & storage
		49313 Farm product warehousing & storage	**493130** Farm product warehousing & storage
		49319 Other warehousing & storage	**493190** Other warehousing & storage

North American Industry Classification System (NAICS)

51 – Information

Sub-Sector	Industry Group	NAICS Industry	National Industry
511 Publishing Industries excl Internet	**5111** Newspaper, periodical, book & directory publishers	**51111** Newspaper publishers	**511110** Newspaper publishers
		51112 Periodical publishers	**511120** Periodical publishers
		51113 Book publishers	**511130** Book publishers
		51114 Directory & mailing list publishers	**511140** Directory & mailing list publishers
		51119 Other publishers	**511191** Greeting card publishers
			511199 All other publishers
	5112 Software publishers	**51121** Software publishers	**511210** Software publishers
512 Motion picture & Sound recording industries	**5121** Motion picture & video industries	**51211** Motion Picture & video industries	**512110** Motion picture & video industries
		51212 Motion picture & video distribution	**512120** Motion picture & Video distribution
		51213 Motion picture & video exhibition	**512131** Motion picture theaters excl drive-ins
			512132 Drive-in motion picture theaters
		51219 Postproduction services & other motion picture & video industries	**512191** Teleproduction & other post production services
			512199 Other motion picture & video industries
	5122 Sound recording industries	**51221** Record production	**512210** Record production
		51222 Integrated record production/distribution	**512220** Integrated record production/distribution
		51223 Music publishers	**512230** Music publishers
		51224 Sound recording studios	**512240** Sound recording studios
		51229 Other sound recording industries	**512290** Other sound recording industries
515 Broadcasting Ex-Internet	**5151** Radio & television broadcasting	**51511** Radio broadcasting	**515111** Radio networks
			515112 Radio stations
		51512 Television broadcasting	**515120** Television broadcasting

North American Industry Classification System (NAICS)

Sub-Sector	Industry Group	NAICS Industry	National Industry
	5152 Cable & other subscription programming	**51521** Cable & other subscription programming	**515120** Cable & other subscription programming
517 Telecommunications	**5171** Wired telecommunications carriers	**51711** Wired telecommunications carriers	**517110** Wired telecommunications carriers
	5172 Wireless telecommunications carriers excl satellite	**51721** Wireless telecommunications carriers excl satellite	**517210** Wireless telecommunications carriers excl satellite
	5174 Satellite telecommunications	**51741** Satellite telecommunications	**517410** Satellite telecommunications
	5179 Other telecommunications	**51791** Other telecommunications	**517911** Other telecommunications
			517919 All other telecommunications
518 Data Processing, Hosting & Related Services	**5182** Data processing, hosting & related services	**51821** Data processing, hosting & related services	**518210** Data processing, hosting & related services
519 Other Information Services	**5191** Other information services	**51911** News syndicates	**519110** News syndicates
		51912 Libraries & archives	**519120** Libraries & archives
		51913 Internet publishing & broadcasting & web reference search portals	**519130** Internet publishing & broadcasting & web reference search portals
		51919 All other information services	**519190** All other information services

52 – Finance & Insurance

Sub-Sector	Industry Group	NAICS Industry	National Industry
521 Monetary authorities – central bank	**5211** Monetary authorities – central bank	**52111** Monetary authorities – central bank	**521110** Monetary authorities – central bank
522 Credit Intermediation & Related Activities	**5221** Depository credit intermediation	**52211** Commercial banking	**522110** Commercial banking
		52212 Savings institutions	**522120** Savings institutions
		52213 Credit unions	**522130** Credit unions
		52219 Other depository credit intermediation	**522190** Other depository credit intermediation
	5222 Non-depository credit intermediation	**52221** Credit card issuing	**522210** Credit card issuing

North American Industry Classification System (NAICS)

Sub-Sector	Industry Group	NAICS Industry	National Industry
		52222 Sales financing	**522220** Sales financing
		52229 Other non-depository Credit intermediation	**522291** Consumer lending
			522292 Real estate credit
			522293 International trade financing
			522294 Secondary market financing
			522298 All other non-depository credit intermediation
	5223 Activities related to credit intermediation	**52231** Mortgage & non-mortgage loan brokers	**522310** Mortgage & non-mortgage loan brokers
		52232 Financial transactions processing, reserve & clearinghouse activities	**522320** Financial transactions processing, reserve & clearinghouse activities
		52239 Other activities related to credit intermediation	**522390** Other activities related to credit Intermediation
523 Securities, Commodity Contracts & Other Financial Investments & Related Activities	**5231** Securities & commodity contracts intermediation & brokerage	**52311** Investment banking & securities dealing	**523110** Investment banking & securities dealing
		52312 Securities brokerage	**523120** Securities brokerage
		52313 Commodity contracts dealing	**523130** Commodity contracts dealing
		52314 Commodity contracts brokerage	**523140** Commodity contracts brokerage
	5232 Securities & commodity exchanges	**52321** Securities & commodity exchanges	**523210** Securities & commodity exchanges
	5239 Other financial investment activities	**52391** Miscellaneous intermediation	**523910** Miscellaneous intermediation
		52392 Portfolio management	**523920** Portfolio management
		52393 Investment advice	**523930** Investment advice
		52399 All other financial investment activities	**523991** Trust, fiduciary & custody activities
			523999 Miscellaneous financial investment activities
524 Insurance Carriers & Related Activities	**5241** Insurance carriers	**52411** Direct life, health & medical insurance carriers	**524113** Direct life insurance carriers

North American Industry Classification System (NAICS)

Sub-Sector	Industry Group	NAICS Industry	National Industry
			524114 Direct health & medical insurance carriers
		52412 Direct insurance excl life, health & medical carriers	**524126** Direct property & casualty insurance carriers
			524127 Direct title insurance carriers
			524128 Other direct insurance excl life, health & medical carriers
		52413 Reinsurance carriers	**524130** Reinsurance carriers
	5242 Agencies, brokerages & other Insurance related activities	**52421** Insurance agencies & brokerages	**524210** Insurance agencies & brokerages
		52429 Other insurance related activities	**524291** Claims adjusting
			524292 Third party administration of insurance & pension funds
			524298 All other insurance related activities
525 Funds, Trusts & Other Financial Vehicles	**5251** Insurance & employee benefit funds	**52511** Pension funds	**525110** Pension funds
		52512 Pension funds	**525120** Pension funds
		52519 Other insurance funds	**525190** Other insurance funds
	5259 Other investment pools & funds	**52591** Open-end investment funds	**525910** Open-end investment funds
		52592 Trusts, estates & agency accounts	**525920** Trusts, estates & agency accounts
		52599 Other financial vehicles	**525990** Other financial vehicles

53 – Real Estate & Rental & Leasing

Sub-Sector	Industry Group	NAICS Industry	National Industry
531 Real Estate	**5311** Lessors of real estate	**53111** Lessors of residential buildings & dwellings	**531110** Lessors of residential buildings & dwellings
		53112 Lessors of non-residential buildings excl mini-warehouses	**531120** Lessors of non-residential buildings excl mini-warehouses
		53113 Lessors of mini-warehouses & self-storage units	**531130** Lessors of mini-warehouses & self-storage units

North American Industry Classification System (NAICS)

Sub-Sector	Industry Group	NAICS Industry	National Industry
		53119 Lessors of other real estate property	531190 Lessors of other real estate property
	5312 Offices of real estate agents & brokers	53121 Offices of real estate agents & brokers	531210 Offices of real estate agents & brokers
	5313 Activities related to real estate	53131 Real estate property managers	531311 Residential property managers
			531312 Nonresidential property managers
		53132 Offices of real estate appraisers	531320 Offices of real estate appraisers
		53139 Other activities related to real estate	531390 Other activities related to real estate
532 Rental & Leasing Services	5321 Automotive equipment rental & leasing	53211 Passenger car rental & leasing	532111 Passenger car rental
			532112 Passenger car leasing
		53212 Truck, utility trailer & rv rental & leasing	532120 Truck, utility trailer & rv rental & leasing
	5322 Consumer goods rental	53221 Consumer electronics & appliances rental	532210 Consumer electronics & appliances rental
		53222 Formal wear & costume rental	532220 Formal wear & costume rental
		53223 Video tape & disc rental	532230 Video tape & disc rental
		53229 Other consumer goods rental	532291 Home health equipment rental
			532292 Recreational goods rental
			532299 All other consumer goods rental
	5323 General rental centers	53231 General rental centers	532310 General rental centers
	5324 Commercial & industrial machinery & equipment rental & leasing	53241 Construction, transportation, mining & forestry machinery & equipment rental & leasing	532411 Commercial air, rail & water transportation equipment rental & leasing
			532412 Commercial air, rail & water transportation equipment rental & leasing

North American Industry Classification System (NAICS)

Sub-Sector	Industry Group	NAICS Industry	National Industry
532 Rental & Leasing Services	**5324** Commercial & industrial machinery & equipment rental & leasing	**53242** Office machinery & equipment rental & leasing	**532420** Office machinery & equipment rental & leasing
		53249 Other commercial & industrial machinery & equipment rental & leasing	**532490** Other commercial & industrial machinery & equipment rental & leasing
533 Lessors of Non-financial Intangible Assets Ex-Copyrighted Works	**5331** Lessors of non-financial intangible assets excl copyrighted works	**53311** Lessors of non-financial intangible assets excl copyrighted works	**533110** Lessors of non-financial intangible assets excl copyrighted works

54 – Professional, Scientific & Technical Services

Sub-Sector	Industry Group	NAICS Industry	National Industry
541 Professional, Scientific & Technical Services	**5411** Legal services	**54111** Offices of lawyers	**541110** Offices of lawyers
		54112 Offices of notaries	**541120** Offices of notaries
		54119 Other legal services	**541191** Title abstract & settlement offices
			541199 All Other legal services
	5412 Accounting, tax preparation, bookkeeping & payroll services	**54121** Accounting, tax preparation, bookkeeping & payroll Services	**541211** Offices of certified public accountants
			541213 Tax preparation services
			541214 Payroll services
			541219 Other accounting services
	5413 Architectural, engineering & related services	**54131** Architectural services	**541310** Architectural services
		54132 Landscape architectural services	**541320** Landscape architectural services
		54133 Engineering services	**541330** Engineering services
		54134 Drafting services	**541340** Drafting services
		54135 Building inspection services	**541350** Building inspection services

North American Industry Classification System (NAICS)

Sub-Sector	Industry Group	NAICS Industry	National Industry
		54136 Geophysical surveying & mapping services	**541360** Geophysical surveying & Mapping services
		54137 Surveying & mapping ex-geophysical services	**541370** Surveying & mapping excl geophysical services
		54138 Testing laboratories	**541380** Testing laboratories
	5414 Specialised design services	**54141** Interior design services	**541410** Interior design services
		54142 Industrial design services	**541420** Industrial design services
		54143 Graphic design services	**541430** Graphic design services
		54149 Other specialised design services	**541490** Other specialised design services
541 Professional, Scientific & Technical Services	**5415** Computer systems design & related services	**54151** Computer systems design & related services	**541511** Custom computer programming services
			541512 Computer systems design services
			541513 Computer facilities management services
			541519 Other computer related services
	5416 Management, scientific & technical consulting services	**54161** Management consulting services	**541611** Administrative management & general management consulting services
			541612 Human resources consulting services
			541613 Marketing consulting services
			541614 Process, physical distribution & logistics consulting services
			541618 Other management consulting services
		54162 Environmental consulting services	**541620** Environmental consulting services
		54169 Other scientific & technical consulting services	**541690** Other scientific & technical consulting services
	5417 Scientific research & development services	**54171** Research & development in the physical, engineering & life sciences	**541711** Research & development in biotechnology

North American Industry Classification System (NAICS)

Sub-Sector	Industry Group	NAICS Industry	National Industry
			541712 Research & development in the physical, engineering & life sciences excl biotechnology
		54172 Research & development in the social sciences & humanities	**541720** Research & development in the social sciences & humanities
	5418 Advertising, public relations & related services	**54181** Advertising agencies	**541810** Advertising agencies
		54182 Public relations agencies	**541820** Public relations agencies
		54183 Media buying agencies	**541830** Media buying agencies
		54184 Media representatives	**541840** Media representatives
		54185 Outdoor advertising	**541850** Outdoor advertising
		54186 Direct mail advertising	**541860** Direct mail advertising
		54187 Advertising material distribution services	**541870** Advertising material distribution services
		54189 Other services related to advertising	**541890** Other services related to advertising
	5419 Other professional, scientific & technical services	**54191** Marketing research & public opinion polling	**541910** Marketing research & public opinion polling
		54192 Photographic services	**541921** Photography studios, portrait
			541922 Commercial photography
		54193 Translation & interpretation services	**541930** Translation & interpretation services
		54194 Veterinary services	**541940** Veterinary services
		54199 All other professional, scientific & technical services	**541990** All other professional, scientific & technical Services

55 – Management of Companies & Enterprise

Sub-Sector	Industry Group	NAICS Industry	National Industry
551 Management of Companies & Enterprises	**5511** Management of companies & enterprises	**55111** Management of companies & enterprises	**551111** Offices of bank holding companies
			551112 Offices of other holding companies
			551114 Corporate, subsidiary & regional managing offices

North American Industry Classification System (NAICS)

56 – Administrative & Support & Waste Management & Remediation Services

Sub-Sector	Industry Group	NAICS Industry	National Industry
561 Administrative & Support Services	**5611** Office administrative services	**56111** Office administrative services	**561110** Office administrative services
	5612 Facilities support services	**56121** Facilities support services	**561210** Facilities support services
	5613 Employment services	**56131** Employment placement agencies & executive search services	**561311** Employment placement agencies
			561312 Executive search services
		56132 Temporary help services	**561320** Temporary help services
		56133 Professional employer organisations	**561330** Professional employer organisations
	5614 Business support services	**56141** Document preparation services	**561410** Document preparation services
		56142 Telephone call centers	**561421** Telephone answering services
			561422 Telemarketing bureaus & other contact centers
		56143 Business service centers	**561431** Private mail centers
			561439 Other business service centers & copy shops
		56144 Collection agencies	**561440** Collection agencies
		56145 Credit bureaus	**561450** Credit bureaus
		56149 Other business support services	**561491** Repossession services
			561492 Court reporting & stenotype services
			561499 All other business support services
	5615 Travel arrangement & reservation services	**56151** Travel agencies	**561510** Travel agencies
		56152 Tour operators	**561520** Tour operators
		56159 Other travel arrangement & reservation services	**561591** Convention & visitors bureaus
			561599 All other travel arrangement & reservation services

North American Industry Classification System (NAICS)

Sub-Sector	Industry Group	NAICS Industry	National Industry
	5616 Investigation & security services	**56161** Investigation, guard & armoured car services	**561611** Investigation services
			561612 Security guards & patrol services
			561613 Armoured car services
		56162 Security systems services	**561621** Security systems services excl locksmiths
			561622 Locksmiths
561 Administrative & Support Services	**5617** Services to buildings & dwellings	**56171** Exterminating & pest control services`	**561710** Exterminating & pest control services
		56172 Janitorial services	**561720** Janitorial services
		56173 Landscaping services	**561730** Landscaping services
		56174 Carpet & upholstery Cleaning services	**561740** Carpet & upholstery cleaning services
		56179 Other services to buildings & dwellings	**561790** Other services to buildings & dwellings
	5619 Other support services	**56191** Packaging & labeling services	**561910** Packaging & labeling services
		56192 Convention & trade show organisers	**561920** Convention & trade show organisers
		56199 All other support services	**561990** All other support services
562 Waste Management & Remediation Services	**5621** Waste collection	**56211** Waste collection	**562111** Solid waste collection
			562112 Hazardous waste collection
			562119 Other waste collection
	5622 Waste treatment & disposal	**56221** Waste treatment & disposal	**562211** Hazardous waste treatment & disposal
			562212 Solid waste landfill
			562213 Solid waste combustors & incinerators
			562219 Other nonhazardous waste treatment & disposal
	5629 Remediation & other waste management services	**56291** Remediation services	**562910** Remediation services

North American Industry Classification System (NAICS)

Sub-Sector	Industry Group	NAICS Industry	National Industry
		56292 Materials recovery facilities	562920 Materials recovery facilities
		56299 All other waste management services	562991 All other waste management services
			562998 All other miscellaneous waste management services

61 – Educational Services

Sub-Sector	Industry Group	NAICS Industry	National Industry
611 Educational Services	6111 Elementary & secondary schools	61111 Elementary & secondary schools	611110 Elementary & secondary schools
	6112 Junior colleges	61121 Junior colleges	611210 Junior colleges
	6113 Colleges, universities & professional schools	61131 Colleges, universities & professional schools	611310 Colleges, universities & professional schools
	6114 Business schools & computer & management training	61141 Business & secretarial schools	611410 Business & secretarial schools
		61142 Computer training	611420 Computer training
		61143 Professional & management development training	611430 Professional & management development training
	6115 Technical & trade schools	61151 Technical & trade schools	611511 Cosmetology & barber schools
			611512 Flight training
			611513 Apprenticeship training
			611519 Other technical & trade schools
611 Educational Services	6116 Other schools & instruction	61161 Fine arts schools	611610 Fine arts schools
		61162 Sports & recreation instruction	611620 Sports & recreation instruction
		61163 Language schools	611630 Language schools
		61169 All other schools & instruction	611691 Exam preparation & tutoring
			611692 Automobile driving schools

North American Industry Classification System (NAICS)

Sub-Sector	Industry Group	NAICS Industry	National Industry
			611699 All other miscellaneous schools & instruction
	6117 Educational support services	**61171** Educational support services	**611710** Educational support services

62 – Health Care & Social Assistance

Sub-Sector	Industry Group	NAICS Industry	National Industry
621 Ambulatory Health Care Services	**6211** Offices of physicians	**62111** Offices of physicians	**621111** Offices of physicians excl mental health specialists
			621112 Offices of physicians, Mental Health specialists
	6212 Offices of dentists	**62121** Offices of dentists	**621210** Offices of dentists
	6213 Offices of other health practitioners	**62131** Offices of chiropractors	**621310** Offices of chiropractors
		62132 Offices of optometrists	**621320** Offices of optometrists
		62133 Offices of mental health practitioners ex-physicians	**621330** Offices of mental health practitioners excl physicians
		62134 Offices of physical, occupational & speech therapists & audiologists	**621340** Offices of physical, occupational & speech therapists & audiologists
		62139 Offices of all other health practitioners	**621391** Offices of podiatrists
			621399 Offices of all other Miscellaneous health practitioners
	6214 Outpatient care centers	**62141** Family planning centers	**621410** Family planning centers
		62142 Outpatient mental health & substance abuse centers	**621420** Outpatient mental health & substance abuse centers
		62149 Other outpatient care centers	**621491** HMO medical centers
			621492 Kidney dialysis centers
			621493 Freestanding ambulatory surgical & emergency centers
			621498 All other outpatient care centers
	6215 Medical & diagnostic laboratories	**62151** Medical & diagnostic laboratories	**621511** Medical laboratories

North American Industry Classification System (NAICS)

Sub-Sector	Industry Group	NAICS Industry	National Industry
			621512 Diagnostic imaging centers
	6216 Home health care services	**62161** Home health care services	**621610** Home health care services
	6219 Other ambulatory health care services	**62191** Ambulance services	**621910** Ambulance services
		62199 All other ambulatory health care services	**621991** Blood & organ banks
			621999 All other miscellaneous ambulatory health care services
622 Hospitals	**6221** General medical & surgical hospitals	**62211** General medical & surgical hospitals	**622110** General medical & surgical hospitals
	6222 Psychiatric & substance abuse hospitals	**62221** Psychiatric & substance abuse hospitals	**622210** Psychiatric & substance abuse hospitals
	6223 Specialty excl psychiatric & substance abuse hospitals	**62231** Specialty excl psychiatric & substance abuse hospitals	**622310** Specialty excl psychiatric & substance abuse hospitals
623 Nursing & Residential Care Facilities	**6231** Nursing care facilities (skilled nursing facilities)	**62311** Nursing care facilities (skilled nursing facilities)	**623110** Nursing care facilities (skilled nursing facilities)
	6232 Residential intellectual & developmental disability, mental health & substance abuse facilities	**62321** Residential intellectual & developmental disability facilities	**623210** Residential intellectual & developmental disability Facilities
		62322 Residential mental health & substance abuse facilities	**623220** Residential mental health & substance abuse facilities
	6233 Continuing care retirement communities & assisted living facilities for the elderly	**62331** Continuing care retirement communities & assisted living facilities for the elderly	**623311** Continuing care retirement communities
			623312 Assisted living facilities for the elderly
	6239 Other residential care facilities	**62399** Other residential care facilities	**623990** Other residential care facilities

North American Industry Classification System (NAICS)

Sub-Sector	Industry Group	NAICS Industry	National Industry
624 Social Assistance	**6241** Individual & family services	**62411** Child & youth services	**624110** Child & youth services
		62412 Services for the elderly & persons with disabilities	**624120** Services for the elderly & persons with disabilities
		62419 Other individual & family services	**624190** Other individual & family services
	6242 Community food & housing & emergency & other relief services	**62421** Community food services	**624210** Community food services
		62422 Community housing services	**624221** Temporary shelters
			624229 Other community housing services
		62423 Emergency & other relief services	**624230** Emergency & other relief services
	6243 Vocational rehabilitation services	**62431** Vocational rehabilitation services	**624310** Vocational rehabilitation services
	6244 Child day care services	**62441** Child day care services	**624410** Child day care services

71 – Arts, Entertainment, & Recreation

Sub-Sector	Industry Group	NAICS Industry	National Industry
711 Performing Arts, Spectator Sports & Related Industries	**7111** Performing arts companies	**71111** Theater companies & dinner theaters	**711110** Theater companies & dinner theaters
		71112 Dance companies	**711120** Dance companies
		71113 Musical groups & artists	**711130** Musical groups & artists
		71119 Other performing arts companies	**711190** Other performing arts companies
711 Performing Arts, Spectator Sports & Related Industries	**7112** Spectator sports	**71121** Spectator sports	**711211** Sports Teams & Clubs
			711212 Racetracks
			711219 Other spectator sports
		71131 Promoters of performing arts sports, & similar events with facilities	**711310** Promoters of performing arts sports, & similar events with facilities

North American Industry Classification System (NAICS)

Sub-Sector	Industry Group	NAICS Industry	National Industry
	7113 Promoters of performing arts, sports & similar even	**71132** Promoters of performing arts, sports & similar events without facilities	**711320** Promoters of performing arts, sports & similar events without facilities
	7114 Agents & managers for artists, Athletes, entertainers & other public figures	**71141** Agents & managers for artists, athletes, entertainers & Other public figures	**711410** Agents & managers for artists, athletes, entertainers & other public figures
	7115 Independent artists, writers & performers	**71151** Independent artists, writers & performers	**711510** Independent artists, writers & performers
712 Museums, Historical Sites & Similar Institutions	**7121** Museums, historical sites & similar institutions	**71211** Museums	**712110** Museums
		71212 Historical sites	**712120** Historical sites
		71213 Zoos & botanical gardens	**712130** Zoos & botanical gardens
		71219 Nature parks & other similar institutions	**712190** Nature parks & other similar institutions
713 Amusement, Gambling & Recreation Industries	**7131** Amusement parks & arcade	**71311** Amusement & theme parks	**713110** Amusement & theme parks
		71312 Amusement arcades	**713120** Amusement arcades
	71312 Amusement arcades	**71321** Casinos excl casino hotels	**713210** Casinos excl casino hotels
		71329 Other gambling industries	**713290** Other gambling industries
	7139 Other amusement & recreation industries	**71391** Golf courses & country clubs	**713910** Golf courses & country clubs
		71392 Skiing facilities	**713920** Skiing facilities
		71393 Marinas	**713930** Marinas
		71394 Fitness & recreational sports centre	**713940** Fitness & recreational Sports centre
		71395 Bowling centres	**713950** Bowling centres
		71399 All other amusement & recreation industries	**713990** All other amusement & recreation industries

North American Industry Classification System (NAICS)

72 – Accommodation & Food Services

Sub-Sector	Industry Group	NAICS Industry	National Industry
721 Accommodation	**7211** Traveler accommodation	**72111** Hotels excl casino hotels & motels	**721110** Hotels excl casino hotels & motels
		72112 Casino hotels	**721120** Casino hotels
		72119 Other traveler accommodation	**721191** Bed & breakfast inns
			721199 All other traveler accommodation
	7212 RV (recreational vehicle) parks & recreational camps	**72121** RV (recreational vehicle) parks & recreational camps	**721211** RV (recreational vehicle) parks & campgrounds
			721214 Recreational & vacation camps excl campgrounds
	7213 Rooming & boarding houses	**72131** Rooming & boarding houses	**721310** Rooming & boarding houses
722 Food Services & Drinking Places	**7223** Special food services	**72231** Food service contractors	**722310** Food service contractors
		72232 caterers	**722320** Caterers
		72233 Mobile food services	**722330** Mobile food services
	7224 Drinking places (alcoholic beverages)	**72241** Drinking places (alcoholic beverages)	**722410** Drinking places (alcoholic beverages)
	7225 Restaurants & other eating places	**72251** Restaurants & other eating places	**722511** Full service restaurants
			722513 Limited service restaurants
			722514 Cafeterias, grill buffets & buffets
			722515 Snack & non-alcoholic beverage bars

81 – Other Services Excluding Public Administration

Sub-Sector	Industry Group	NAICS Industry	National Industry
811 Repair & Maintenance	**8111** Automotive repair & maintenance	**81111** Automotive mechanical & electrical repair & maintenance	**811111** General automotive repair
			811112 Automotive exhaust system repair
			811113 Automotive transmission repair

North American Industry Classification System (NAICS)

Sub-Sector	Industry Group	NAICS Industry	National Industry
			811118 Other automotive mechanical & electrical repair & maintenance
		81112 Automotive body, paint, interior & glass repair	**811121** Automotive body, paint & Interior repair & maintenance
			811122 Automotive glass replacement shops
		81119 Other automotive repair & maintenance	**811191** Automotive oil change & lubrication shops
			811192 Car washes
			811199 All other automotive repair & maintenance
811 Repair & Maintenance	**8112** Electronic & precision equipment repair & maintenance	**81121** Electronic & precision equipment repair & maintenance	**811211** Consumer electronics repair & maintenance
			811212 Computer & office machine repair & maintenancec
			811213 Communication equipment repair & maintenance
			811219 Other electronic & precision equipment repair & maintenance
	8113 Commercial & industrial machinery & equipment excl automotive & electronic repair & maintenance	**81131** Commercial & industrial machinery & equipment excl automotive & electronic repair & maintenance	**811310** Commercial & industrial machinery & equipment excl automotive & electronic repair & maintenance
	8114 Personal & household goods repair & maintenance	**81141** Home & garden equipment & appliance repair & maintenance	**811411** Home & garden equipment repair & maintenance
			811412 Appliance repair & maintenance
		81142 Re-upholstery & furniture repair	**811420** Re-upholstery & furniture repair
		81143 Footwear & leather goods repair	**811430** Footwear & leather goods repair
		81149 Other personal & household goods repair & maintenance	**811490** Other personal & household goods repair & maintenance

North American Industry Classification System (NAICS)

Sub-Sector	Industry Group	NAICS Industry	National Industry
812 Personal & Laundry Services	**8121** Personal care services	**81211** Hair, nail & skin care services	**812111** Barber shops
			812112 Beauty salons
			812113 Nail salons
		81219 Other personal care services	**812191** Diet & weight reducing centers
			812199 Other personal care services
	8122 Death care services	**81221** Funeral homes & funeral services	**812210** Funeral homes & funeral services
		81222 Cemeteries & crematories	**812220** Cemeteries & crematories
	8123 Dry-cleaning & laundry services	**81231** Coin-operated laundries & drycleaners	**812310** Coin-operated laundries & drycleaners
		81232 Dry-cleaning & laundry services excl coin-operated	**812320** Dry-cleaning & laundry services excl coin-operated
		81233 Linen & uniform supply	**812331** Linen supply
			812332 Industrial launderers
	8129 Other personal services	**81291** Pet care excl veterinary services	**812910** Pet care excl veterinary services
		81292 Photofinishing	**812921** Photofinishing laboratories excl one-hour
			812922 One hour photofinishing
		81293 Parking lots & garages	**812930** Parking lots & garages
		81299 All other personal services	**812990** All other personal services
813 Religious, Grant making, Civic, Professional & Similar Organisations	**8131** Religious organisations	**81311** Religious organisations	**813110** Religious organisations
	8132 Grant making & giving services	**81321** Grant making & giving services	**813211** Grant making foundations
			813212 Voluntary health organisations
			813219 Other grant making & giving services
	8133 Social advocacy organisations	**81331** Social advocacy organisations	**813311** Grant making foundations

North American Industry Classification System (NAICS)

Sub-Sector	Industry Group	NAICS Industry	National Industry
			813312 Environment, conservation & wildlife organisations
			813319 Other social advocacy organisations
813 Religious, Grant making, Civic, Professional & Similar Organisations	**8134** Civic & social oirganisations	**81341** Civic & social organisations	**813410** Civic & social organisations
		81391 Business associations	**813910** Business associations
	8139 Business, professional, labor, political & similar organisations	**81392** Professional organisations	**813920** Professional organisations
		81393 Labor unions & similar Labor organisations	**813930** Labour unions & Similar Labour organisations
		81394 Political organisations	**813940** Political organisations
		81399 Other similar organisations excl business, professional, labor & political organisations	**813990** Other similar organisations excl business, professional, labour & political organisations
814 Private Households	**8141** Private households	**81411** Private households	**814110** Private households

92 – Public Administration

Sub-Sector	Industry Group	NAICS Industry	National Industry
921 Executive, Legislative & Other General Government Support	**9211** Executive, legislative & other general government support	**92111** Executive offices	**921110** Executive offices
		92112 Legislative bodies	**921120** Legislative bodies
		92113 Public finance activities	**921130** Public finance activities
		92114 Executive & legislative offices, combined	**921140** Executive & legislative offices, combined
		92115 American indian & alaska native tribal governments	**921150** American indian & alaska native tribal governments
		92119 Other general government support	**921190** Other general government support
922 Justice, Public Order & Safety Activities	**9221** Justice, public order & safety activities	**92211** Courts	**922110** Courts
		92212 Police protection	**922120** Police protection

North American Industry Classification System (NAICS)

Sub-Sector	Industry Group	NAICS Industry	National Industry
		92213 Legal counsel & prosecution	**922130** Legal counsel & prosecution
		92214 Correctional institutions	**922140** Correctional institutions
		92215 Parole offices & probation offices	**922150** Parole offices & probation offices
		92216 Fire protection	**922160** Fire protection
		92219 Other justice, public order & safety activities	**922190** Other justice, public order & safety activities
923 Administration of Human Resource Programs	**9231** Administration of human resource programs	**92311** Administration of education programs	**923110** Administration of education programs
		92312 Administration of public health programs	**923120** Administration of public health programs
		92313 Administration of human resource programs excl education, public health & veterans affairs programs	**923130** Administration of human resource programs excl education, public health & veterans affairs programs
		92314 Administration of veterans affairs	**923140** Administration of veterans affairs
924 Administration of Environmental Quality Programs	**9241** Administration of environmental quality programs	**92411** Administration of air & water resource & solid waste management programs	**924110** Administration of air & water resource & solid waste management programs
		92412 Administration of conservation programs	**924120** Administration of conservation programs
925 Administration of Housing Programs, Urban Planning & Community Development	**9251** Administration of housing programs, urban planning & community development	**92511** Administration of housing programs	**925110** Administration of housing programs
		92512 Administration of urban planning & community & rural development	**925120** Administration of urban planning & community & rural development
926 Administration of Economic Programs	**9261** Administration of economic programs	**92611** Administration of general economic programs	**926110** Administration of general economic programs
		92612 Regulation & administration of transportation programs	**926120** Regulation & administration of transportation programs
		92613 Regulation & administration of communications, electric, gas & other utilities	**926130** Regulation & administration of communications, electric, gas & other utilities
		92614 Regulation of agricultural marketing & commodities	**926140** Regulation of agricultural marketing & commodities

North American Industry Classification System (NAICS)

Sub-Sector	Industry Group	NAICS Industry	National Industry
		92615 Regulation, licensing & inspection of miscellaneous Commercial sectors	**926150** Regulation, licensing & inspection of miscellaneous commercial sectors
927 Space Research & Technology	**9271** Space research & technology	**92711** Space research & technology	**927110** Space research & technology
928 National Security & International Affairs	**9281** National security & international affairs	**92811** National security	**928110** National security
		92812 International affairs	**928120** International affairs

Standard Industrial Classification (SIC)

In brief

The Standard Industrial Classification (SIC) is an industrial classification system used by US government agencies. The SIC system is also used by agencies in other countries, such as the UK's Companies House. SIC codes are assigned on the basis of common characteristics in the products, services, production and delivery system of a business.

SIC codes are used by the US Census Bureau, the Bureau of Labor Statistics, the Internal Revenue Service (IRS) and Social Security Administration as well as by academic and business sectors. The Bureau of Labor Statistics updates the codes every three years and uses SIC codes to report on workforce, wages and pricing issues. The Social Security Administration assigns SIC codes to businesses based on the descriptions provided by employers under the primary business activity entry on employer ID applications.

SIC issuer

US Department of Labor –
    Occupational Safety & Health Administration
200 Constitution Avenue NW
Washington, DC 20210
United States of America
Tel: +1 800 321 6742
www.osha.gov/pls/imis/sic_manual.html

History

SIC codes were developed in the 1930s when the US government needed standardised and meaningful ways in which to measure, analyze and share data across its various agencies. The new system was first released in 1937. Although certain US government departments and agencies, such as the US Securities and Exchange Commission (SEC), still use SIC codes, the newer six-digit North American Industry Classification System (NAICS code), developed under the auspices of the Office of Management and Budget and adopted in 1997, has largely superseded their use.

In recent years SIC codes' limitations have become increasingly apparent. Business has changed considerably, from manufacturing-based to mostly service-based, while SIC codes were developed for traditional, pre-1970 industries. The SIC has also been slow to recognise new and emerging industries, such as those in the technology sector. By contrast, the expanded six-digit NAICS provides more flexibility in handling emerging industries. NAICS was implemented in Canada and the United States in 1997 and in Mexico the following year.

Structure

SIC codes begins with general characteristics and narrows down to the specifics. The first two digits of the code represent the major industry sector to which a business belongs. The third and fourth digits describe the sub-classification of the business group and specialisation, respectively. For example, "36" refers to a business that deals in "Electronic and other equipment." Adding "7" as a third digit to get "367" indicates that the business operates in "Electronic, component and accessories." The fourth digit distinguishes the specific industry sector, so a code of "3672" indicates that the business is concerned with "Printed circuit boards."

Each division encompasses a range of SIC codes:

0100 to 0999	Agriculture, forestry and fishing
1000 to 1499	Mining
1500 to 1799	Construction
1800 to 1999	Unused
2000 to 3999	Manufacturing
4000 to 4999	Transportation, communications, electric, gas & sanitary services
5000 to 5199	Wholesale trade
5200 to 5999	Retail trade
6000 to 6799	Finance, insurance & real estate
7000 to 8999	Services
9100 to 9729	Public administration.

Codes starting 99 represent non-classified businesses.

Company Registration Codes

Virtually every nation in the world has an office in which commercial organisations are registered. Some nations, such as the US, have company registration offices in their individual states.

The codes generated in these registration offices are vital for domestic and, especially, international investors. Company registration codes help investors to find official information about securities and to conduct research into potential invesments.

In addition, company registration codes comprise a crucial database for building the Global LEI. Official records help local operating units to issue LEIs for local companies requesting one.

Please note: There is no comprehensive list of company registration offices worldwide.

Australia-Australian Business Register (ABR)

The Australian Business Number (ABN) is a single identifier for all business dealings with the Australian Taxation Office (ATO) and for dealings with other government departments and agencies. An ABN is allocated when an entity is entered into the ABR. The ABN is a unique 11-digit number formed from a nine-digit identifier prefixed by two check digits. The two leading check digits are derived from the subsequent nine-digit identifier using a modulus 89 check digit calculation.

http://www.abn.business.gov.au/

Austria: Firmenbuch

Austria's Ministry of Justice maintains official information in the companies register, or Firmenbuch. The Firmenbuch is the public directory of companies in Austria in which the main details and legal relationships of companies and other institutions that are subject to the commercial law are registered. A

Firmenbuch number (Firmenbuchnummer, or FN) has a maximum length of six digits.

http://www.firmenbuch.at/

Belgium: Crossroads Bank for Enterprises

Belgium's national registry is the Crossroads Bank for Enterprises (Banque-Carrefour des Entreprises/KruispuntBank van Ondernemigen), a department of the federal Ministry of Economy. Banque Carrefour des Entreprises is the EBR member for Belgium. The CBE, or enterprise number, is a unique number that identifies companies in respect of the Belgian administrative services and consists of 10 digits. The first digit is 0.

http://economie.fgov.be/fr/

Canada: regional registries

In Canada, the business number (BN) is the common identifier assigned to businesses to simplify their dealings with federal, provincial, and municipal governments. A BN is nine digits in length.

In addition, companies incorporated in Quebec are assigned a Quebec Enterprise Number (NEQ) when registered with the Registraire des Entreprises. A NEQ is ten digits.

http://www.cra-arc.gc.ca/bn/

http://www.registreentreprises.gouv.qc.ca/en/

Chile: Servicio de Impuestos Internos

There is no equivalent of a Companies House registration number in Chile. Instead the tax number or Rol Único Tributario (RUT) assigned by the Servicio de Impuestos Internos (Inland Revenue) serves as the unique identifier for all registered companies. The RUT comprises two parts: an eight-digit identification number and a check digit separated by a hyphen. The check digit is derived using the module 11 algorithm.

Company Registration Codes

http://www.sii.cl/contribuyentes/contribuyentes_individuales/chilenos_extranjero/rol_unico_tributario.htm

Czech Republic: Czech Statistical Office Register

The Identifikační Čislo Osoby or Company Identification Number (ICO) is issued by the Czech Statistical Office to identify businesses domiciled in the Czech Republic, including entrepreneurs and sole traders. This identification number remains associated with a commercial company or other legal entity even if it changes its trade name or location. The ICO is an eight-digit number where the first seven digits represent the entity and the eighth digit is a check digit. ICOs are assigned sequentially and no ICO is re-used even after dissolution of a company.

http://www.vyhledavace.cz/firmy/ico.html

Denmark: Danish Commerce & Companies Agency

The central business register (Det Centrale Virtsomhedsregister, or CVR) of the Danish Ministry of Commerce is the central register containing primary data on all businesses in Denmark, regardless of economic and organisational structure. The CVR covers both public and private businesses. The CVR number is eight digits long and again is effectively also a VAT number for tax purposes.

https:///www.datacvr.virk.dk/data/

Estonia: Centre of Registers & Information Systems (RIK)

Estonia's Centre of Registers and Information Systems (RIK) is a state agency working under the Ministry of Justice. The Central Commercial Register is an online service is based on the central database of registration departments of the courts. This central database includes the data of the commercial register, the register of non-profit associations and foundations and the commercial pledge register. The Estonian company registration number is eight digits in length.

http://www.rik.ee/en

Finland: Finnish Patent & Registration Office

The National Board of Patents and Registration of Finland (PRH) is the official company registrar for Finnish companies. The PRH gives businesses and organisations their business identity code. It replaces the trade register number, foundation register number and business code used before. The business ID consists of seven digits, a dash and check digit, e.g. 1234567-8.

http://www.prh.fi/en/index.html

France: Register of Commerce & Companies

France's Register of Commerce and Companies (Registre National du Commerce et des Sociétés or RNCS) assigns a SIREN (business identification directory system) number to all registered businesses regardless of their legal form. It consists of nine digits; the first eight are assigned sequentially (except for public bodies starting with 1 or 2), the ninth is a check digit (modulo 10 following Luhn algorithm). For example, SIREN 404 833 048 represents an enterprise with the national number 404 833 04 and a check digit of 8.

In France both annual accounts and other corporate documents are collected and made available by the 190 or so commercial court registries (Greffes des Tribunaux de Commerce) distributed throughout France. Each registry collects the data for enterprises in its own area. To collect and circulate the data, they use a common technical platform, Infogreffe.

https://www.infogreffe.fr/societes/

Germany: Commercial Register

Germany's commercial register, or Handelsregister, is a public register that contains details of all trades people and legal entities in the district of the registrar (generally the Amtsgericht or local district court) of the place where the Landgericht (superior court)) is also situated. The Handelsregister comprises two sections or departments: one (Handelsregister Abteilung A or HRA) for partnerships, sole traders and registered associations (Vereine) without share capital; and one for all incorporated companies with share capital (Handelsregister Abteilung B or HRB). A Handelsregister number is

Company Registration Codes

five digits in length prefixed by either HRA or HRB depending on an entity's legal status.

https://www.handelsregister.de/rp_web/welcome.do

Greece: Athens Chamber of Commerce & Industry (EBEA)

The Athens Chamber of Commerce and Industry (ACCI) is the European Business Register (EBR) member for Greece. Greece does not yet have a unified national business registry, as local registers are the chambers of commerce. ACCI is the largest chamber in Greece. In general, company registration numbers are six digits in length.

http://www.acci.gr/acci/shared/index.jsp?context=101

Hungary: Courts of Company Registration

In Hungary registry courts maintain the registers of companies. Company registry numbers are 10 digits in length in the format XX-XX-XXXXXX. For example, company registry number 08-09-013097 represents the company Buda Invest Hungary 5000.

http://www.companyincorporationhungary.com/court-company-registration-hungary
https://www.companyregister.hu/

Iceland: Directorate of Internal Revenue

Iceland's public and private limited companies are registered with the Register of Limited Companies operated by the Directorate of Internal Revenue. The kennitala (plural: kennitölur; abbreviated to kt.) is a unique national identification number used by the Icelandic government to identify individuals and organisations in Iceland, administered by the National Registry (Þjóðskrá). Kennitölur are composed of ten digits and are often written with a hyphen following the first six digits, For example, 630109-1080 represents the company Reginn hf.

https://www.rsk.is/

Ireland: Companies Registration Office (CRO)

Ireland's Companies Registration Office, An Oifig um Chlárú Cuideachtaí (CRO), is the central repository of public statutory information on Irish companies and business names. The CRO operates under the aegis of the Department of Jobs, Enterprise and Innovation. CRO numbers are allocated sequentially and are generally five or six digits in length.

https://www.cro.ie/

Israel: Ministry of Justice

The Ministry of Justice acts as the registrar of companies in Israel. Company registration numbers are nine digits in length.

http://www.justice.gov.il/MOJEng/

Italy: Italian Chambers of Commerce

Italian companies are registered with the Register of Enterprises (Registro delle Imprese) at the local chamber of commerce. The Italian Chambers of Commerce (Società Consortile di Informatica delle Camere di Commercio Italiane per Azioni) operates the national system linking the regional chambers of commerce via its InfoCamere IT system. A typical registry number (numero di iscrizione nel Registro delle Imprese) is composed of a sequence of characters and digits conveying the province of registration, the year of registration and the identification number of the company or enterprise.

http://www.registroimprese.it/
http://www.infocamere.it/

Luxembourg: Registre du Commerce et des Sociétés du Grand-Duché de Luxembourg (RCSL)

The Registre du Commerce et des Sociétés du Grand-Duché de Luxembourg (RCSL), Luxembourg's Register of Commerce, is the country's EBR member. RCSL numbers are generally five or six digits in length prefixed by one of the letters A to J representing the type of entity. The most common

Company Registration Codes

prefix is the letter B representing a commercial organisation (Societé Commerciale).

https://www.rcsl.lu/mjrcs/jsp/IndexActionNotSecured.action?-time=1406739358486&loop=2

Mexico: Public Registry of Commerce

The Public Registry of Commerce (Registro Publico del Comercio) is responsible for the registration of companies in Mexico. All companies are also required by law to register with, and to update financial and other information annually in, the Government's National Business Information Registry (Sistema de Información Empresarial Mexicano, or SIEM). Companies are assigned a Registro Federal del Contribuyentes (RFC) number which is 12 characters in length. The first three characters represent the business name, the next six characters represent the company's registration date (YYMMDD) and the last three characters are assigned randomly by the tax authority.

http://www.buromexico.mx/registro-publico-de-la-propiedad-y-del-comercio/
http://www.siem.gob.mx/siem/

Netherlands: Netherlands Chamber of Commerce

All Dutch companies are obliged to enter their key details in the trade register managed by the Netherlands Chamber of Commerce (KvK). Companies required to file a financial report with the Chamber of Commerce each financial year include private limited liability companies (BVs), public limited liability companies limited by shares (NVs), cooperatives and mutual benefit companies. The KvK number is eight digits in length.

http://www.kvk.nl/english/

New Zealand: Companies Office

In New Zealand, companies are registered in the companies register of the New Zealand Companies Office (NZCO). NZCO numbers are assigned sequentially and at present can be up to seven digits in length.

In addition, the NZCO now issues all registered companies with a New Zealand Business Number (NZBN). The NZBN is an initiative to assign a single identifying number to all businesses, government agencies and commercial entities in New Zealand. The NZBN is a 13-digit number, starting with the two digits ID for New Zealand, 94, followed by a 10-digit business ID and finally a check digit.

http://www.business.govt.nz/companies/

Norway: Ministry of Trade & Industry

The Brønnøysund Register Centre is a government body under the Norwegian Ministry of Trade and Industry. The Register of Business Enterprises registers all Norwegian and foreign business enterprises in Norway. Registered companies are issued with a nine-digit company number.

http://www.brreg.no/english/

Poland: Ministry of Justice

The Ministry of Justice maintains the Polish National Court Trade Registry (KRS). KRS numbers are 10 digits in length.

http://ms.gov.pl/en/national-registers/national-court-register/general-information-on-the-national-court-register/

Portugal: Commercial Registry

Companies must register with the Commercial Registry (Registo Comercial) maintained by the Institute of Registration and Notary Affairs (Instituto dos Registos e do Notoriado). It assigns companies a nine-digit registration number, or Número de Identificação de Pessoa Colectiva (NIPC), which doubles up as a fiscal number for tax purposes. The ninth digit is a check digit calculated using the modulo 11 algorithm.

http://www.irn.mj.pt/IRN/sections/inicio

Company Registration Codes

Slovakia: Identifikačné Číslo Organizácie/Company (ICO)

The Identifikačné Číslo Organizácie, or company identification number (ICO), is issued by the Statistical Office of the Slovak Republic to identify businesses domiciled there. The ICO is an eight-digit number (older numbers may be only six digits) where the first seven digits represent the entity and the eighth digit is a check digit. ICOs are assigned sequentially and no ICO is re-used even after dissolution of a company.

http://portal.statistics.sk/showdoc.do?docid=2844

Slovenia: AJPES

The Agency of the Republic of Slovenia for Public Legal Records and Related Services (AJPES) manages the Slovenian business register, the central public database of legal entities (companies and their subsidiaries, subsidiaries of foreign companies, co-operatives, public and private institutes, public agencies and other legal entities) registered to trade in Slovenia. AJPES business identification numbers are seven digits in length.

http://www.ajpes.si/Default.asp?language=english&mdres=1

Spain: Central Business Register

Spain's companies are registered with the commercial registrar in their province. Information is supplied to the Central Business Register (Registro Mercantil Central). Companies are assigned a Código de Identificación Fiscal (CIF) by the tax authorities, which doubles up as the company registration number and VAT registration number for tax purposes. A CIF consists of nine characters. The first is a letter that represents the type of entity or the legal status of a company. The next two characters are a numerical two-digit code that represents the province where the entity or company is registered. The next five digits (positions 4 to 8) constitute a serial number for registration of the entity or company in the provincial registry, and the last character (position 9) is a control or check character which can be a number or a letter. A CIF must match the final abbreviation, i.e. the type of company, according to the Spanish listing of civil societies and corporations.

http://www.rmc.es/Home.aspx?lang=en

Sweden: Companies Registration Office

In Sweden companies register with the Companies Registration Office (Bolagsverket), which is affiliated to the Swedish Enterprise Energy and Transportation Ministry. A Bolagsverket registration number is 10 digits in length in the format XXXXX-XXXX.

http://www.bolagsverket.se/en

Switzerland: Federal Commercial Registry Office

Switzerland's federal commercial registry office maintains the Central Business Names Index (ZEFIX) which includes details of all companies listed in the Swiss Commercial Register (Registre du Commerce in French, or Handelsregister in German). A total of 28 Swiss commercial registers are administered by 26 cantons, under the supervision of the Swiss Confederation.

All commercial entries are published in the Swiss Official Gazette of Commerce (SOGC) after having been checked and approved by the federal commercial registry office. Every company must be assigned a uniform identification number (UID). A UID has the format CHE-123.456.789. In addition, for a company that is registered for Swiss tax purposes, the Swiss VAT number is CHE-123.456.789 MWST i.e. the new format of the VAT number is the UID with MWST appended.

http://www.zefix.ch/zfx-cgi/hrform.cgi/hraPage?alle_eintr=on&pers_sort=-original&pers_num=0&language=4&col_width=366&amt=007

Turkey: Ministry of Commerce and Industry

Following the introduction of the new Turkish commercial code in July 2012, the Central Registry Record System (Merkezi Sicil Kayıt Sistemi, or MERSIS) was established by the Ministry of Commerce and Industry and the Union of Chambers and Commodity Exchanges of Turkey. All commercial enterprises, equity companies and their branch offices are given a unique MERSIS number upon registration, which is not subject to change.

http://www.mersissorgulama.com/

Company Registration Codes

United Kingdom: UK Company Registration Number

The UK Company Registration Number, or UKREG, is a unique identifier applied by Companies House in its capacity as the United Kingdom registrar of companies, to all companies registered to do business in the United Kingdom. All forms of companies (as permitted by the Companies Act) are incorporated and registered with Companies House and file specific details as required by the current Companies Act 2006. The United Kingdom has had a system of company registration since 1844.

In addition, Companies House has a simple Uniform Resource Identifier (URI) for all companies on its register. The URI is permanent and represents the company. When used as an internet address, it will return basic company details in a format appropriate for the requesting system.

English and Welsh companies have registration numbers that consist of eight digits. Companies registered in Scotland and Northern Ireland and those registered by the Financial Services Authority have a 1 or 2 character alphabetic prefix. The following are possible values for the prefix.

Value	Description
AC	Assurance Company England & Wales
FC	Foreign Company England & Wales
GE	European Economic Interest Grouping (EEIG) England & Wales
GN	EEIG Northern Ireland
GS	EEIG Scotland
IC	Investment Company with Variable Capital (ICVC) England & Wales
IP	Industrial & Provident England & Wales
LP	Limited Partnership England & Wales
NA	Assurance Company Northern Ireland
NF	Foreign Company Northern Ireland
NI	Northern Ireland Company
NL	Limited Partnership Northern Ireland
NO	Other Northern Ireland
NP	Industrial & Provident Northern Ireland
NR	Royal Charter Northern Ireland
NZ	Not Companies Act Northern Ireland
OC	Other England & Wales (only used for LLP cases in liquidation)
R	Northern Ireland Company registered pre-partition of Ireland in 1922
RC	Royal Charter England & Wales
SA	Assurance Company Scotland
SC	Scottish Company
SF	Foreign Company Scotland
SI	Investment Company with Variable Capital (ICVC) Scotland
SL	Limited Partnership Scotland (companies registered not liable to Corporation Tax)
SO	Other Scotland (only used for LLP cases in liquidation)
SP	Industrial / Provident Scotland
SR	Royal Charter Scotland
SZ	Not Companies Act Scotland
ZC	Not Companies Act England & Wales

http://www.companieshouse.gov.uk/

Company Registration Codes

United States: State Governments

US state governments are responsible for companies' incorporation, and detailed requirements vary according to state law. A corporation doing business in another state will need to register there as a foreign corporation. In general, there is no harmonised identification number system. Companies can be identified by the employer identification number (EIN) issued by the Internal Revenue Service for tax purposes, the alphanumeric SWIFT BIC or the Business Identifier Code (sometimes referred to as the Business Entity Identifier or BEI). Publicly traded companies are also assigned a CUSIP or a CINS.

https://www.gov.uk/government/publications/overseas-registries/overseas-registries#registries-in-the-united-states-of-america

Regulator Codes

Every country with a financial service sector will have a regulation(s).

At a national level, regulator codes are codes issued and managed by the securities somissions in each jurisdiction. These commissions have the power of enforcement related to their country's financial sector.

Internationally, the International Organization of Securities Commissions (IOSCO) brings together the world's securities regulators. It is recognised as the global standard-setter for the securities sector. IOSCO develops, implements and promotes adherence to internationally recognised standards for securities regulation. It works intensively with the G20 and the Financial Stability Board (FSB) on the global regulatory reform agenda.

IOSCO contact
Oquedo 12
28006 Madrid
Spain
Tel: +34 91 417 55 49
Fax: +34 91 555 93 68
Email: info@iosco.org
www.iosco.org

Australia: Securities & Investments Commission

The Australia Securities & Investments Commission (ASIC) regulates Australia's corporate, markets and financial services sectors. The ASIC issues a unique eight-digit number (known as a "corporate key") to all registered companies with an Australian company number (ACN) or an Australian business number (ABN).

https://www.acnpacific.com/

Regulator Codes

https://abr.gov.au/For-Business,-Super-funds---Charities/Applying-for-an-ABN/Apply-for-an-ABN/

Austria: Financial Market Authority

The Financial Market Authority (FMA) is the supervisory authority for the Austrian financial market, established as an institution by the Financial Market Authority Act of 2002. It is responsible for the supervision of credit institutions, insurance undertakings, pension funds, staff provision funds, investment funds, investment service providers, companies listed on the stock exchange, and stock exchanges themselves. The FMA issues a seven-digit data processing register number (DVR) to all entities for which it is the supervisory authority.

http://www.fma.gv.at/en

Belgium: Financial Services & Markets Authority

The Belgian FSMA Storage of Regulated Information (STORI) includes information about issuers whose securities are traded on a regulated market, and for which Belgium is the home member state. Within the context of their obligations regarding periodic and certain ongoing information, It also holds information on issuers whose securities are admitted to trading on Alternext (operated by Euronext Brussels NV/SA). Issuers are not assigned a separate FSMA identification number for the purpose of filings. All items are filed using the company enterprise number or the ISIN.

http://www.fsma.be/en.aspx

Canada: Regional Securities Commissions

Unlike other major federations, Canada does not have a federal securities regulatory authority. Canadian securities regulation is managed through laws and agencies established by Canada's 13 provincial and territorial governments. Each province and territory has a securities commission or equivalent authority and its own piece of provincial or territorial legislation. The largest of the provincial regulators is the Ontario Securities Commission. Other significant provincial regulators are the British Columbia Securities Commission, the Alberta Securities Commission and the Autorité des Marchés Financiers (Québec).

Public companies are required to file their financial statements and other disclosure documents on the System for Electronic Disclosure Analysis and Retrieval (SEDAR). Items are filed by name and CUSIP number.

http://www.osc.gov.on.ca/, http://www.bcsc.bc.ca/,
http://www.albertasecurities.com/Pages/home.aspx
http://www.lautorite.qc.ca/en/index.html

Chile: Superintendencia de Valores y Seguros

The Superintendent of Securities and Insurance (Superintendencia de Valores y Seguros, or SVS) is the regulator for the financial industry and markets in Chile. The SVS does not assign a registration number to companies for the purpose of filing financial or other price-sensitive information. Instead, the tax number, or Rol Único Tributario (RUT) assigned by the Servicio de Impuestos Internos (Inland Revenue), serves as the unique identifier for all registered companies. The RUT comprises two part: an eight-digit identification number and a check digit separated by a hyphen. The check digit is derived using the module 11 algorithm.

http://www.svs.cl/portal/principal/605/w3-channel.html

Czech Republic: Czech National Bank

The Czech National Bank employs an eight-digit company identification number, or Identifikační Číslo Osoby (ICO), in its capacity as the regulator of the securities market. The ICO is the main key for the identification of all issuer filings submitted to its central storage of regulated information.

https://www.cnb.cz/en/

Denmark: Financial Supervisory Authority

The Danish Financial Supervisory Authority (Finanstilsynet, or DFSA) assigns a sequential five-digit identification to all regulated issuers. This identification

Regulator Codes

number together with the eight-digit Central Business Register (CVR) number is used as the key identification number for issuer filings on the regulatory database.

https://www.finanstilsynet.dk/da/

Estonia: Financial Supervision Authority

Estonia's Financial Supervision Authority (Finantsinspektioon, or FI) is responsible for the supervision of its securities market. The FI uses the eight-digit company registration number as its main identification number for issuer filings and other purposes.

http://www.fi.ee/?id=580

Finland: Financial Supervision Authority

The Financial Supervisory Authority (Finanssivalvonta, or FIN-FSA) is responsible for the supervision and regulation of the Finnish financial and insurance markets. It supervises banks, investment firms, fund management companies, the Helsinki Stock Exchange, insurance and pension companies, as well as other companies operating in the insurance sector.

http://www.finanssivalvonta.fi/fi/Pages/Default.aspx

France: Autorité des Marchés Financiers

The Financial Markets Authority (Autorité des Marchés Financiers, or AMF) is responsible for the supervision and regulation of the financial markets in France. The AMF verifies company disclosure of financial information and approves prospectuses for public offerings and/or requests for admission of securities to a regulated market. The ISIN is the accepted identification number for the filing of financial reports and price-sensitive information.

http://www.amf-france.org/en_US/?langSwitch=true

Germany: Bundesanstalt für Finanzdienstleistungsaufsicht

Germany's Federal Financial Supervisory Authority (Bundesanstalt für Finanz-dienstleistungsaufsicht, or BaFin) is responsible for the supervision of financial markets and listed companies. All financial institutions must be registered in the BAFin database before they can commence operations – a requirement which encompasses banks, financial services providers, asset management companies, insurers and pension funds. BaFin ID numbers are up to eight digits in length and allocated sequentially.

http://www.bafin.de/EN/Homepage/homepage_node.html

Greece: Hellenic Republic Capital Market Commission/Bank of Greece

The Hellenic Republic Capital Market Commission (HCMC) and the Bank of Greece act as the financial regulators for Greece. The HCMC supervises securities laws. The Bank of Greece is a treasurer and fiscal agent that supervises private insurance companies. In general, the ISIN is the main identification number used to fulfill reporting requirements.

http://www.hcmc.gr

Hungary: Central Bank of Hungary

Following its merger with the Hungarian Financial Supervisory Authority, the Central Bank of Hungary, or Magyar Nemzeti Bank, became Hungary's national regulatory body for financial markets. The 10-digit company registry number is the main identification number for reporting requirements.

http://english.mnb.hu/

Iceland: Financial Supervisory Authority

All entities engaged in financial activities are regulated by the Financial Supervisory Authority, or Fjármálaeftirlitið. It regulates stock exchanges, commercial banks, savings banks, credit institutions, securities firms, insurance companies, pension funds and UCITs. Companies use 10-digit Kennitölur registration numbers for the purposes of reporting.

Regulator Codes

http://www.fme.is/

Ireland: Central Bank of Ireland

The Central Bank of Ireland oversees the circulation of information about traded securities, monitors the market for misreporting or the manipulation of the market, and supervises the corporate governance of organised markets. The Central Bank of Ireland's registers contain individual registers for all financial service providers and collective investment schemes. It also includes details of other types of financial service providers which it is required to disclose on its registers. The Central Bank issues unique reference numbers to all registered entities.

http://www.centralbank.ie/Pages/home.aspx

Israel: Israel Securities Authority

The Israel Securities Authority (ISA), established in 1968, sees its mandate as ensuring that the country has an efficient capital market based on transparency and fairness. The nine-digit company register number is used for reports that must be filed with the ISA, the Tel Aviv stock exchange and the registrar of companies.

http://www.isa.gov.il/sites/ISAEng/Pages/default.aspx

Italy: Commissione Nazionale per le Società e la Borsa

The Commissione Nazionale per le Società e la Borsa (CONSOB) is the public authority which regulates Italy's securities market. CONSOB is responsible for: transparency by securities market participants; the disclosure of accurate information by listed companies; the accuracy of prospectuses relating to offerings of transferable securities; and compliance with regulations by auditors entered in the register. CONSOB assigns numerical sequential codes to all the entities it regulates.

http://www.consob.it/

Japan: Financial Services Agency

Japan's Financial Services Agency (FSA) oversees the country's banking, securities and insurance industries. The agency reports to the Ministry of Finance. The FSA assigns numerical sequential codes to all entities it regulates.

http://www.fsa.go.jp/en/

Korea: Financial Services Commission/Financial Supervisory Service

The Financial Services Commission (FSC) and its executive arm, the Financial Supervisory Service (FSS), supervise the Korean banking and financial sector, are usually assigned following the completion of the full-scope examination of the subject financial services firm's head office.

http://www.fsc.go.kr/eng/
http://english.fss.or.kr/fss/en/main.jsp

Luxembourg: Commission de Surveillance du Secteur Financier

The Commission de Surveillance du Secteur Financier (CSSF) is responsible for the supervision of credit institutions, securities firms, investment fund managers, undertakings for collective investment, pension funds, SICARs, securitisation undertakings issuing securities to the public on a continuous basis, regulated securities markets and their operators, multilateral trading facilities, payment institutions and electronic money institutions. RCSL (Registre de commerce et de Sociétés) numbers are used as the main identifier for periodic and other regulatory reporting.

http://www.cssf.lu/en/

Mexico: Comisión Nacional Bancaria y de Valores

The Comisión Nacional Bancaria y de Valores (CNBV), Mexico's banking and securities regulator, supervises and regulates all financial institutions including banks, non-banking financial companies, brokerage houses and mutual fund companies. The National Securities Registry (Registro Nacional de Valores or

Regulator Codes

RNV), run by the CNBV, contains entries for all regulated entities. Registration numbers are numerical in format and sequential.

http://www.cnbv.gob.mx/Paginas/default.aspx

Netherlands: Authority for the Financial Markets

The Netherlands Authority for the Financial Markets (Autoriteit Financiële Markten) is Holland's financial services regulatory agency. Its registers contain licences that have been granted by De Nederlandsche Bank (DNB) or by the Authority for the Financial Markets (AFM). Financial undertakings require a DNB or AFM licence to pursue their business in the Netherlands. The licensed undertakings are subject to ongoing DNB or AFM supervision. The registers use the eight-digit numbers, Kamer van Koophandel (KvK) which are used as the main identifier for all the companies.

http://www.afm.nl/en

New Zealand: Financial Markets Authority

New Zealand's Financial Markets Authority (FMA) regulates all financial market participants and exchanges, and the setting and enforcing of financial regulations. Issuers are identified by their NZCO number. Financial service providers and advisers are assigned a five- or six-digit FSP number.

http://www.fma.govt.nz/

Norway: Financial Supervisory Authority

Norway's Financial Supervisory Authority, or Finanstilsynet, is the igovernment agency responsible for supervising all financial institutions and markets: banks, finance companies, mortgage companies, insurance companies, pension funds, investment firms, market conduct in the securities market, securities registers, estate agencies, debt collection agencies, external accountants and auditors. Companies are identified by their nine-digit company registration number.

http://www.finanstilsynet.no/en/

Poland: Financial Supervision Authority

The Polish Financial Supervision Authority (KNF) supervises the country's financial services industry. This includes credit institutions, insurance firms, investment companies, exchanges, pension schemes, payment institutions and credit unions. For the purposes of disclosure and supervision, entities and registered service providers are identified by one of three registration numbers – the National Court Register Number (KRS), the Taxpayer Identification Number (NIP) or the National Business Registry Number (REGON).

http://www.knf.gov.pl/en/index.html

Portugal: Comissão do Mercado de Valores Mobiliários

The Portuguese Securities Market Commission (Comissão do Mercado de Valores Mobiliários, or CMVM) is responsible for the supervision and regulation of the securities industry and other financial markets. For the purposes of disclosure and supervision, entities and registered service providers are identified by the nine-digit NIPC number issued by the commercial registry.

http://www.cmvm.pt/en

Slovakia: National Bank of Slovakia

In 2006, Slovakia's Financial Market Authority was dissolved by law and all its powers and responsibilities were transferred to the National Bank of Slovakia. The NBS is now solely responsible for financial market supervision. It maintains the Central Register of Regulated Information database of regulated information that issuers of traded securities must submit to the National Bank of Slovakia pursuant to the Stock Exchange Act. Issuers are identified by their eight-digit Identifikačné Číslo Organizácie, or company identification number, issued by the Statistical Office.

http://www.nbs.sk/en/home

Slovenia: Agencija Za Trg Vrednostnih Papirjev

The Securities Market Agency (Agencija Za Trg Vrednostnih Papirjev) supervises and regulates the securities industry and other financial markets in

Regulator Codes

Slovenia. The agency maintains lists and registers of issued licences issued to brokerage companies, stock exchanges, management companies and investment funds, clearing and depository houses and mutual pension funds and their managers. It also maintains a register of public companies, authorises prospectuses for public securities offerings for admission to trading, and issues authorisations for takeover bids. Entities are identified by TIN a seven-digit number which defines the taxpayer (individuals and legal entities).

http://www.a-tvp.si/

Spain: Comisión Nacional del Mercado de Valores

The Comisión Nacional del Mercado de Valores (CNMV) is the agency in charge of supervising and inspecting the Spanish stockmarket and its participants. For the purposes of disclosure and supervision, entities and regulated individuals are identified by ISINs (listed companies), the CIF (Certificado de Identificación Fiscal) business tax ID number for all companies or the NIF (Número de Identificación Fiscal) individual tax ID number. For Spaniards, it's the DNI (documento nacional de identidad) plus one letter; for foreigners, it is the NIE (Número de Identidad de Extranjero).

https://www.cnmv.es/portal/home.aspx?lang=en

Sweden: Finansinspektionen

Sweden's Finansinspektionen supervises and regulates the securities industry and other financial companies. It issues entities with their 10-digit Bolagsverket registration number.

http://www.fi.se/

Switzerland: Swiss Financial Market Supervisory Authority

The Swiss Financial Market Supervisory Authority (FINMA) is an independent institution responsible for implementing Switzerland's Financial Market Supervision Act and financial market legislation. Swiss supervision of the stock exchange and market supervision are based on the principle of self-regulation. FINMA is in charge of the overall supervision of the stock exchanges and markets. FINMA-maintained registers generally use the uniform identification numberfor entity identification. Insurance and other financial intermediaries (Vermittler) are assigned a five-digit number. Other companies are assigned a thirteen-digit number issued by the Commercial Registery (Zefix).

http://www.finma.ch/e/Pages/default.aspx

Turkey: Capital Markets Board

The Capital Markets Board of Turkey (CMB) is the regulatory and supervisory authority in charge of the securities markets. It gives unique numbers to all commercial enterprises, equity companies and their branch offices; these numbers are used for identification purposes.

http://www.cmb.gov.tr/

United Kingdom: Financial Conduct Authority

The UK's Financial Services Register provides a public record of all firms and individuals in the financial services industry regulated by the Financial Conduct Authority (FCA). An FCA firm reference number is six or seven digits in length. Each entry on the FCA database is allocated the next vacant number when it is added to the system. The reference numbers allocated to authorised firms are not necessarily consecutive because not all firms that apply for FCA authorisation complete the registration process.

When a firm changes its legal status, the new entity is authorised in its own right and allocated a new reference number. Previously, an organisation had a permanent relationship with its firm reference number irrespective of whether it moved, changed its name, moved regulator, became incorporated or returned to being authorised following a non-authorised period. Under the new system, this no longer applies.

https://register.fca.org.uk/

Regulator Codes

United States: Securities and Exchange Commission

The US Securities and Exchange Commission (SEC) assigns a Central Index Key (CIK), or identification code, to corporations and individuals identified on regulatory filings. The CIK can be used to search for company or fund filings on the Electronic Data Gathering, Analysis and Retrieval (EDGAR) system of submissions by companies and others who are required by law to file with the SEC. The CIK is a 10-digit identification code assigned sequentially. For example, the CIK for Apple Inc. is 0000320193.

http://www.sec.gov/edgar/searchedgar/cik.htm#.U9lFl8toyic

Proprietary

Several companies have devised their own coding which has been used widely within the financial services industry. Often, they require licensing relying either on copyright, trademark or the database directive.

CUSIP Avox Business Reference Entity Identifier

Introduction

The Avox International Business Entity Identifier (AVID) is an identifier assigned by Avox Limited. Avox assigns a unique identifier to each business entity it validates for its clients. Avox maps each client's existing internal business entity identifier to the AVID so it is not necessary for Avox community members to physically add another identifier to their infrastructure.

AVID issuer

Avox
55 Water Street
    New York City, NY 10041
United States of America
Tel: +1 212 855 8099
Email: entitydata@dtcc.com
www.dtcc.com

History

Avox Limited, a wholly owned subsidiary of The Depository Trust & Clearing Corporation (DTCC), provides legal entity data services. The company was founded in 2003 in cooperation with several financial institutions that required a more efficient mechanism for delivering better data in a timely manner. The Avox International Business Entity Identifier (AVID) is a unique identifier assigned by Avox to each business entity it validates for its clients. The AVID can be delivered back to the client upon request. Avox maps each client's existing internal business entity identifier to the AVID so it is not necessary for Avox community members to physically add another identifier to their infrastructure. Avox collaborates with a variety of industry participants to ensure the AVID is consistent with the global identification standards of the International Business Ethics Institute (IBEI) and to facilitate fast and reliable identification of all parties involved in any transaction process.

CUSIP Avox Business Reference Entity Identifier

In 2009, Avox and Cusip Global Services (CGS), joined forces to create a universal identification system for global business entities known as the Cusip Avox Business Reference Entity identifier (CABRE). The new standard 10-character code is assigned and maintained for issuers, obligors and counterparties on a global basis. Customers can submit and track entity challenges at http://www.avoxdata.com/portal

Structure

AVIDs are eight-digit codes assigned sequentially to business entities upon request. CABREs are 10-digit codes also assigned sequentially.

For more information

https://www.avoxdata.com/portal/
https://www.cusip.com/cusip/cabre.htm

Compustat ID

In brief

The Global Company Key or GVKEY is a unique six-digit number key assigned to each company (issue, currency, index) in the Capital IQ Compustat database. It is a company identifier similar to a TICKER symbol. It represents the primary key for a company that is an index constituent.

GVKEY issuer

S&P Capital IQ Compustat
55 Water Street
    New York, NY 10041
United State of America
Tel: +1 877 863 1306

20 Canada Square, Canary Wharf
    London, UK E14 5LH
United Kingdom
Tel: +44 20 7176 1234
Unit 01, Level 69

International Commerce Centre
1 Austin Road West
Kowloon
Hong Kong
Tel: +852 2533 3565

http://www.marketintelligence.spglobal.com

History

Compustat is a database, owned by S&P, of financial, statistical and market information on active and inactive global companies throughout the world. The service began in 1962. The principal contents of the data files are items reported by companies in standard financial reports, such as quarterly and annual income statements, balance sheets and cash flow statements. Separate files in the North American database cover US and Canadian firms, while the global files cover companies in more than 80 other countries.

Compustat provides a broad range of information products for institutional investors, universities, bankers, advisors, analysts, and asset/portfolio managers in corporate, M&A, private capital, equity and fixed income markets. The database covers 99% of the world's total market capitalisation with annual company data history available back to 1950 and quarterly available back to 1962 (depending when that company was added to the database).

The Compustat Global Company Key, or GVKEY, is a proprietary identifier assigned to each company in the Standard & Poor's Capital IQ Compustat database. The GVKEY can be used to track a company continuously regardless of whether the company name, CUSIP or ticker changes over time.

Structure

The GVKEY is a unique six-digit number key assigned to each company (issue, currency, and index) in the Compustat database. It represents the primary key for a company that is an index constituent. The GVKEY can be used to track a company in the database in perpetuity, even if the company changes its name, CUSIP or ticker.

For more information

https://www.capitaliq.com/home/what-we-offer/information-you-need/financials-valuation/compustat-financials.aspx

Data Universal Numbering System (DUNS)

In brief

The Data Universal Numbering System (DUNS or D-U-N-S) is a coding system developed and maintained by Dun & Bradstreet (D&B). DUNS assigns a unique numeric identifier (a "DUNS number") to a single business entity. DUNS numbers are used for a variety of purposes, including establishing business credit and applying for government contracting opportunities.

DUNS issuer
Dun & Bradstreet
103 JFK Parkway
    Short Hills, NJ 07078
New Jersey
United States of America
    Tel: +1 973 921 5500
www.dnb.com

History

Introduced in 1963 to support D&B's credit reporting practice, DUNS has become a common worldwide standard. DUNS users include the European Commission, the United Nations and the United States government. More than 50 global, industry and trade associations recognise, recommend or require DUNS. The DUNS database contains over 100 million entries for businesses throughout the world.

Structure

The DUNS number is a nine-digit number assigned to each business location in the D&B database. The DUNS number is random and the digits have no apparent significance. Until around December 2006, the DUNS number contained a mod-10 check digit to support error detection. Discontinuing the check digit increased the inventory of available DUNS numbers by 800 million. Unlike national employer identification numbers, a DUNS number

Data Universal Numbering System (DUNS) ━━━

may be issued to any business worldwide. Certain US government agencies require that a vendor have a DUNS number as well as a US employer identification number (EIN).

Other agencies, such as some United Nations offices and Australian government agencies, require certain businesses to have a DUNS number. DUNS numbers are now available to individuals; previously, DUNS numbers could only be obtained by corporations or other organisations.

A DUNS number is sometimes formatted with embedded dashes to promote readability, such as "15-048-3782". Modern usage typically omits dashes and shows the number as in the form "150483782". The dashes are not part of D&B's official definition of the DUNS number.

Depository Trust Corporation Participant Account (DTCPA)

Depository Trust Corporation Participant Account (DTCPA)

In brief

The DTCC provides clearing, settlement and information series for equities, bonds and government- and mortgage backed securities, money market instruments and other financial instruments.

DTCC issuer

Depository Trust and Clearing Corporation
140 58th St.
Brooklyn NY 11220
United States of America
Tel: +1 718 439 3784
www.dtcc.com

History

The Depository Trust and Clearing Corporation (DTCC) was established in 1999 as a holding company combining the Depository Trust Company (DTC) and the National Securities Clearing Corporation (NSCC). Through its subsidiaries, the DTCC provides clearing, settlement and information services for equities, corporate and municipal bonds, government- and mortgage-backed securities, money market instruments and over-the-counter derivatives. In addition, the DTCC is a leading processor of mutual funds and insurance transactions, linking funds and carriers with their distribution networks.

The Depository Trust Corporation Participant Account (DTCPA) code is used by the DTCC to identify participating depository institutions.

Factiva Data Symbol (FDS)

In brief

The Factiva Data Symbol (FDS) is a code applied to quoted and unquoted companies referenced in Factiva's database of business information.

> **FDS Issuer**
>
> Dow Jones & Company
> 1211 Avenue of the Americas
> New York, NY 10036
> United States of America
> *Email: service@dowjones.com*
> *www.dowjones.com*

History

Now wholly-owned by Dow Jones & Company, Factiva was originally founded as a joint venture between Reuters and Dow Jones & Co in May 1999. Factiva provides business news and information from over 10,000 licensed and free sources, such as the *Wall Street Journal*, the *Financial Times*, Dow Jones, Reuters and the Associated Press, as well as Reuters Fundamentals and Dun & Bradstreet (D&B) company profiles. It also provides access to more than 36,000 sources, including more than 400 newswires, local newspapers, journals and magazines, from almost 200 countries in 28 languages.

Structure

An FDS is a unique alphabetic code of between two and six characters in length. Each code represents one company, which may be public or private. Codes generally bear some resemblance to the company name. Codes are assigned to all independent companies, quoted subsidiaries, 50/50 joint ventures, mutual funds and investment trusts, consortia and a controlled list of unquoted subsidiaries which attract significant news coverage on Factiva services.

Fitch Issuer Identification Number (FIID)

In brief

The FIID applies to issuers of debt rated by Fitch Ratings Inc, a subsidiary of Hearst Corporation and the smallest of three US statistical rating organisations approved by the SEC.

Fitch issuer
33 Whitehall Street
New York NY 10004
United State of America
Tel: +1 212 908 0500

30 North Colonnade, Canary Wharf
London E14 5GN
United Kingdom
Tel: +44 20 3530 1000
www.fitchratings.com

History

Fitch Ratings Inc is a wholly owned subsidiary of Hearst Corporation. Founded by John Knowles Fitch in New York in 1913 as the Fitch Publishing Company, it merged with London-based IBCA Ltd in December 1997. In 2000 Fitch acquired both Chicago-based Duff & Phelps Credit Rating Co and Thomson Financial BankWatch. Fitch Ratings is the smallest of the three nationally recognised statistical rating organisations (NRSROs) designated by the US Securities and Exchange Commission in 1975.

Structure

The Fitch Issuer Identification Number (FIID) is a unique proprietary 12-digit tracking number applied to each issuer of debt rated by Fitch Ratings. Fitch Ratings is an independent global credit rating agency.

Moody's Issuer Number (MIN)

In brief

The MIN is a 10-digit code issued to issuers of debt rated by Moody's Investor Services.

MIN issuer

Moody's Investor Services
One International Place
100 Oliver Street, Suite 1400
Boston MA 02110
United States of America

One Canada Square
London E14 5FA
United Kingdom
Tel: +44 20 772 1000

10th Floor, Tower D
Beijing China Merchants International Finance Center
156 Fuxingmen Nei Street
Beijing 100031
China

www.moodys.com

History

Moody's Investors Service, often referred to as Moody's, is the bond credit rating business of Moody's Corporation. Moody's was founded by John Moody in 1909 to produce manuals of statistics related to stocks and bonds and bond ratings. In 1975, the company was identified as a nationally recognised statistical rating organisation (NRSRO) by the US Securities and Exchange Commission. Following several decades of ownership by Dun & Bradstreet, Moody's Investors Service became a separate company in 2000.

Moody's Issuer Number (MIN)

Moody's Investors Service rates debt securities in several market segments related to public and commercial securities in the bond market. These include government, municipal and corporate bonds; managed investments such as money market funds, fixed-income funds and hedge funds; financial institutions including banks and non-bank finance companies; and asset classes in structured finance.

Structure

The Moody's Issuer Number (MIN) is a unique 10-digit identifier applied to each issuer of debt rated by Moody's Investor Services.

Moody's KMV Identifier

In brief

Moody's KMV is a six-digit code applied to companies covered by Moody's credit assessment service.

> **KMV issuer**
>
> Moody's Investor Services
> One International Place
> 100 Oliver Street, Suite 1400
> Boston, MA 02110
> United States of America
>
> One Canada Square
> London, E14 5FA
> United Kingdom
> Tel: +44 20 772 1000
>
> 10th Floor, Tower D
> Beijing China Merchants International Finance Center
> 156 Fuxingmen Nei Street
> Beijing, 100031
> China
> **www.moodys.com**

History

Moody's Investors Service, described above, is the bond credit rating business of Moody's Corporation. In 2002, Moody's acquired KMV (Kealhofer, McQuown and Vasicek). KMV's product, CreditEdge, delivers forward-looking daily public firm Expected Default Frequency (EDF) credit measures to support credit risk assessment and investment decisions.

Moody's KMV Identifier

Structure

The Moody's KMV unique company identifier, PID or MKMV ID, is a six-digit number applied to companies covered by Moody's CreditEdge Plus service.

For more information

http://www.moodysanalytics.com/About-Us/History/KMV-History

Markit codes

In brief

IHS Markit provides three codes: the MEI, which identifies entities in the loan market; LoanX ID, which applies to syndicated loans; and CLIP, used in the financial derivatives market.

> **Markit codes issuer**
> HIS Markit
> 25 Ropemarker St
> London EC2Y 9LY
> United Kingdom
> Tel: +44 20 7260 2000
> *www.markit.com/Product/Reference-Data-CDS*

History

Markit Ltd was founded in 2003 as independent source of credit derivative pricing. The company provides independent data, trade processing of derivatives, foreign exchange and loans, customised technology platforms and managed services. LoanX Inc, a US provider of syndicated loan data, was acquired by Markit in December 2003. In 2016, Markit merged with IHS to form IHS Markit.

Structure

Six-digit RED credit agreement codes uniquely identify the reference credit agreement. Nine-digit RED pair codes uniquely identify each "ranking" by linking reference credit agreement – lien – reference obligations. Nine-digit Markit Loan IDs (MLIDs) are uniquely assigned to each facility. Mapping between MLID and Markit Cash Loan Identifier LX (previously LoanX) identifiers allows users to easily compare cash and synthetic loan information. Markit RED is an integral part of DTCC, trading platforms and processing systems.

Markit codes

Markit Entity Identifier (MEI)

The Markit Entity Identifier (MEI) uniquely identifies entities in the loan market including counterparties, issuers, funds, sub-funds and borrowers. The primary objective of MEIs is to provide global coverage of entities in the loan market and their relationships. MEIs link disparate identifiers including Markit RED and Markit LoanX IDs and other standard identifiers facilitating straight-through-processing and improving transparency and operational efficiency in the syndicated loan market. Approximately 18,000 MEIs have been issued, covering counterparties, funds, sub-funds and borrowers.

LoanX ID (LXID)

The Markit LoanX ID (LXID) is a unique identifier applied to syndicated loans to facilitate straight-through-processing. Syndicated loans are credits granted by a group of banks to a borrower. They are hybrid instruments that combine features of relationship lending and publicly traded debt. They allow the sharing of credit risk between various financial institutions without the disclosure requirements faced by bond issuers. Syndicated credits are a significant source of international financing, accounting for around a third of all international financing, including bond, commercial paper and equity issues. In a syndicated loan, two or more banks agree jointly to make a loan to a borrower. Every syndicate member has a separate claim on the debtor, although there is a single loan agreement contract.

CUSIP Linked MIP (CLIP)

The CUSIP-linked MIP code – with MIP meaning Markit Partners – is used in the financial derivatives markets to identify the reference entity of a credit default swap. Called CLIP, it is mainly used as a key field in Markit's reference entity database (RED). Each CLIP is linked with one or more CUSIPs each representing a reference entity obligation (securities). For example, the CLIP of WESTLAB AG (reference entity) is 'DMFCCI'. There are multiple issues from WESTLAB AG, each with different CUSIPs: D96637AG4, D96637AH2, D96637AK5, etc. CLIP is known under multiple names such as Markit RED code, RED CLIP or simply CLIPS. S&P and Markit Partners introduced the CLIP concept , with the S&P CUSIP bureau generating entity CLIP codes and assigning them to each entity name individually. CLIP codes are used for electronic matching on DTCC and have been integrated in various online platforms.

For more information

www.ihsmarkit.com/

Section 2
Security Codes

Securities industry professionals and investors alike require unique security identifiers to distinguish between the numerous and varied securities issuers and individual securities issues with which they work on a daily basis. The most widely used security identifiers are exchange ticker symbols, International Securities Identification Numbers (ISINs), CUSIPs and London Stock Exchange SEDOLs. The two main proprietary security identification systems are the Reuters Instrument Code (RIC) and the Bloomberg Global ID (BBGID).

Ticker symbols are the most widely used identifiers in the broker and investor community, as they are easily recognised and remembered. Ticker symbols, via their additional-letter codes, also communicate important information to investors about the trading status of the security or the issuer. Although tickers identify a security, they are exchange-dependent, generally limited to stocks, and can change. This limitation has led to the development of other codes such as the International Securities Identifying Number (ISIN) to identify securities for clearing and settlement purposes. ISINs are assigned to a wide range of financial instruments and uniquely identify an individual security.

International Codes

CUSIP International Numbering System (CINS)

In brief

A CUSIP is a nine-character alphanumeric code that identifies a North American financial security for the purposes of facilitating clearing and settlement of trades.

CUSIP is operated by S&P Capital IQ and owned by the American Bankers Association.

CUSIP issuer
CUSIP Global Services
55 Water Street, 45th Floor
New York NY 10041
United State of America
Tel: +1 609 426 7358
+1 212 438 6500
Email: cusip.custservice@cusip.com
www.cusip.com

History

The CUSIP International Numbering System (CINS) was conceived in the 1980s as part of an effort to extend the CUSIP system to international securities. CUSIP's operating body, CUSIP Global Services (CGS), serves as the national numbering agency (NNA) for North America. It also serves as the National Securities Identification Number (NSIN) for products issued from both the United States and Canada. In its role as the NNA, CUSIP Global Services (CGS) also assigns all US-based ISINs.

Currently, the CINS system contains entries for approximately 1.3 million different securities. Just as with CUSIP numbers, CINS numbers consist of nine characters. Each issuer is assigned a unique six-digit number. The next two characters uniquely identify the security issue. As with CUSIP numbers, the final character is a check digit.

CUSIP International Numbering System (CINS)

Structure

The CINS number consists of nine characters – for instance, Z 23456 78 9.

A unique feature of the CINS system is that the first character is always a letter signifying the domicile country of the issuer.

A = Austria
B = Belgium
C = Canada
D = Germany
E = Spain
F = France
G = United Kingdom
H = Switzerland
J = Japan
K = Denmark
L = Luxembourg
M = Middle East
N = Netherlands
P = South America
Q = Australia
R = Norway
S = South Africa
T = Italy
U = United States
V = Africa-Other
W = Sweden
X = Europe-Other
Y = Asia

The 1st position "Z" denotes the country or origin or the geographical region of the issuer as per the list above. The next five positions identify the issuer. Positions 7 and 8 identify the issue or security type and position 9 is the check digit calculated using the same methodology as for a standard CUSIP number.

CUSIP International Numbering System (CINS)

Issuer number

A five-digit issuer number preceded by the country or regional code is assigned to each issuer in alphabetical order. Only one identifier will be assigned to an issuer, except in those few cases where the issue identifiers are not sufficient to accommodate all outstanding issues. In such cases one or more additional issuer numbers will be assigned.

Unlike the standard CUSIP numbering system, there is no provision within the CINS for user number assignments throughout the sequence. Numbers 90 to 99 in the 5th and 6th positions of the issuer number are used by the CINS. However, to accommodate a limited amount of user defined international assets, the last 3,000 plus issuer numbers within each country or region have been allocated as user numbers and will not be assigned as official CINS issuer numbers.

This uniquely identifies each individual issue of an issuer and consists of two numeric characters for equities and two alphabetic characters or one numeric and one alphabetic character for fixed income securities. Issue numbers are assigned in sequence as each issue is originated. However, in the setting up of the CINS and in the assignment of numbers to issues then in existence, numbers were assigned on the basis of rate and maturity and no consideration was given to the original date of the issue.

Issue numbers for equities

The first issue number for an issuer's equity securities is 10. The unit position of the equity number is used to identify rights, warrants and so on and is assigned on an as available basis.

Issue numbers for fixed income securities

Issue numbers for fixed income securities may consist of two alphabetic characters e.g. AA, one alphabetic character followed by one digit, e.g. A1, or one digit followed by an alphabetical character, e.g. 1A, assigned in that order. Debt securities are sorted in order by their maturity dates.

CUSIP International Numbering System (CINS)

Check digit calculation

The 9th digit is an automatically generated check digit using the "Modulus 10 Double Add Double" technique. To calculate the check digit every second digit is multiplied by two. Letters are converted to numbers based on their ordinal position in the alphabet, starting with A equal to 10 and finishing with Z equal to 35.

For example, for issuer number A12345 and issue number 12, i.e. A1234512, digits in the 1st, 3rd, 5th and 7th positions are multiplied by 1 and digits in the 2nd, 4th, 6th and 8th positions are multiplied by 2. This results in the sequence 10-2-2-6-4-10-1-4. Adding up the sequence 1+0+2+2+6+4+1+0+1+4 results in a figure of 21. It is the complement of the last digit of the sum that becomes the check digit. The complement of 1 is 9, hence the full CUSIP number with the check digit is A12345129.

Corporate actions and CINs

In general, CUSIP Global Services determines whether a new CINS is required as a result of a proposed corporate action. Actions which normally result in the allocation of a new CINS include a change in company name, a reorganisation, a merger, a forward stock split, a reverse split or emergence from bankruptcy.

For more information

https://www.cusip.com/cusip/about-cgs-identifiers.htm

Common code

In brief

The common code is used to uniquely identify individual securities for clearing and settlement purposes between the two International Central Securities Depositories (ICSDs), Clearstream Banking and Euroclear Bank, and their participants.

> ### Common code issuer
> CEDEL – Euroclear
> 60 Wall Street, Suite 23-E
>   New York NY 10005
>   United States of America
> Tel: +1 212 655 9541
>
> Vicarage House
>   58 Kensington Church St
>   London W8 4DB
> United Kingdom
>   Tel: +44 207 993 80 49
>
> Two Exchange Square
>   8 Connaught Place Central
> Hong Kong
>   Tel: +852 3008-5655
> *http://www.clearstream.com/clearstream-en/prod-ucts-and-services/issuance--1-/issuance-services/code-allocation*

History

In January 1991, common codes replaced the earlier, then-separate CEDEL and Euroclear codes. These codes were used by the European depository banks, Clearstream and Euroclear, respectively. The use of one code allowed for inter-operability.

Common code

Structure

The common code is a nine-digit code allocated sequentially. Until 1999, when the second digit became a significant digit, the leading two digits were set to zero. In November 2013, it was anticipated that the current common code format would reach the highest possible number of possible codes. It was therefore announced that all digits would be significant for all securities accepted after this point, for example 100002874. No changes are to be made to existing codes.

International Securities Identification Number (ISIN)

In brief

An International Securities Identification Number, or ISIN, uniquely identifies a securitiy. Securities for which ISINs are issued include bonds, commercial paper, stocks and warrants. The ISIN code is a 12-character alphanumerial code that does not contain information characterising financial information, but provides uniform identification of securities at trading and settlement.

ISIN issuer

Each country's national numbering agency issues ISINs as described by the ISO 6166 standard and the classification of financial instruments code as described by the ISO 10962 standard. The role of the NNA is typically assigned to the national stock exchange, central bank or financial regulatory, but can also be a financial data provider or clearing and custodian organisation.

Anna issuer
http://www.anna-web.orgw

History

Although the structure of the International Securities Identification Number (ISIN) code was defined by the International Standards Organisation (ISO) in the late 1970s, ISINs were not widely accepted until 1989, following the recommendation of the G-30 countries. In 1992, the Association of National Numbering Agencies (ANNA) was founded by 22 national numbering agencies. Two years later, the Global ISIN Access Mechanism (GIAM) was developed to facilitate the electronic exchange of ISIN information across the different NNAs.

Operating under Belgian law, ANNA oversees the use of ISINs for the uniform identification of financial instruments. At the initial stage of the Association's activity its members worked on the standardisation of the accompanying

International Securities Identification Number (ISIN)

algorithm, which is the basis of ISIN. The work also included defining the regulatory framework related to allocation of ISINs by financial institutions founded and operating in different countries. Subsequently, ISO appointed ANNA as an authorised registering and maintaining agency on standards of numbers ISIN (ISO 6166). ISIN and CFI information (see next chapter) can be accessed through the ANNA Service Bureau, run by Standard and Poor's and SIX Financial Information.

In North America, the NNA is the CUSIP organisation, meaning that CUSIPs can easily be converted into ISINs by adding the US or CA country code to the beginning of the existing CUSIP code and adding an additional check digit at the end. In the United Kingdom and Ireland, the NNA is the London Stock Exchange (See Appendix A) and the NSIN is the SEDOL, converted in a similar fashion. Swiss ISINs are issued by SIX Financial Information and are based on the VALOR number. Most other countries use similar conversions, but if no country NNA exists then regional NNAs are used instead.

Structure

The structure of International Securities Identification Numbers (ISINs) is defined by the international standard ISO 6166. ISINs uniquely identify a security and not the exchange (if any) on which it trades; it is not a ticker symbol. Fungible securities are identified by one ISIN. For instance, although Daimler AG stock trades through almost 30 trading platforms and exchanges worldwide and is priced in five different currencies, it has the same ISIN on each, but not the same ticker symbol. An ISIN does not convey details of the trading location. To do this, another identifier, such as the Market Identification Code or MIC (ISO 10383) would be needed in addition to the ISIN. The currency of the trade may also be required to uniquely identify the instrument.

ISINs consist of 12 characters. The first two characters represent the country code as issued in accordance with the international standard ISO 3166 of the country where the issuer of securities, other than debt securities, is legally registered or in which it has legal domicile. For debt securities, the relevant country is that of the ISIN-allocating national numbering agency (NNA). In the case of depository receipts, such as ADRs, the country code is that of the organisation who issued the receipt instead of the one who issued the underlying security. The next nine characters are taken up by the local number of

International Securities Identification Number (ISIN)

the security concerned. Where the national number consists of fewer than nine characters, zeros are inserted in front of the number so that the full nine spaces are used. The final character is a check digit computed according to the "Modulus 10 Double Add Double" formula.

Generally ISINs are never re-used. Where re-use is unavoidable, a 10-year period must elapse between the deactivation of the ISIN and its re-use. This applies to all financial instruments with the exception of options, futures and other short-term money market instruments. In these cases re-use is permitted one year after the expiration date of the instrument.

Specific Cases Relating to Fungibility

Situation	Fungible – Yes/No
Different marketplaces	Yes, if the security is traded in different marketplaces
Rights difference between different marketplaces with respect to corporate actions, interest payment or dividends	Yes, if it is only a technical difference No, if the securities are lodged in different codes to distinguish the different rights between holders of the various market places
Subsequent tranches	Yes, if the securities have identical terms and may be used to settle trades in either tranches, forms or markets No, in other cases until assimilation
Securities issued in bearer and/or registered form	Yes, if the securities are fully exchangeable No, if the securities are not fully exchangeable
Change of issue from bearer to registered form or vice versa at the behest of the issuer	No, if the holder does not have the same rights until the exchange
Representative certificates	Yes, in France Euroclear France is allowed to rematerialise French securities to be delivered in some foreign countries No, if dematerialised (e.g. German, Swiss, Dutch certificates) or materialized (e.g. IDR, ADR) secondary paper is issued Yes, if no secondary paper is issued
Corporate actions	Yes, if the securities confer to the new holders that same rights (e.g. subscription of shares with the same rights as the old shares) subscription of shares with the same rights as the old shares) No, if the new shares are not fully exchangeable or if an exchange or a future assimilation is required
Partly paid/Fully paid/Nil paid	No, until the full payment if an additional payment is required

International Securities Identification Number (ISIN)

Exceptional Assignment Rules

Situation	Rule
Allocation of ISINs to debt instruments issued with warrants	Debt instruments cum- and ex-warrant(s) must be registered separately; hence, at least three ISINs are assigned: one for the debt instrument cum-warrant(s); one for the debt instrument ex-warrant(s); and one for each warrant
Issues composed of both domestic and international tranches	If the tranches are not fungible, two ISINs are assigned
Partial reimbursement of capital when repayment equally to all holders at the same time	No need to assign new ISINs even if the payment effects a change of denomination amount
Issues with different denominations	Where different categories of shares are issued, each will be assigned its own ISIN Where certificates consist of multiple shares, only one ISIN is assigned For bonds, only one ISIN for different denominations if fungible
Taxable/non-taxable securities	If the securities are fungible, tax considerations will not affect the assignment of ISINs
ISINs for rights	ISINs are assigned to rights in accordance with ISO 6166
Issues with two or more tranches	Tranches with different issue prices are assigned separate ISINs, but will be assimilated after the first coupon payment
Warrants issued by foreign branches of banks	Where branches have no separate legal entity, the ISIN prefix will be that of the headquarters country; where the branch is a separate legal entity, the country of the branch will be used in assigning the ISIN prefix
Issues of the European Union	Financial instruments issued by the European Union but not relating to a specific EU country (e.g. European indices and interest rates) are assigned an ISIN with the prefix EU by WM Datenservice
Preferred shares	Preferred shares issued in unit form that are being treated as debt will be assigned ISINs by the NNA in the issuer's country of incorporation and set up as equity Preferred shares issued in nominal form that are being treated as debt will be assigned a XS ISIN and set up as bonds Preferred shares that are being treated as equity will be assigned ISINs by the NNA in the issuer's country of incorporation and set up as equity
RegS/144A debt issues	If the RegS and/or 144A portion is deposited with a US CSD, the ISIN will have a US prefix If the RegS and/or 144A portion is deposited with Euroclear/Clearstream, the ISIN will have a XS prefix In case of a bifurcated structure or split note, between two and four ISINs will be assigned by the relevant NNA in accordance with the place of deposit
RegS/144A for warrants	Where RegS/144A rules apply to warrants they will exceptionally be assigned a US prefix without reference to the country of the issuer, as this is normally the case for instruments referenced under the category "rights"

International Securities Identification Number (ISIN)

Situation	Rule
Common investment funds	The ISIN prefix will be the country where the fund is registered; if this information is not available at the time of the ISIN allocation, the country where tax is to be paid will be used
Depository receipts representing a debt instrument	Standard rules for debt instruments apply
Structured products	Currently there is no consistent rule. Euroclear/Clearstream, Spain and Germany use debt rule; UK uses country of incorporation; Switzerland uses domicile of lead manager

Exceptional Country Assignment Rules

Country	Rule
Australia	Delisted instruments: a temporary ISIN can be assigned when a security is delisted from the ASX Re-use of ISINs for warrants: re-use can occur after 45 days as the ISIN comprises the ASX code for the issuer and the characteristics of the warrant
Hong Kong	Securities issued in the Dual Tranche Dual Counter model (i.e. a simultaneous offering and listing of a tranche of RMB-traded shares and HKD-traded shares by the same issuer, with the option of transferability post-issuance) will be assigned two separate ISINs, one for each tranche, to allow for identification between the two counters in post trade settlement and position management
Italy	Different tranches of Italian debt securities subject to pro rata temporis taxation under the provisions of Legislative Decree 239/96 are only fungible, and can only bear the same ISIN, if the issue and redemption prices and the issue and redemption dates to be used for tax purposes are identical
Russia	Separate ISINs assigned to new issues of equities with the same rights until they are merged with the principal shares
US	Assign ISIN codes to bank loans

Other Financial Instruments

Instrument	Rules	Examples
Currencies	For single currencies, ISIN bears the prefix of the issuer country; for cross rates ISIN prefix is the issuer country of the fixed currency of the ratio	Euro: EU0009656420 USD: US9117941131
Indices	Stock exchange indices bear the prefix of the domicile of the exchange Other indices bear the prefix of the country of the calculating agent	FTSE 100: GB0001383545 S&P 500: US78378X1072

International Securities Identification Number (ISIN)

Instrument	Rules	Examples
Interest rates	Interest rates bear the prefix of the originator's country	1Y MIBOR: ES0S00000018 12M LIBOR: GB00B5M93442
Commodities	A single ISIN is assigned per commodity and domicile of the exchange even if multiple exchanges exist in the same country	Lampante Olive Oil: ES0SM00032042
Traded options	Each contract defined by expiration date, options type, strike price, currency and underlying instrument is assigned an ISIN with the prefix of the country of the exchange issuing the option	
Financial futures	Each contract defined by expiration date, currency and underlying instrument is assigned an ISIN with the prefix of the country of the exchange issuing the contract	
Contracts for differences (CfDs)	Each CfD defined by a standard contract specification and traded on an organised exchange or marketplace is assigned an ISIN with the prefix of the country of the exchange issuing the option	

Additional Information

Corporate Action Effects on ISINs

Event	Rules for Paperless Securities	Rules for Physical Certificates
Change of domicile	No change of ISIN	New ISIN assigned if the old security is exchanged for a new one
Merger by absorption	ISINs of shares of former companies will become inactive after a certain period	ISINs of shares of former companies will become inactive after a certain period
Merger by amalgamation	New ISIN assigned to the shares of the new company; former ISINs will become inactive	New ISIN assigned to the shares of the new company; former ISINs will become inactive
Assimilation	The ISIN of the new stock will become inactive when old and new shares become fungible unless a reuse is planned	The ISIN of the new stock will become inactive when old and new shares become fungible unless a reuse is planned

International Securities Identification Number (ISIN)

Event	Rules for Paperless Securities	Rules for Physical Certificates
Redemption	ISIN will become inactive after redemption date unless bonds are in default For convertible bonds, at the end of the conversion period, when the last conversion date is after maturity	ISIN will become inactive after redemption date unless bonds are in default For convertible bonds, at the end of the conversion period, when the last conversion date is after maturity
Bankruptcy	The ISIN will become inactive after deletion of the company from the register of commerce	The ISIN will become inactive after deletion of the company from the register of commerce
Increase of share capital by issue of additional stock	A new ISIN will only be assigned to stock with different rights	A new ISIN will only be assigned to stock with different rights
Increase of share capital by change of nominal value	ISIN remains unchanged	A new ISIN is assigned in case of exchange of the old certificates
Decrease of share capital by change of nominal value	ISIN remains unchanged	A new ISIN is assigned in case of exchange of the old certificates
Liquidation	The ISIN will become inactive after deletion of the company from the register of commerce	The ISIN will become inactive after deletion of the company from the register of commerce
Change of name	For both shares and debt securities the ISIN remains unchanged except for those where CUSIP is the relevant NNA	For both shares and debt securities a new ISIN is assigned in case of exchange of the old certificates
Stock split/sub-division	ISIN only changed if necessary for technical reasons	A new ISIN is assigned in case of exchange of the old certificates
Reverse split/consolidation	ISIN only changed if necessary for technical reasons	A new ISIN is assigned in case of exchange of the old certificates
Renewal of coupons	Not applicable	No new ISIN is assigned provided certificates do not need to be exchanged
Official stripping	ISIN will bear the prefix as determined by the allocation rules for debt instruments	ISIN will bear the prefix as determined by the allocation rules for debt instruments
Unofficial stripping	ISIN will bear the prefix of the country in which the entity performing the coupon strip is legally domiciled	ISIN will bear the prefix of the country in which the entity performing the coupon strip is legally domiciled

International Securities Identification Number (ISIN)

Event	Rules for Paperless Securities	Rules for Physical Certificates
Change of primary place of deposit	No ISIN change	A new ISIN is assigned in case of exchange of the old certificates
Change of issuer	No ISIN change	A new ISIN is assigned in case of exchange of the old certificates

For more information

http://www.isin.org/

http://www.anna-web.org/index.php

Classification of Financial Instruments (CFI) (ISO 10962)

CFI stands for Classification of Financial Instruments, a coding system developed to address the problem of inconsistent classification of financial instruments. CFIs are assigned by the same national numbering agencies responsible for the allocation of ISINs. Where no national numbering agency exists, the designated substitute agency will assign CFIs.

CFI issuer
http://www.anna-web.orgw

History

With the growth of cross-border trading, new instruments and new features attached to existing financial instruments, many market participants were using the same descriptions for financial instruments in different countries that in fact had significantly different attributes. In addition, the translation of financial terminology across multiple foreign markets, and the customs and practices in those markets for instrument classification, created confusion as to the exact nature of specific instruments.

The answer was the creation of a coding system which clearly classifies financial instruments with similar attributes, in conjunction with a glossary of common terms and definitions which allows market participants to understand what was what.

The structure of the CFI was designed to provide as much information possible, whilst maintaining manageability. Classification is determined by the characteristics of a financial instrument and not by the instrument name or terms that may differ in meaning from one country to another. The aim was to remove any confusion resulting from linguistic interpretation, thus providing an objective comparison of instruments across all domestic markets.

Classification of Financial Instruments (CFI) (ISO 10962)

Structure

ISO 10962 **defines the structure and format for classification of financial instruments** approved by the **International Organization for Standardization** (ISO). These instruments are used for saving, investing, trading, hedging and speculating and are generally organised in groups called "asset classifications".

The **alphabetical characters** in each position of this six-character code reflect specific characteristics intrinsic to the financial instruments that are defined at the issue of the instrument, and which in most cases remain unchanged during the lifetime of the instrument.

The CFI code is a six-character alpha code where the first character indicates the highest level of classification and differentiates between eight generic categories – (i) equities, (ii) debt instruments, (iii) entitlements, e.g. rights, (iv) options, (v) futures, (vi) structured products, (vii) referential instruments and (viii) others. The second character indicates sub-divisions within each category. For example, equities are sub-divided into common/ordinary shares, preferred shares, preference shares, convertible shares, preferred convertible shares, preference convertible shares, units (i.e. unit trusts/mutual funds/OPCVM/OICVM), and others. Debt instruments are sub-divided into bonds, convertible bonds, bonds with warrants, medium term notes, money market instruments, asset-backed securities, mortgage-backed securities and others.

Characters three to six indicate the most important attributes applicable to each category. For example, for equities, voting rights, ownership/transfer restrictions, payment status and form are common attributes whereas for options, underlying instruments, delivery, standardised/non-standardised and type of scheme apply.

Where information is not available or applicable at the time of assigning a code the letter "X" is used for the respective character in the code.

Category Codes

E – Equities – Exxxxx
D – Debt Instruments – Dxxxxx
R – Entitlements (Rights) – Rxxxxx

Classification of Financial Instruments (CFI) (ISO 10962)

O – Options – Oxxxxx

F – Futures – Fxxxxx

S – Structured Products/Hybrids – Sxxxxx

T – Referential Instruments – Txxxxx

M – Others (Miscellaneous) – Mxxxxx

Category Sub-Divisions and Attributes

Equities

Equity Type	1st Attribute	2nd Attribute	3rd Attribute	4th Attribute
S – Common/ Ordinary Shares – ESxxxx	**Voting Rights**	**Ownership/Transfer Restrictions**	**Payment Status**	**Form**
	V – Voting – ESVxxx	T – Restricted ownership or transfer – ESxTxx	O – Nil paid – ESxxOx	B – Bearer – ESxxxB
	N – Non-voting – ESNxxx	U – Unrestricted – ESxUxx	P – Partly paid – ESxxPx	R – Registered – ESxxxR
	R – Restricted voting – ESRxxx		F – Fully paid – ESxxFx	N – Bearer/registered – ESxxxN
	E – Enhanced voting – ESExxx			Z – Bearer depository receipt – ESxxxZ
				A – Registered depository receipt – ESxxxA
				G – SEC Regulation 144A – ESxxxG
				S – SEC Regulation S – ESxxxS
P – Preferred shares – EPxxxx	Identical to common/ordinary shares – replace second character "S" with "P"	**Redemption**	**Income**	Identical to common/ordinary shares – replace second character "S" with "P"
		R – Redeemable – EPxRxx	F – Fixed rate – EPxxFx	
		E – Extendible – EPxExx	C – Cumulative – EPxxCx	

Classification of Financial Instruments (CFI) (ISO 10962)

Equity Type	1st Attribute	2nd Attribute	3rd Attribute	4th Attribute
		T – Redeemable/extendible – EPxTxx	P – Participating income – EPxxPx	
		G – Exchangeable – EPxGxx	Q – Cumulative, participating income – EPxxQx	
		A – Redeemable/exchangeable/extendible – EPxAxx	A – Adjustable rate income – EPxxAx	
		C – Redeemable/exchangeable – EPxCxx	N – Normal rate income – EPxxNx	
		N – Non-redeemable – EPxNxx	U – Auction rate income – EPxxUx	
R – Preference Shares – ERxxxx	Identical to preferred shares – replace second character "P" with "R"	Identical to preferred shares – replace second character "P" with "R"	Identical to preferred shares – replace second character "P" with "R"	Identical to preferred shares – replace second character "P" with "R"
C – Convertible Shares – ECxxxx	Identical to common/ordinary shares – replace second character "S" with "C"	Identical to common/ordinary shares – replace second character "S" with "C"	Identical to common/ordinary shares – replace second character "S" with "C"	Identical to common/ordinary shares – replace second character "S" with "C"
F – Preferred Convertible Shares – EFxxxx	Identical to preferred shares – replace second character "P" with "F"	Identical to preferred shares – replace second character "P" with "F"	Identical to preferred shares – replace second character "P" with "F"	Identical to preferred shares – replace second character "P" with "F"
V – Preference Convertible Shares – EVxxxx	Identical to preferred shares – replace second character "P" with "V"	Identical to preferred shares – replace second character "P" with "V"	Identical to preferred shares – replace second character "P" with "V"	Identical to preferred shares – replace second character "P" with "V"
U – Units (unit trusts/mutual funds/OPCVM/OICVM) – EUxxxx	Closed/Open-End	Distribution Policy	Assets	Strategy
	C – Closed – EUCxxx	I – Income funds – EUxIxx	R – Real estate – EUxxRx	H – Hedge fund – EUxxxH
	O – Open-end – EUOxxx	G – Growth funds – EUxGxx	S – Securities – EUxxSx	B – Balanced – EUxxxB

Classification of Financial Instruments (CFI) (ISO 10962)

Equity Type	1st Attribute	2nd Attribute	3rd Attribute	4th Attribute
		M – Mixed funds – EUxMxx	B – Debt instruments – EUxxBx	E – Exchange traded funds – EUxxxE
			E – Equities – EUxxEx	S – Sector fund – EUxxxS
			V – Convertible securities – EUxxVx	M – Mid-cap fund – EUxxxM
			N – Money market instruments – EUxxNx	L – Large-cap fund – EUxxxL
			M – Mixed general – EUxxMx	I – High yield fund – EUxxxI
			C – Commodities – EUxxCx	A – Small-cap fund – EUxxxA
			D – Derivatives –	M – Others – EU
M – Others (miscellaneous including baskets) – EMxxxx	X – Not applicable/undefined – EMXxxx	X – Not applicable/undefined – EMxXxx	X – Not applicable/undefined – EMxxXx	Syntax as for common/ordinary shares – replace second character "S" with "M"

Debt Instruments

Debt Instrument Type	1st Attribute	2nd Attribute	3rd Attribute	4th Attribute
B – Bonds – DBxxxx	Type of Interest	Guarantee	Redemption/ Reimbursement	Form
	F – Fixed rate – DBFxxx	T – Government / Treasury guarantee – DBxTxx	F – Fixed maturity – DBxxFx	B – Bearer – DBxxxB

Classification of Financial Instruments (CFI) (ISO 10962)

Debt Instrument Type	1st Attribute	2nd Attribute	3rd Attribute	4th Attribute
	Z – Zero rate/discounted – DBZxxx	G – Guaranteed – DBxGxx	G – Fixed maturity with call – DBxxGx	R – Registered – DBxxxR
	V – Variable – DBVxxx	S – Secured – DBxSxx	C – Fixed maturity with put – DBxxCx	N – Bearer/registered – DBxxxN
		U – Unsecured / Unguaranteed – DBxUxx	D – Fixed maturity with put and call – DBxxDx	Z – Bearer depository receipt – DBxxxZ
		P – Negative pledge – DBxPxx	A – Amortisation plan – DBxxAx	A – Registered depository receipt – DBxxxA
		J – Junior/subordinated – DBxJxx	B – Amortisation plan with call – DBxxBx	G – SEC Regulation 144A – DBxxxG
		N – Senior – DBxNxx	T – Amortisation plan with put – DBxxTx	S – SEC Regulation S – DBxxxS
			L – Amortisation plan with put and call – DBxxLx	
			P – Perpetual – DBxxPx	
			Q – Perpetual with call – DBxxQx	
C – Convertible Bonds – DCxxxx	Identical to bonds – replace second character "B" with "C"	Identical to bonds – replace second character "B" with "C"	Identical to bonds – replace second character "B" with "C"	Identical to bonds – replace second character "B" with "C"
W – Bonds with Warrants – DWxxxx	Identical to bonds – replace second character "B" with "W"	Identical to bonds – replace second character "B" with "W"	Identical to bonds – replace second character "B" with "W"	Identical to bonds – replace second character "B" with "W"
T – Medium Term Notes – DTxxxx	Identical to bonds – replace second character "B" with "T"	Identical to bonds – replace second character "B" with "T"	Identical to bonds – replace second character "B" with "T"	Identical to bonds – replace second character "B" with "T"
Y – Money Market Instruments – DYxxxx	Identical to bonds – replace second character "B" with "Y"	Identical to bonds – replace second character "B" with "Y"	X – Not applicable/undefined – DYxxXx	Identical to bonds – replace second character "B" with "Y"
A – Asset-Backed Securities – DAxxxx	Identical to bonds – replace second character "B" with "A"	Identical to bonds – replace second character "B" with "A"	Identical to bonds – replace second character "B" with "A"	Identical to bonds replace second character "B" with "A"

Classification of Financial Instruments (CFI) (ISO 10962)

Debt Instrument Type	1st Attribute	2nd Attribute	3rd Attribute	4th Attribute
G – Mortgage-Backed Securities – DGxxxx	Identical to bonds – replace second character "B" with "G"	Identical to bonds – replace second character "B" with "G"	Identical to bonds – replace second character "B" with "G"	Identical to bonds – replace second character "B" with "G"
M – Others (miscellaneous) – DMxxxx	Identical to bonds – replace second character "B" with "M"	Identical to bonds – replace second character "B" with "M"	Identical to bonds – replace second character "B" with "M"	Identical to bonds – replace second character "B" with "M"

Entitlements (Rights)

Entitlement Type	1st Attribute	2nd Attribute	3rd Attribute	4th Attribute
A – Allotment/ Bonus Rights – RAxxxx	X – Not applicable/undefined – RAXxxx	X – Not applicable/undefined – RAxXxx	X – Not applicable/undefined – RAxxXx	Form
				B – Bearer – RAxxxB
				R – Registered – RAxxxR
				N – Bearer/registered – RAxxxN
				Z – Bearer depository receipt – RAxxxZ
				A – Registered depository receipt – RAxxxA
				G – SEC Regulation 144A – RAxxxG
				S – SEC Regulation S – RAxxxS
S – Subscription Rights – RSxxxx	**Underlying Assets**	X – Not applicable/undefined – RSxXxx	X – Not applicable/undefined – RSxxXx	Identical to Allotment/Bonus Rights – replace second character "A" with "S"
C – Convertible Bonds – DCxxxx	Identical to bonds – replace second character "B" with "C"	Identical to bonds – replace second character "B" with "C"	Identical to bonds – replace second character "B" with "C"	Identical to bonds – replace second character "B" with "C"
W – Bonds with Warrants – DWxxxx	Identical to bonds – replace second character "B" with "W"	Identical to bonds – replace second character "B" with "W"	Identical to bonds – replace second character "B" with "W"	Identical to bonds – replace second character "B" with "W"

Classification of Financial Instruments (CFI) (ISO 10962)

Entitlement Type	1st Attribute	2nd Attribute	3rd Attribute	4th Attribute
T – Medium Term Notes – DTxxxx	Identical to bonds – replace second character "B" with "T"	Identical to bonds – replace second character "B" with "T"	Identical to bonds – replace second character "B" with "T"	Identical to bonds – replace second character "B" with "T"
Y – Money Market Instruments – DYxxxx	Identical to bonds – replace second character "B" with "Y"	Identical to bonds – replace second character "B" with "Y"	X – Not applicable/undefined – DYxxXx	Identical to bonds – replace second character "B" with "Y"
A – Asset-Backed Securities – DAxxxx	Identical to bonds – replace second character "B" with "A"	Identical to bonds – replace second character "B" with "A"	Identical to bonds – replace second character "B" with "A"	Identical to bonds – replace second character "B" with "A"
G – Mortgage-Backed Securities – DGxxxx	Identical to bonds – replace second character "B" with "G"	Identical to bonds – replace second character "B" with "G"	Identical to bonds – replace second character "B" with "G"	Identical to bonds – replace second character "B" with "G"
M – Others (miscellaneous) – DMxxxx	Identical to bonds – replace second character "B" with "M"	Identical to bonds – replace second character "B" with "M"	Identical to bonds – replace second character "B" with "M"	Identical to bonds – replace second character "B" with "M"

Options

Option Type	1st Attribute	2nd Attribute	3rd Attribute	4th Attribute
C – Call Options – OCxxxx	Type of Scheme	Underlying Assets	Delivery	Standardised/ Non-Standardised
	E – European – OCExxx	B – Basket – OCxBxx	P – Physical – OCxxPx	S – Standardised – OCxxxS
	A – American – OCAxxx	S – Stock equities – OCxSxx	C – Cash – OCxxCx	N – Non-standardised – OCxxxN
	B – Bermuda – OCBxxx	D – Debt instruments/Interest – OCxDxx	N – Non-delivering – OCxxNx	F – Flexible – OCxxxF
		T – Commodities – OCxTxx		
		C – Currencies – OCxCxx		
		I – Indices – OCxIxx		
		O – Options – OCxOxx		
		F – Futures – OCxFxx		
		W – Swaps – OCxWxx		

Classification of Financial Instruments (CFI) (ISO 10962)

Option Type	1st Attribute	2nd Attribute	3rd Attribute	4th Attribute
		N – Interest rates – OCxNxx		
		M – Others – OCxMxx		
P – Put Options – OPxxxx	Identical to call options – replace second character "C" with "P"	Identical to call options – replace second character "C" with "P"	Identical to call options – replace second character "C" with "P"	Identical to call options – replace second character "C" with "P"
M – Others (Miscellaneous) – OMxxxx	X – Not applicable/undefined – OMXxxx	X – Not applicable/undefined – OMxXxx	X – Not applicable/undefined – OMxxXx	X – Not applicable/undefined – OMxxxX

Futures

Futures Type	1st Attribute	2nd Attribute	3rd Attribute	4th Attribute
	Underlying Assets	Delivery	Standardized/Non-Standardized	Strategy
F – Financial Futures – FFxxxx	B – Basket – FFBxxx	P – Physical – FFxPxx	S – Standardized – FFxxSx	S – Spread – FFxxxS
	S – Stock equities – FFSxxx	C – Cash – FFxCxx	N – Non-standardized – FFxxNx	W – Swaps – FFxxxW
	D – Debt instruments/Interest – FFDxxx	N – Non-delivering – FFxNxx	F – Flexible – FFxxFx	O – Outright – FFxxxO
	C – Currencies – FFCxxx			
	I – Indices – FFIxxx			
	O – Options – FFOxxx			
	F – Futures – FFFxxx			
	W – Swaps – FFWxxx			
	N – Interest rates – FFNxxx			
P – Put Options – OPxxxx	Identical to call options – replace second character "C" with "P"	Identical to call options – replace second character "C" with "P"	Identical to call options – replace second character "C" with "P"	Identical to call options – replace second character "C" with "P"
M – Others (Miscellaneous) – OMxxxx	X – Not applicable/undefined – OMXxxx	X – Not applicable/undefined – OMxXxx	X – Not applicable/undefined – OMxxXx	X – Not applicable/undefined – OMxxxX

Classification of Financial Instruments (CFI) (ISO 10962)

Structured Products/Hybrids

Product Type	1st Attribute	2nd Attribute	3rd Attribute	4th Attribute
W – With Capital Protection – SWxxxx	Underlying Assets	Distribution	Repayment	Strategy
	S – Stock equities – SWSxxx	F – Fixed interest payments – SWxFxx	F – Fixed cash repayment – SWxxFx	K – Knock-out/in – SWxxxK
	D – Debt instruments/Interest – SWDxxx	D – Fixed dividend payments – SWxDxx	V – Variable cash repayment – SWxxVx	S – Stop loss – SWxxxS
	T – Commodities – SWTxxx	P – Fixed premium payments – SWxPxx	S – Repayment in stock – SWxxSx	R – Outright – SWxxxR
	C – Currencies – SWCxxx	I – Fixed interest and premium payments – SWxIxx	C – Repayment in stock and cash – SWxxCx	A – Accelerated tracker – SWxxxA
	I – Indices – SWIxxx	T – Fixed interest and dividend payments – SWxTxx	T – Repayment in stock or cash – SWxxTx	B – Bonus tracker – SWxxxB
	R – Ratings – SWRxxx	V – Variable interest payments – SWxVxx	N – No repayment – SWxxNx	D – Discount tracker – SWxxxD
	M – Others – SWMxxx	E – Variable dividend payments – SWxExx	M – Others – SWxxMx	M – Other conditions – SWxxxM
		R – Variable premium payments – SWxRxx		
		N – Variable interest and premium payments – SWxNxx		
		A – Variable interest and dividend payments – SWxAxx		
		Y – No payments – SWxYxx		
		M – Others – SWxMxx		
O – Without Capital Protection – SOxxxx	Identical to structured products with capital protection – replace second character "W" with "O"	Identical to structured products with capital protection – replace second character "W" with "O"	Identical to structured products with capital protection – replace second character "W" with "O"	Identical to structured products with capital protection – replace second character "W" with "O"

Classification of Financial Instruments (CFI) (ISO 10962)

Referential Instruments

Instrument Type	1st Attribute	2nd Attribute	3rd Attribute	4th Attribute
C – Currencies – RCxxxx	Type	X – Not applicable/undefined – RCxXxx	X – Not applicable/undefined – RCxxXx	X – Not applicable/undefined – RCxxxX
	N – National currency – RCNxxx			
	S – Spot rate – RCSxxx			
	F – Forward – RCFxxx			
	C – Coins – RCCxxx			
	M – Others – RCMxxx			
T – Commodities – RTxxxx	Underlying Assets	X – Not applicable/undefined – RTxXxx	X – Not applicable/undefined – RTxxXx	X – Not applicable/undefined – RTxxxX
	E – Extraction resources – RTExxx			
	A – Agriculture, forestry and fishing – RTAxxx			
	I – Industrial products – RTIxxx			
	S – Services – RTSxxx			
O – Without Capital Protection – SOxxxx	Identical to structured products with capital protection – replace second character "W" with "O"	Identical to structured products with capital protection – replace second character "W" with "O"	Identical to structured products with capital protection – replace second character "W" with "O"	Identical to structured products with capital protection – replace second character "W" with "O"

Others (Miscellaneous)

Instrument Type	1st Attribute	2nd Attribute	3rd Attribute	4th Attribute
C – Combined Instruments – MCxxxx	Type of Component	X – Not applicable/undefined – MCxXxx	X – Not applicable/undefined – MCxxXx	X – Not applicable/undefined – MCxxxX
	S – Combination of shares – MCSxxx			

Classification of Financial Instruments (CFI) (ISO 10962)

Instrument Type	1st Attribute	2nd Attribute	3rd Attribute	4th Attribute
	B – Combination of bonds – MCBxxx			
	H – Share(s) and bond(s) – MCHxxx			
	A – Share(s) and warrant(s) – MCAxxx			
	W – Warrant and warrant(s) – MCWxxx			
	R – Share(s), bond(s) and warrant(s) – MCRxxx			
	M – Other combinations – MCMxxx			
M – Other Assets – MMxxxx	**Further Grouping**	X – Not applicable/undefined – MMxXxx	X – Not applicable/undefined – MMxxXx	X – Not applicable/undefined – MMxxxX
	R – Real estate deeds – MMRxxx			
	I – Insurance policies – MMIxxx			
	E – Escrow receipts – MMExxx			
	F – Forwards – MMFxxx			
	P – Precious metal receipts – MMPxxx			
	M – Others – MMMxxx			

Examples

BT Group plc Ord 5p

ISIN: GB0030913577
CFI: ESVUFR where E = Equities, S = Shares, V = Voting, U = Unrestricted, F = Fully paid and R = Registered

Lloyds Banking Group 9.25% Preference Shares

Classification of Financial Instruments (CFI) (ISO 10962)

ISIN: GB00B3KS9W93

CFI: ERNNNR where E = Equities, R= Preference, N = Non-voting, N = Non-redeemable, N = Normal Rate and R = Registered

For more information

http://www.anna-web.org

Market Identifier Code (MIC) (ISO 10383)

In brief

The Market Identifier Code (MIC) (ISO 10383) is a unique identification code which identifies securities trading exchanges and regulated and non-regulated trading markets. ISO 10383 is the international standard for the identification of exchanges, trading platforms, regulated or non-regulated markets and trade reporting facilities as sources of prices and related information in order to facilitate automated processing. SWIFT is the registration authority for ISO 10383.

MIC issuer
S.W.I.F.T SCRL
Avenue Adele 1
B-1310 La Hulpe
Belgium
Tel: +32 2 655 31 11
Fax: +32 2 655 32 26
www.swift.com

Registration takes place through *www.iso10383.org* for the creation, modification or deactivation of a MIC. They can be registered only by the authorised contact person/s of the related market organisation.

To download the list of Market Identifier Codes:

Excel	PDF	Annexes	Publication date	Modifications implementation date	Next publication date
Download	Download	Download	13 February 2017	27 February 2017	13 March 2017

The list is also available here: *https://www.iso20022.org/sites/default/files/ ISO10383_MIC/ISO10383_MIC.xls*

History

The first edition of ISO 10383 was published in 1992. The third edition, published October 2012, altered the structure of MICs through the introduction of the concept of operating exchange level MICs and market segment MICs. The old and new versions of ISO 10383 co-existed until August 2013.

MIC lists are published monthly on the second Monday of the month or the following business day if it falls on a public holiday in the country of the registration authority. Changes apply from the fourth Monday of the month.

Each monthly list includes all requests for changes or new MICs received by the first Monday of the month, after validation by the registration authority. Requests received after the first Monday of the month and before publication are, if possible, incorporated in that month's publication.

Structure

With the exception of the German 360T, all MICs are comprised of four letters. Original exchange MICs tend to begin with the letter "X". For example, the exchange level MIC for the London Stock Exchange is "XLON". An additional market segment MIC "XLOD" exists for London Stock Exchange derivatives.

A MIC expires at the request of the organisation itself or if SWIFT becomes aware that the market or market segment no longer exists. Specific events such as mergers or acquisitions may mean that an existing MIC or MICs is/are transferred to the new market organisation.

For more information

http://www.iso15022.org/MIC/homepageMIC.htm

Alternative Instrument Identifier (Aii)

Alternative Instrument Identifier (Aii)

In brief

In transaction reporting, the Alternative Instrument Identifier (Aii) is used where the ISIN is not the industry method of identification. This consists of six separate mandatory elements, known collectively as the Aii.

> ## Aii contact
> Financial Conduct Authority
> 25 The North Colonnade
> London E14 5HS
> United Kingdom
> Tel: +44 207 066 1000
> *www.fca.org.uk*

History

In 2009, the Committee of European Securities Regulators (CESR) issued a consultation paper concerning the classification and identification of OTC derivative instruments for the purpose of the exchange of transaction reports amongst its members. This followed the introduction of the Transaction Reporting Exchange Mechanism (TREM) in 2007, which organised the exchange of transaction reports amongst European financial regulators under the Market in Financial Instrument Directive (MiFID). At the time, TREM was limited to the exchange of transaction reports on instruments admitted to trading in Europe and required modification to facilitate the exchange of transaction reports on OTC derivative instruments amongst CESR members. It was the lack of ISINs for several groups of derivatives (and the cost involved in assigning and maintaining them) that led to the creation of the Alternative Instrument Identifier (Aii) for MiFID reporting purposes.

Structure

In line with the requirements of the European Securities and Markets Authority (ESMA), the Aii is composed of six elements:

— ISO 10383 Market Identifier Code (MIC) of the regulated market where the derivative is traded.
— Exchange product code: the code assigned to the derivative contract by the regulated market where it is traded.
— Derivative type: identifying whether the derivative is an option or a future.
— Put/call identifier: mandatory where the derivative is an option.
— Expiry date: exercise date/maturity date of the derivative.
— Strike price: mandatory where the derivative is an option.
  For example, a transaction in a Vodafone option traded on the NYSE Liffe market will be reported as follows:

MIC code: XLIF

Exchange Product Code: VOD

Derivative type: O

Put/call Identifier: C

Expiry date: 2014-03-21

Strike price: 2.00

For more information

https://www.fca.org.uk/firms/gabriel

Unique Swap Identifier (USI)

In brief

The Unique Swap Identifier (USI) is assigned by the US Commodities Futures Trading Commission to all swap transactions. The USI identifies the transaction (the swap and its counterparties) uniquely throughout its duration.

USI issuer

Us Commodities Futures Trading Commission
1155 21st St NW
Washington, DC 20581
United States of America
Tel: +1 202 418 5000
www.cftc.gov

History

The creation and use of the USI is mandated by the Commodity Futures Trading Commission (CFTC) and Securities and Exchange Commission (SEC) as part of the Dodd-Frank Act. Under the so-called "namespace" method, the first characters of each USI consist of a unique code that identifies the registered entity, creating the USI given to the registered entity by the Commission during the registration process. The remaining characters of the USI consist of a code created by the registered entity that must be unique with respect to all other USI's created by that registered entity.

The aim of the initiative is to facilitate consistency in the creation and use of USIs among Swap Execution Facilities (SEFs), Swap Data Repositories (SDRs), Designated Contract Markets (DCMs), Derivatives Clearing Organizations (DCOs), Major Swap Participants (MSPs), and Swap Dealers (SDs).

Structure

The first component of the USI or "namespace" is a ten-digit alphanumeric identifier that consists of a three-digit prefix followed by a seven-digit identifier unique to each three-character prefix. The three-digit prefix range of 101-119 is reserved for the use of the CFTC; hence the prefix range available to other entities that could issue USIs in the future is 120-ZZZ. In addition, the three-digit alphanumeric prefix may not begin with a zero or the letters "I" or "O".

The second component of the USI is the transaction identifier. This is a unique identifier of variable length, to a maximum of 32 alphanumeric characters, for the swap transaction as assigned by the entity reporting swap data to the Swap Data Repository (SDR). Transaction identifiers can include an additional set of "special" characters permissible as internal delimiters such as colon, hyphen (minus), period (full stop) and underscore. However, they may not start or end with a special character or comprise sequences of multiple consecutive special characters. The namespace together with the transaction identifier make up the USI.

Creation

USIs are created at these points in the lifecycle of a trade:

— Point of execution: a new USI is assigned by the Swap Dealer (SD), Major Swap Participant (MSP) or Swap Execution Facility (SEF).
— Allocation: USIs for each individual allocation at the account level are assigned by the SD, MSP, SEF or agent assigning one side of the swap to client or customer accounts of one of the counterparties. The USI of the replaced trade must be included when reporting to the SDR.
— Clearing: pairs of USIs are assigned for each cleared trade assigned by the Derivative Clearing Organisation (DCO).
— Compression/netting: a new USI is assigned to the netted trade and the USIs of all replaced trades must be reported to the SDR.
— Continuation: when a trade is novated, a new USI is created for the trade between the transferee and transferor. A second new USI is created for the new contract between the remaining party and the transferee. Both must include the original trade USI in reports to the SDR.

Unique Swap Identifier (USI)

The aim of the USI is to facilitate aggregation of all data concerning a given swap (including creation data, continuation data and error corrections as reported by execution platforms, clearing houses and counterparties) into a single data record that tracks the swap during its lifetime. As well as giving regulators the ability to track swap transactions throughout their lives, USIs provide an efficient means of assuring that transactions are not double-counted when producing summary reports. This is particularly important where transactions may be reported to multiple swap data repositories (SDRs) – for example, where a counterparty may be required to report a transaction to a foreign SDR.

Because the USI is created when the swap is executed, all market participants involved with the swap, from counterparties to platforms to clearinghouses to SDRs, will have the same USI for the swap at the earliest possible point. This reduces potential errors and delays in submitting an executed swap for clearing and minimises the need to alter pre-existing records on the swap.

For more information
http://www.cftc.gov/ucm/groups/public/@swaps/documents/dfsubmission/ usidatastandards100112.pdf

Unique Trade Identifier (UTI)

In brief

The Unique Trade Identifier (UTI) is an identifier at the transaction level, and remains throughout the lifecycle of a trade. It helps to ensure the uniqueness of contract information and helps to avoid double reporting due to the different reporting requirements of distinct jurisdictions.

UTI issuer

ISDA
360 Madison Avenue, 16th Floor
New York NY 10017
United States of America
Tel: +1 212 901 6000
Fax: +1 212 901 6001
Email: isda@isda.org

One Bishops Square
London E1 6AD
United Kingdom
Tel: + 44 20 3808 9700
Fax: + 44 20 3808 9755
Email: isdaeurope@isda.org

Suite 1602, 16th Floor, China Building
29 Queen's Road Central
Central Hong Kong
Hong Kong
Tel: 852 2200 5900
Fax: 852 2840 0105
Email: isdaap@isda.org
www.isda.org

Unique Trade Identifier (UTI)

History

In order to address the roots of the 2008 financial crisis, the G20 countries agreed to address risks related to derivative markets. The introduction of EU Regulation 648/2012 of the European Parliament and Council or European Market Infrastructures Regulation (EMIR) on OTC derivatives, central counterparties (CCPs) and trade repositories (TRs) requires trading counterparties to allocate a Unique Trade Identifier (UTI) to each transaction. UTIs are generated, communicated and then matched, for both ongoing business and historical data subject to reporting obligations.

The regulation introduces provisions to improve transparency and reduce the risks associated with the OTC derivatives market and establishes common rules for CCPs and for TRs. EMIR was adopted in July 2012 and entered into force on 16 August 2012. It commenced for all asset classes from 1 January 2014.

Structure

Like the Unique Swap Identifier (USI), a Unique Trade Identifier (UTI) is comprised of two parts: (i) a UTI prefix that is unique to the party generating the UTI; and (ii) a transaction identifier. Provided that the UTI generating party ensures it always issues a new transaction identifier in relation to their UTI prefix, each UTI value should be unique. Note: if a trade requires a Unique Swap Identifier (USI), this will be the UTI.

Initially, the preferred code for the UTI prefix for non-CFTC registered reporting counterparties was the 18-character legal entity identifier (LEI). However, during industry discussions it became clear that many FX systems could only accommodate up to, and including, a 10-character prefix. Hence, although the LEI system is used as a foundation for the UTI prefix, only the first 10 characters, characters 7-16, of the entity-specific portion are used (characters 7-18 form the alphanumeric, randomly generated entity-specific portion of the 20 character global LEI number allocation scheme). Note that where a counterparty already has CFTC USI namespace, or any other mandated namespace from a regulator, this will be used as the UTI prefix.

The second component of the UTI is the transaction identifier. This is a unique identifier of variable length, to a maximum of 32 alphanumeric characters with leading zeros, for the transaction as assigned by the entity reporting the transaction. The UTI prefix, together with the transaction identifier, make up the UTI.

UTI creation

UTI generation, communication and matching should occur at the earliest possible point in the lifecycle of the trade. The ideal order is:

— Centrally executed trades: reference is generated and communicated at the point of execution on a platform that can generate a UTI and ensure its uniqueness.
— Up-front affirmed: reference is generated and communicated at the point of submission.
— Back-end confirmation matched (post-trade): reference is generated at submission and communicated at point of matching.
— Paper trades: unless otherwise communicated, a reference is generated by individual firms which share via paper and update their reporting to reference the UTI for the trade once agreed by counterparties.
Like the USI initiative, the aim of a UTI is to facilitate aggregation of all data concerning a transaction (including creation data, continuation data and error corrections as reported by execution platforms, clearing houses and counterparties) into a single data record that tracks the transaction during its lifetime. As well as giving regulators the ability to track transactions throughout their lives, UTIs provide an efficient means of assuring that transactions are not double-counted when producing summary reports.

As with the USI, a UTI is created at the point of execution, meaning that all market participants from counterparties to platforms to clearinghouses will have the same UTI at the earliest possible point. Although the development of a unique trade identifier was initiated with the Unique Swap Identifier (USI) (because CFTC reporting developed before comparable reporting in other jurisdictions), the UTI is the primary value for global reporting, with the USI in reality a subset of the UTI.

Unique Trade Identifier (UTI)

For more information

http://www2.isda.org/search?headerSearch=1&keyword=unique+trade+identifier

National Codes

CUSIP

In brief

The Committee on Uniform Security Identification Procedures, or CUSIP, is owned by the American Bankers Association, while the CUSIP distribution system is operated by Standard & Poor's. CUSIP Global Services acts as the national numbering agency (NNA) for North America. CUSIPs serve as the national securities identification number for products issued in both the United States and Canada and are therefore the basis for the generation of international security identification numbers (ISINs) for US and Canadian incorporated securities. CUSIP Global Services provides reference data on more than nine million securities issued by corporations, municipalities and government agencies including derivatives and syndicated loans. Various organisations use CUSIPs to aid security identification in their financial business activities such as portfolio valuation, trade execution, processing datafeeds and as a cross reference to other identifiers and price validation.

CUSIP issuer

CUSIP Global Services
55 Water Street, 45th Floor
New York NY 10041
United State of America
Tel: +1 609 426 7358
+1 212 438 6500
Email: cusip.custservice@cusip.com
www.cusip.com

History

Development of the CUSIP numbering system began in 1962 when the New York Clearing House Association established a committee to look into the feasibility of developing a uniform securities identification system. In 1964, the American Bankers Association Committee on Uniform Security Identification Procedures, or CUSIP, was born. In developing the identification system, the committee identified two criteria: (i) the identifier needed to be as short as possible; and (ii) it should be linked to an alphabetical sequence of issuer names. The identifier also had to be adaptable to the internal systems of all users; capable of meeting both present and future operating requirements; and have a structure that would allow each user to assign identifiers to securities or other assets not covered by the CUSIP system.

In the 1980s there was an attempt to expand the CUSIP code system for international securities. The resulting CUSIP international numbering system (CINS) has seen little use, as it was introduced at about the same time as the international security identification Number (ISIN) system.

Structure

The CUSIP code is a nine-character alphanumeric code. The first six characters form the base or issuer number (also known as the CUSIP-6), and uniquely identify the issuer. The 7th and 8th digits identify the exact issue. The 9th digit is an automatically generated checksum.

Issuer number

A six-digit issuer number is assigned to each corporate, municipal and governmental issuer in alphabetical order. Only one identifier is assigned to an issuer, except in those few cases where the issue identifiers are not sufficient to accommodate all outstanding issues with their various rates and maturities, such as US governments and certain municipalities or states. In such instances, one or more additional issuer identifiers is assigned.

Issuer numbers are assigned alphabetically from a series that includes deliberate built-in "gaps" for future expansion. Issuer numbers 900 to 989 in each group of 1,000 numbers have been reserved for overflow. These overflow numbers will be assigned in ascending sequence to any new issuer that cannot be accommodated at the proper alphabetical position in the preceding group of issuer numbers. Such names are always in a positively identifiable position as the number assigned will contain a 9 in the hundreds position.

Issuer numbers 990 to 999 and 99A to 99Z in each group of 1,000 numbers have also been reserved for the user's own assignment. This allows a user to assign an issuer number to any issuer that might be relevant to his holdings

CUSIP

but does not qualify for coverage under the CUSIP numbering system. Other issuer numbers (990000 to 999999 and 99000A to 99999Z) are also reserved for the user so that they may be assigned to non-security assets or for other internal operating purposes. Thus, with the addition of at least two numeric digits in the issue number field, a minimum of three million numbers are available to the user for numbering miscellaneous assets. The alphabetic character Z in the 5th and 6th position has been reserved for use by the Canadian Depository for Securities.

This uniquely identifies each individual issue of an issuer and consists of two numeric characters for equities and two alphabetic characters or one numeric and one alphabetic character for fixed income securities. Issue numbers are assigned in sequence as each issue is originated. However, in the setting up of the CUSIP numbering system and in the assignment of numbers to issues then in existence, numbers were assigned on the basis of rate and maturity. No consideration was given to the original date of the issue.

Issue numbers for equities

The first issue number for an issuer's equity securities is 10. The unit position of the equity number is used to identify rights, warrants and so on and is assigned on an as available basis. When there are insufficient tens positions available for all individual issues, the necessary additional numbers are found through the use of the first open two-position digit in reverse sequence starting with 88 and assigned in descending order. Issue numbers 00 to 09 are reserved for future use. Issue number 01 is used for an issuer's options and issue number 89 is reserved for overflow linkage and is not assigned to a specific issue.

Issue numbers for fixed income securities

Issue numbers for fixed income securities may consist of two alphabetic characters, e.g. AA, one alphabetic character followed by one digit, e.g. A1. Alternatively, one digit may be followed by an alphabetical character, e.g. 1A, assigned in that order. A separate issue number is assigned to each rate and/or maturity for each issue of bonds. The alphabetic letters "I" and "O" and the numeric "1" and zero are not used. Issue number 9Z is reserved for overflow linkage.

Issue numbers reserved for internal use

Issue numbers 90 to 99 for equities and 9A to 9Y for fixed income securities are reserved for the user for assignment to those issues of an eligible issuer where no CUSIP issue number has been assigned.

Check digit calculation

The 9th digit is an automatically generated check digit using the "Modulus 10 Double Add Double" technique. To calculate the check digit every second digit is multiplied by two. Letters are converted to numbers based on their ordinal position in the alphabet, starting with A equal to 10 and finishing with Z equal to 35.

For example: for issuer number 837649 and issue number 12 i.e. 83764912, digits in the 1st, 3rd, 5th and 7th positions are multiplied by 1 and digits in the 2nd, 4th, 6th and 8th positions are multiplied by 2. This results in the sequence 8-6-7-12-4-18-1-4. Adding up the sequence 8+6+7+1+2+4+1+8+1+4 results in a figure of 42. It is the complement of the last digit of the sum that becomes the check digit. The complement of 2 is 8, hence the full CUSIP number with the check digit is 837649128.

Corporate Action Effects on CUSIPs

In general, CUSIP Global Services determine whether a new CUSIP is required as result of a proposed corporate action. Actions which will normally result in the allocation of a new CUSIP include a change in company name, a reorganisation, a merger, a forward stock split, a reverse split or emergence from bankruptcy.

For more information

https://www.cusip.com/cusip/index.htm

Exchange Ticker Codes

In brief

An exchange ticker code or symbol is an abbreviation used to uniquely identify publicly traded shares of a particular company on a particular stock market. Exchange ticker codes can consist of letters, numbers or a combination of both, depending on the market.

Ticker code issuer

Ticker codes are issued by a country's stock exchange.

History

The first stock price ticker system using a telegraphic printer was invented in the 1860s by Edward A Calahan, an employee of the American Telegraph Company. The term "ticker symbol" originally referred to the symbols printed on ticker tape. Ticker tape was the earliest digital electronic communications medium that transmitted stock price information over telegraph lines from around 1870 to 1970. It consisted of a paper strip which ran through a ticker-tape machine, which printed abbreviated company names as alphabetic symbols followed by numeric stock transaction price and volume information. The term "ticker" came from the sound made by the machine as it printed. The symbols were kept as short as possible to reduce the number of characters that had to be printed on the ticker tape and to make it easy to recognise by traders and investors.

Structure

The allocation of symbols and formatting convention is specific to each stock exchange. In the US, for example stock tickers are typically between 1 and 5 letters and represent the company name as closely as possible. For example, Apple Inc. traded on NASDAQ has the symbol AAPL, while Ford traded on the New York Stock Exchange has the single letter ticker F.

In Europe most exchanges now use the International Securities Identification Number (ISIN) as the main security identifier for trading and data distribution although alpha and alphanumeric mnemonics are also assigned. In Asia numbers are more often used as stock tickers to avoid issues for international investors when using non-Latin-scripts. For example, the Hong Kong Stock Exchange uses a five-digit code, whilst the Chinese and Indian exchanges use a six-digit code. New Zealand and Australia both use traditional alpha ticker codes in conjunction with ISINs.

In the United Kingdom prior to 1996, stock codes were known as EPICs, named after the London Stock Exchange's Exchange Price Information Computer. Although still widely referred to as EPICs, EPICs were renamed Tradable Instrument Display Mnemonics (TIDMs), following the introduction of the Sequence trading platform.

Extensions and specific conventions

NYSE "Behind the Dot" or NASDAQ 5th Letter Codes
A – Class A
B – Class B
C – Exempt from NASDAQ
D – New issue or reverse split
E – Delinquent SEC filings
F – Foreign
G – First convertible bond
H – Second convertible bond
I – Third convertible bond
J – Voting
K – Non-voting common
L – Miscellaneous situation
M – Fourth class preferred share
N – Third class preferred share
O – Second class preferred share
P – First class preferred share
Q – In bankruptcy
R – Rights
S – Shares of beneficial interest
T – With warrants or rights
U – Units

Exchange Ticker Codes

V – When issued and when distributed
W – Warrants
X – Mutual fund
Y – American depositary receipt (ADR)
Z – Miscellaneous situation

Canadian symbology

Common shares will have a one-, two- or three-letter root with no extension.

Class A shares may or may not have an .A after the root. If there are two classes of common shares for the same company, the extension will be on the Class A. If there is only one class of share, this extension is not necessarily the case.

.E – Equity dividend.

.W – "When issued shares"; if more than one "when issued", the second one is .I.

.L – Legended shares.

.M – Booms.

.NT, NO and NS – Notes.

P – Capital pool – venture.

H – NEX – junior venture market.

.R – Subscription receipts; second set of subscription receipts the symbol is .N; third, symbol is .o.

.S – Special US trading terms.

.T – Second special US trading terms.

.U – US funds; for second issue trading in US funds .V is used; .U is used exclusively for US funds following a common, preferred, warrant or debenture extension.

Y – Redeemable common.

.PR – Preferred shares or priority equity; following the .PR there will be a one letter extension from A–Z; with the exception of the .U and .V extensions, the letter may not have any meaning except for distinguishing one preferred from another.

.UN – Units, true regardless of whether it is an equity, trust, or partnership unit; there can be no other letter after the .UN.

.WT – Warrants, can be followed with a letter from A–Z if the company lists more than one warrant.

.RT – Rights; like warrants this can be followed with a letter from A–Z if the company lists more than one warrant.

.IR – Installment receipts.

.DB – Debentures; a letter from A–Z can follow if there is more than one debenture for a company or if the debentures are US or when issued.

Hong Kong Symbology

00001 to 09999: securities listed on the Main Board and Growth Enterprise Market (GEM); information pages are sub-divided as follows:

02800 to 02849 and 03000 to 03199: Exchange Traded Funds (ETFs)

04000 to 04199: Hong Kong Monetary Authority Exchange Fund Notes

04200 to 04299: HKSAR government bonds

04300 to 04329, 04500 to 04599 and 05900 to 06029: Other debt securities

06200 to 06499: Hong Kong depositary receipts (HDRs)

06300 to 06399: Restricted HDRs

08000 to 08999: GEM securities and information pages

Exchange Ticker Codes

10000 to 29999: Derivative warrants with the subset 10000 to 10999 reserved for derivative warrants with underlying assets listed outside Hong Kong, basket warrants and exotics

60000 to 69999: Callable bull/bear contracts

80000 to 89999: Products traded in Renminbi sub-divided as follows:

80000 to 83999: Equity, equity warrants and ETFs listed on the Main Board and GEM

82800 to 82849 and 83000 to 83199: ETFs

83900 to 83999: Temporary counters

84000 to 86999: Debt securities

85900 to 86029: Other debt securities

86600 to 86799: Ministry of Finance of People's Republic of China Bonds

87000 to 87999: Real Estate Investment Trusts (REITs), unit trusts, mutual funds other than ETFs

89000 to 89999: Derivative warrants

Note 30000 to 59999, 70000 to 79999, 87100 to 87999 and 90000 to 99999 are all reserved for future use within relevant categories.

Ticker symbols are easily recognised and remembered, and are key to facilitating the huge number of trades that occur around the world every day. Without them, brokers and investors would likely confuse issuers, securities and different securities from the same issuer. Ticker symbols, via their additional-letter codes, also communicate important information to investors about the trading status of the security or the issuer.

Although tickers identify a security, they are exchange-dependent, generally limited to stocks and can change. This limitation has led to the development of other codes such as the International Securities Identifying Number (ISIN) to identify securities for clearing and settlement purposes. ISINs are assigned to a wide range of financial instruments and uniquely identify an individual security.

However, the ISIN does not replace the ticker symbol; it identifies the security, not the exchange (if any) on which it trades. For instance, Daimler AG stock trades on 22 different stock exchanges worldwide, and is priced in five different currencies; it has the same ISIN on each stock exchange, though not the same ticker symbol. The ISIN cannot specify a trade on a particular exchange; another identifier, typically the exchange MIC, will have to be specified in addition to the ISIN.

For more information

http://en.wikipedia.org/wiki/Ticker_symbol

Options Symbology Initiative (OSI)

Options Symbology Initiative (OSI)

In brief

The Options Symbology Initiative (OSI) was undertaken by the Option Clearing Corporation (OCC) to address limitations in the 25-year-old conventional method of identifying US/Canadian listed options contracts during back-office processing. Introduced in February 2010, the OSI replaced the previous five-character options symbols with a 21-character identifier that fully describes the underlying option. Its intention was to match options symbols with the underlying security symbol, in order to reduce corporate action symbol conversions, eliminate the need for wrap symbols and the LEAPS rollover process and reduce errors in back-office processes.

OSI issuer

Option Clearing Corporation (OCC)
One North Wacker Drive, Suite 500
    Chicago, IL 60606
United State of America
Tel: +1 312 322 6200
Fax: +1 312 977 0611
Email: investorservices@theocc.com
www.optionsclearing.com

History

In 2005 the OCC opened discussions with industry representatives with the aim of eliminating the use of the Options Price Reporting Authority codes in the listed options market. The following year, working groups comprised of brokers, exchanges, clearing houses and vendors, representing both the US and Canadian securities industries, were formed in order to develop a new coding system for identifying listed options.

The traditional way of representing options was usually a five-character code where the first one to three characters (depending on the length of the underlying symbol) identified the underlying security; the fourth character identified the expiration month and call/put indicator and the fifth character, the strike price expressed in whole numbers or decimals. Under this system the letters A to L represented call options for the months January to December and the letters M to X identified put options from January to December. Strike price codes were as follows:

Code	Strike Prices						Code	Strike Prices					
A	5	105	205	305	405	505	N	70	170	270	370	470	570
B	10	110	210	310	410	510	O	75	175	275	375	475	575
C	15	115	215	315	415	515	P	80	180	280	380	480	580
D	20	120	220	320	420	520	Q	85	185	285	385	485	585
E	25	125	225	325	425	525	R	90	190	290	390	490	590
F	30	130	230	330	430	530	S	95	195	295	395	495	595
G	35	135	235	335	435	535	T	100	200	300	400	500	600
H	40	140	240	340	440	540	U	7.5	37.5	67.5	97.5	127.5	157.5
I	45	145	245	345	445	545	V	12.5	42.5	72.5	102.5	132.5	162.5
J	50	150	250	350	450	550	W	17.5	47.5	77.5	107.5	137.5	167.5
K	55	155	255	355	455	555	X	22.5	52.5	82.5	112.5	142.5	172.5
L	60	160	260	360	460	560	Y	27.5	57.5	87.5	117.5	147.5	177.5
M	65	165	265	365	465	565	Z	32.5	62.5	92.5	122.5	152.5	182.5

Structure

The new 21-character options symbology key introduced in February 2010 as OSI comprises four data elements arranged in logical order, each with a defined field size. The first element, the option root symbol, is the underlying equity ticker symbol for the contract. This is up to six characters in length and may contain digits. If the symbol is less than six characters, spaces are suffixed to equal the six-character length. The second element is the expiration date of the option expressed in the format YYMMDD.

The third element is the call/put indicator expressed as a single character: "C" for call and "P" for put. The final element is the strike price comprised of eight characters with leading 0s expressed as the price x 1000 i.e. without a decimal point. For instance, MSFT131221C00038000 is a call option on the underlying security Microsoft with a strike price of USD 38.00 expiring on 21 December 2013.

Options Symbology Initiative (OSI)

The most recent development in the OSI came into effect in March 2013, when the Chicago Board Options Exchange (CBOE) introduced mini-options for trading on a select group of securities: Amazon (AMZN), Apple (AAPL), Google (GOOG), the SPDR Gold Trust ETF (GLD), and the SPDR S&P 500 ETF Trust (SPY). Mini-options contracts feature specifications identical to those of standard-sized options contracts, except mini-options contracts represent 10 shares of the underlying security instead of the 100 shares for standard-sized options contracts. In terms of symbology, mini-options have the number "7" at the end of the security symbol to differentiate them from standard contracts. For example, the Apple mini-options symbol is AAPL7.

In addition to standard monthly expiration dates, non-standard expiration dates, i.e. weeklies options series, quarterlies option series and LEAPS are eligible for mini-options trading.

For more information

http://www.optionsclearing.com/

Stock Exchange Daily Official List Code (SEDOL)

In brief

SEDOL stands for Stock Exchange Daily Official List, a list of security identifiers used in the United Kingdom and Ireland for clearing and settlement purposes. The numbers are assigned at the request of the issuer by the London Stock Exchange (LSE), the National Numbering Agency (NNA) and member of the Association of National Numbering Agencies (ANNA) for the UK and Ireland. SEDOLs serve as the national security identification number (NSIN) for all securities issued in the UK and are therefore the basis for the generation of international security identification numbers (ISINs) for United Kingdom and Ireland incorporated securities.

The SEDOL Masterfile (SMF) provides reference data on over five million global multi-asset securities, including exchange traded derivatives which are each uniquely identified at the market level using a universal SEDOL code. Various organisations use SEDOLs to aid security identification in their financial business activities such as portfolio valuation, trade execution, processing data feeds and as a cross reference to other identifiers and price validation.

SEDOL issuer

London Stock Exchange
10 Paternoster Square
    London, EC4M 7LS
United Kingdom
    Tel: +44 20 7797 1000
**www.londonstockexchange.com/products-and-services/
    reference-data/sedol-master-file/sedol-master-file.htm**

History

SEDOLs were introduced in 1967 to provide a unique instrument identifier for securities appearing in the London Stock Exchange's Daily Official List (DOL) and Weekly Official Intelligence (WOI) publications. In 2004, due to a short-

Stock Exchange Daily Official List Code (SEDOL)

age of remaining numeric SEDOL code combinations available under the previous code allocation system, the LSE introduced a new seven-character alphanumeric code to address the industry need for identification of individual securities and the countries and markets in which they are traded.

Four years later, with increasing regulatory requirements, growing demand from the market for more accurate granular reference data and the emergence of multilateral trading facilities (MTFs) such as BATS Chi-X Europe (formerly Chi-X Europe and BATS Europe) operating outside set geographical boundaries and carrying multiple priced lines of the same security from different markets, the LSE again had to address the limitations of its allocation rules for SEDOLs.

 Up to this point, SEDOLs were assigned to the Official Places of Listing (OPOL) or, in the absence of listings, to the places of trade, but only one SEDOL was allocated per country. There were two exceptions: UK Exchange Trade Funds (ETFs), where a separate SEDOL was allocated for each trading currency on the LSE's trading platform; and Singapore Exchange (SGX) securities, due to a different lot size. This led to the allocation of separate SEDOL codes to identify securities trading in multiple trading currencies on the same platform. It also led to the introduction of market-level SEDOLs assigned to all exchanges and platforms with a separate MIC.

The example below shows how separate SEDOLs are allocated for Royal Dutch Shell plc A share trading on the LSE, NYSE Euronext Amsterdam and the London and Amsterdam segments of the BATS Chi-X trading platform.

Example: Royal Dutch Shell plc A Share

ISIN	MIC	Ticker Code	SEDOL	Currency
GB00B03MLX29	XLON	RDSA	B03MLX2	GBp
GB00B03MLX29	CHIX	RDSAI	B03MLX4	GBp
GB00B03MLX29	XAMS	RDSA	B09CBL4	EUR
GB00B03MLX29	CHIX	RDSAa	B09CBL5	EUR

How does the SEDOL code stack up in comparison with other symbology in terms of providing a unique instrument identifier? The criteria for a unique identifier was outlined in a June 2003 paper, "In Search of a Unique Instru-

Stock Exchange Daily Official List Code (SEDOL)

ment Identifier", published by the Reference Data User Group (RDUG) and the Reference Data Coalition (REDAC). At the time it was recognised that an instrument could be listed in various countries, traded on a number of different exchanges and priced in different currencies.

Now, with the recent introduction of multi-currency and market level SEDOLs and its enormous global coverage, the SEDOL code is close to both providing a unique key for securities reference databases and to fully satisfying the requirements of every party involved in the life of a trade. Proprietary ticker symbology systems such as the Reuters Instrument Code or RIC may be favored by traders and database managers for ease of use and familiarity, but they cannot fulfill the needs of the automated middle and back offices that tend to prefer the precision that a string of digits afford.

The International Security Identification Number or ISIN (ISO 6166), whilst considered the nirvana of codes at the time of its introduction, only identifies the security or issue, and not the exchange or trading platform on which it trades. For example, Daimler AG trades through almost 30 trading platforms and exchanges worldwide and is priced in five different currencies. It has the same ISIN on each, though not the same ticker symbol. ISIN cannot specify a particular trading location in this case; therefore, another identifier, typically the Market Identification Code or MIC (ISO 10383), or the three-letter exchange code, will have to be specified in addition to the ISIN. The currency of the trade will also be required to uniquely identify the instrument using this method.

CUSIP, the numbering standard of the North American naming agency Standard and Poor's, began to expand its allocation in the 1980s to cover international securities with the CUSIP international numbering system or CINS, but it is several leagues behind in terms of coverage. As a result, the international CINS has seen little use. It is also not clear whether it will address the need for multi-currency and market level CINS in its approach to this task.

Stock Exchange Daily Official List Code (SEDOL)

Structure

The new SEDOL code is a seven-character alphanumeric code, although some seven-digit numeric code issued prior to 2004 remain in circulation. SEDOLs are allocated one per country to represent place of listing or in the absence of listing place of trade.

(SEDOLs issued prior to 26 January 2004 were composed only of numbers. For these original SEDOLs, those from Asia and Africa typically begin with 6. Those from the UK and Ireland (until Ireland joined the EU) began with 0 or 3; those from the rest of Europe typically began with 4, 5 or 7; and those from the Americas began with 2.)

The new SEDOL code has the following structure:

1 Alpha
2 Alphanumeric
3 Alphanumeric
4 Alphanumeric
5 Alphanumeric
6 Alphanumeric
7 Numeric check digit

Alpha characters consist of consonants from B–Z, and exclude vowels. Numeric characters are 0–9 and alphanumeric characters are 0–9, B–Z excluding vowels. No SEDOL is issued without an alpha first character.

SEDOL codes are allocated sequentially and with no inherent meaning for each market in which an instrument is traded. Note that no codes are issued with nine as the lead character, as an historic nine series is used as dummy codes.

Stock Exchange Daily Official List Code (SEDOL)

Check digit calculation

The seventh digit of the SEDOL code is a check digit.

Character	Value	Character	Value	Character	Value	Character	Value
B	11	J	19	Q	26	X	33
C	12	K	20	R	27	Y	34
D	13	L	21	S	28	Z	35
F	15	M	22	T	29		
G	16	N	23	V	31		
H	17	P	25	W	32		

To check that a number is reported correctly, each digit is multiplied by a weight and the results are summed. The weight used for each digit is as follows:

Digit	Weight
1st (alpha)	1
2nd (alpha/numeric)	3
3rd (alpha/numeric)	1
4th (alpha/numeric)	7
5th (alpha/numeric)	3
6th (alpha/numeric)	9
7th (numeric check digit)	1

If the sum of the results is a multiple of ten, the number is taken to be correct. If the sum of the results is not a multiple of ten, there is an error.

Deriving the check digit

To derive a check digit for a number, each of the first six digits is multiplied by the corresponding weight. This result is then summed and taken away from the next highest number divisible by 10.

Stock Exchange Daily Official List Code (SEDOL)

Example: (1) SEDOL Number B-123-45

Digit	Weight	Product
B = 11	1	11
1	3	3
2	1	2
3	7	21
4	3	12
5	9	45

Sum = 94. Therefore 94 taken away from a 100 means a check digit of 6.

Additional information

Effects of Corporate Action on SEDOLs

Type of Change	Details	Effect on SEDOL
Name change	Company changes from one name to another with no additional corporate action	A new SEDOL will be allocated if a new ISIN is issued
Change of domicile	Company moves from one country to another	New SEDOL allocated
Merger	Two or more companies merge in their entirety to form a new company	New SEDOL allocated
Simple takeover/acquisition	A company is fully absorbed into another company; no new company is formed	No new SEDOL unless the acquiring company is not on the system
Takeover/reverse takeover	A company is fully absorbed into another	A new SEDOL will be allocated if a new ISIN is issued
De-merger/spinoff	A subsidiary or division of a company is sold as a separate entity	A new SEDOL will be allocated to the new entity, and the parent company SEDOL will be unaffected
Subdivision	When a company increases the number of shares in issue through a subdivision of existing shares	A new SEDOL will be allocated if a new ISIN is issued
Consolidation	When a company decreases the number of shares in issue by consolidating existing shares	A new SEDOL will be allocated if a new ISIN is issued
Share exchange/conversion	When one type of share goes through a mandatory exchange/conversion	Assuming the remaining shares already have a SEDOL, no new SEDOL

Stock Exchange Daily Official List Code (SEDOL)

Type of Change	Details	Effect on SEDOL
Share reclassification/rename	When a class of shares is reclassified/renamed, but the shares fundamentally remain unchanged, e.g. common stock are renamed Class A shares	A new SEDOL will be allocated if a new ISIN is issued
Share reduction	The capital of the company is reduced and the shareholders are compensated	No new SEDOL
Par value change	Change to par value with no additional corporate action	No new SEDOL
Renominalisation	Where par value is recalculated to reflect currency conversion rate	No new SEDOL
Redenomination	Change in currency with no recalculation	No new SEDOL
Strike price change	Where the strike price changes, but the terms remain the same	No new SEDOL
Underlying name change	When the underlying company has a name change, but all other terms of the security remain the same	A new SEDOL will be allocated if a new ISIN is issued
Board lot change	When board lot changes and there is no simultaneous trading period	No new SEDOL
Separate board lot	When different board lots trade simultaneously	A new SEDOL will be allocated to each board lot
Bonus issue/bonus rights	A company issues bonus shares to shareholders	A new SEDOL may be allocated to the bonus shares if a separate ISIN is available, but the parent SEDOL remains unchanged
Rights	A company issues rights to purchase new shares to existing shareholders	A separate SEDOL will be allocated to the rights line, but the parent SEDOL remains unchanged
Deferred shares	Relating to Australian equities, deferred shares trade for a short period of time and then assimilate into the ordinary line	A separate SEDOL will be allocated to the deferred line, but the parent SEDOL remains unchanged
Further tranche/tranche	An additional issue of an existing instrument which increases the amount of outstanding issue	A new SEDOL will be allocated if a new ISIN is issued
Change of security form	Change in the registered form of an instrument, e.g. bearer shares change to registered	A new SEDOL will be allocated if a new ISIN is issued

For more information

http://www.londonstockexchange.com/products-and-services/matching-reconciliation/solutions/data-solutions/sedol-masterfile.pdf

Valoren

In brief

The Valor number is a code used to identify listed securities and financial instruments in Switzerland and Liechtenstein. The word "Valor" is a Swiss-German banking term for a "security", including coins and paper money. In Switzerland, when referring to the code, it is always referred to as the "Valor Nummer", i.e. a security number. In the English-speaking world, the words "Valor" and "Valoren", the plural of Valor, are sometimes used interchangeably. Valor numbers form the basis for the generation of international security identification numbers (ISINs) for Switzerland and Liechtenstein.

Valor issuer

Six Financial Information
Hardturmstrasse 201
8005 Zurich
Switzerland
Tel: +41 58 399 51 11
www.six-financial-information.com

History

Valor numbers were originally introduced by the Swiss Bank Corporation in its role as the manager of the Swiss securities register. Today the numbers are assigned at the request of the issuer by SIX Financial Information, the National Numbering Agency (NNA) and member of the Association of National Numbering Agencies (ANNA) for Switzerland.

Structure

Valor numbers are typically six to nine digits in format and intrinsically have no meaning, i.e. a security's number conveys no additional information such as security type or class. When a new Valor number is needed, the next one from the list is simply allocated. Valor numbers for derivatives may be reused after the derivative expires.

Globally, a Valor number can be allocated for any type of financial instrument which meets the allocation rules. It can be used in conjunction with the MIC and the currency code to uniquely identify a traded instrument. It can be used in transaction reporting and for position keeping.

For more information

https://www.six-group.com/about/en/home.html

Wertpapierkennnummer

In brief

The Wertpapierkennnummer (known as WKN, WPKN, WPK or Werts) is a code used to identify listed securities and financial instruments in Germany. The word Wertpapierkennnummer is a compound word in German comprised of the word "Wertpapier" meaning financial security and "Kennnummer" meaning identity number.

WKN issuer

WM Datenservice
Duesseldorfer Straße 16
Frankfurt am Main, 60329
Germany
Tel: +49 69 2732 100 231
Fax: +49 69 2732 291
Email: service@wmdata.com
www.wmdaten.de

History

The WKN securities identification number was introduced in 1955 in Germany to facilitate an overview of available securities. Historically, WKNs were divided into different number ranges that represented different types of securities such as shares, warrants, funds; however this system representing different classes of securities was abandoned long ago. Today, WKN numbers are assigned at the request of the issuer by WM Datenservice, the National Numbering Agency (NNA) and member of the Association of National Numbering Agencies (ANNA) for Germany. WKN numbers form the basis for the generation of international security identification numbers (ISINs) for Germany and are accredited by the GLEIF (See appendix A).

Structure

WKN numbers comprise six digits or capital letters (excluding I and O). There is no check digit. Although intrinsically WKNs have no meaning, i.e. a security's number conveys no additional information such as security type or class, the first 2 to 4 letters may show the issuer of the instrument. WKN numbers issued prior to 21 July 2003 were numeric only.

For more information

https://www.wmdaten.de/index.php?mid=214

Open Source

Financial Instruments Global Identifier (FIGI)

In brief

A Financial Instruments Global Identifier (FIGI), formerly known as the Bloomberg Global Identifier, is a unique security identifier defined by Bloomberg LP. FIGIs have been created for more than 80 million unique securities, representing most asset classes of the financial markets. Securities to which FIGIs can be issued include common stock, options, derivatives, futures, corporate and government bonds, municipals, currencies, and mortgage products. Unique FIGIs identify securities as well as individual exchanges on which they trade. Composite FIGIs are also issued to represent unique securities across related exchanges. For instance, Apple Inc. common stock trades on 14 exchanges in the United States. Whilst a separate FIGI identifies the common stock on each individual exchange, a composite FIGI represents the company's common stock traded on United States exchanges. Once issued, a FIGI is never reused and represents the same instrument in perpetuity.

FIGI issuer
Bloomberg LP
Bloomberg Tower, 731 Lexington Avenue
New York City, NY 10022
United States of America
Tel: +1 212 318 2000
www.openfigi.com

History

The FIGI was at the heart of Bloomberg's Open Symbology initiative, which it launched in November 2009. Since then, the FIGI has been adopted by 18 exchanges and 28 third-party data providers. For example, FIGIs are distributed by Euronext, along with its own proprietary security identifiers, on all its data products globally. The Financial Industry Regulatory Authority (FINRA) also accepts FIGIs to uniquely identify securities reported to its SEC-mandated Trade Reporting and Compliance Engine (TRACE) program. Elsewhere in

Financial Instruments Global Identifier (FIGI)

the global financial industry, FIGIs have been integrated into exchange trading platforms and distributed as an integral part of exchange data feeds and products.

Structure

A FIGI is a 12-digit alphanumeric randomly generated identification code that does not convey any information about the character of a financial instrument. A FIGI consists of three parts: a three-character "BBG" prefix; an eight-character alphanumeric code which does not contain the English vowels "A", "E", "I", "O", or "U"; and a single check digit. In total, the coding structure has the potential to generate over 852 million codes.

Allocation [IS THIS HEADING CORRECT?]

Entity Level

A FIGI is allocated at the entity level for the following issuer types:

Company
Government
Municipal fundamentals
Municipals
Funds
Fund family
Fund parent
Lead manager
Currency
Commodity
Mortgage

An entity-level FIGI is never reused and does not change once allocated.

Financial Instruments Global Identifier (FIGI)

Entity Level FIGIs and Corporate Actions

Type of Change	Details	Effect on Entity Level FIGI
Name change	Name associated with entity-level FIGI is changed	No change
Acquisition	Acquisition of one company by another	Both the acquired company and the acquiring company retain their original FIGIs
Merger of equals	Merger of two companies	Both companies retain their original FIGIs and a third FIGI is created for the new entity
Integration	Merger where one company is integrated into another with name change	Both companies retain their original FIGIs; a name change occurs to the active company
Reorganisation/formation of holding company	Formation of a holding company above an existing company or change of company into a holding company	Holding company formed above is given its own entity-level FIGI; reorganisation of a listed company into a holding company is treated as a name change and entity-level FIGI becomes that of the holding company; new entity-level FIGI assigned to a subsidiary
Spin-off	Spin-off from existing company creating new company	The newly created company is assigned its own FIGI

Security class level

Multiple listings of the same security share class are assigned the same global identifier at this level. This level of FIGI assignment does not connect all composite global identifiers that represent the same share class as it can be linked to more than one equity ticker, ISIN or other identifier. The share-class-level FIGI Is never reused and does not change once allocated.

Asset class level

Corporates and preferred

FIGIs are allocated to all corporate bonds and preferred securities, active or inactive. For securities with multiple tranches, each tranche is assigned a separate FIGI.

Money market

FIGIs are allocated to both programs and securities. Different program types that are covered under the same document are allocated different FIGIs.

Financial Instruments Global Identifier (FIGI)

Government securities

All securities including bonds, bills and notes are initially assigned a FIGI at the "when-issue" stage. At the time of the auction, if it is determined to be a new issue, a new security is set up and is given a separate FIGI from the "when-issued" security. The "when-issued" security becomes inactive after the first settlement date.

Mortgages

For CMO/ABS/CMBS deals, multiple tranches are assigned a separate FIGI. Where deals have multiple structure changes up to finalisation, FIGIs are not assigned until the deal is completed. If deals amended post-finalisation affect the deal structure, the FIGI is no longer be available for the original class.

Agency-specified pools including Fannie Mae, Freddie Mac, Ginnie Mae, Canadian and SBA Pools are assigned a separate FIGI. Generic mortgages receive a separate FIGI. TBAs (To Be Announced) with delivery dates +/- one year from current month receive a FIGI at the beginning of the month.

Municipals

All securities are assigned a FIGI.

Equities, warrants, funds

Equities, funds and warrants are assigned FIGIs for every exchange within a market and at the composite level.

Asset-Level FIGIs and Corporate Actions

Type of Change	Details	Effect on Asset-Level FIGI
Ticker change	Change of ticker code for a security	The composite FIGI, the primary and each regional exchange FIGI, moves to the new ticker; a FIGI is not assigned to the old ticker
Change in listing	Change in the listing of a security within a market	The composite FIGI remains the same; regional exchange FIGIs become inactive as appropriate
Delisting	Delisting of a security	All FIGIs assigned remain but become inactive

Financial Instruments Global Identifier (FIGI) ▬

Type of Change	Details	Effect on Asset-Level FIGI
Merger/acquisition	Company A buys company B and B delists	All FIGIs assigned remain; FIGI for delisted company becomes inactive
Merger/formation of new company	Company A buys company B and forms new company C	Companies A and B are delisted, FIGIs remain but become inactive; new FIGI assigned to company C
Spin-off	Company A spins off company B	Company A retains existing FIGI and new FIGI is created for company B
When issued	When issued trading before listing	New FIGI assigned to "when-issued" stock; treated as a ticker change when regular trading commences

Indices

All equity indices, active and inactive, are assigned a FIGI at the security level. Indices calculated using different methodologies such as net total return and gross total return are assigned separate FIGIs. Non-equity indices such as bond, commodity, economic and statistical indices, active and inactive, are also assigned FIGIs at the security level. Interest rates such as the LIBOR rate are included in this category.

Futures and options

All futures and options contracts, commodity and financial are assigned a FIGI. Listed FX options are allocated FIGIs at the exchange level. Equity and index options are allocated a FIGI at the composite and exchange level. Upon expiry or maturity, the FIGI becomes inactive.

For equity futures and options, corporate actions on the underlying equity (such as stock splits, reverse stock splits, mergers, cash distributions and cash dividends) all result in changes to contracts. Depending on the exchange, either a new "adjusted" security is created or the adjustment is made to the existing security. If a new "adjusted" ticker is created, the FIGI moves to this new record. If the adjustment is made on a current security, the FIGI will not change. Any new contracts listed as a result of an underlying corporate action are assigned new FIGIs.

Financial Instruments Global Identifier (FIGI)

Spreads, strategies and swaps

A FIGI is allocated for all spreads, futures strategies and swaps.

Forex

The following security types, active and inactive, are allocated a FIGI: Spot, Cross, Forward, Forward Cross, Deposits, IMM Forward, NDF, Onshore Forward, Option Volatility, CDs, Return Indices, Bankers Acceptance, Commercial Paper Promissory Notes, Repo and Treasury Bills. More than one ticker may share the same FIGI.

Reuters Instrument Code (RIC)

In brief

Reuters Instrument Codes (RICs) are proprietary alphanumeric codes used by Thomson Reuters to identify all financial instruments – including stocks, bonds, indices, currencies and commodities – as well as many types of economic data in the various Thomson Reuters financial-information services. The acronym RIC originally stood for Record Identification Code. It later became known as either Reuters Instrument Code or Reuters Identification Code.

RICs provide a structured means of retrieving data from the Thomson Reuters network and can be used to display multiple data items for one financial instrument (aka "Full Quote") or to display key information concerning several financial instruments (aka "Chains and Tiles").

RIC issuer
Thomson Reuters
3 Times Square
New York, NY 10036
United State of America
Tel: +1 646 223 4000
www.thomsonreuters.com

History

Originally defined by Herbie Skeete, a Reuters executive who wrote the original product specifications for the first products on Reuters' Integrated Data Network (IDN), RICs were designed to be logical and intuitive. For equities, RICs were composed of a RIC root, effectively a ticker symbol of one to four characters in length, followed by a period sign, then a one- or two-character (A through Z) code denoting the exchange on which the instrument is traded. Each company was meant to have a unique RIC root regardless of the exchange on which it was traded, e.g. IBM for International Business Machines.

Reuters Instrument Code (RIC)

Skeete intended to make RICs freely available, effectively establishing a potential ISO standard for ticker codes. However, then-Reuters CEO Glen Renfrew vetoed the idea. Although some key elements have changed in recent years, much of Skeete's original work is still contained in the current RIC structure.

Structure

RIC symbols are composed of different elements to avoid duplication of codes and to cater for the diversity of instruments and markets covered by Thomson Reuters' services. These five key components are:

— A RIC root symbol.
— A source code (exchange code, contributor code or market-maker identifier).
— An instrument identifier.
— Period or time intervals.
— One or more delimiters.

The RIC root symbol identifies the most basic aspect of the instrument. For equities, the RIC root for BT Group plc is BT. To differentiate between prices from the different markets where BT is traded, it is necessary to append a source code. For example, the RIC for BT traded on the London Stock Exchange is BT.L and the RIC for BT traded on the Frankfurt Stock Exchange is BT.F.

For foreign exchange or money-market instruments, a period or time interval is added to the RIC root to identify a specific instrument. Examples of periods or time intervals are overnight (ON) or one year (TY).

Delimiters are characters used to separate the different elements of the RIC. For example, the period or dot is used for equities and equity options, while an equals sign is used for foreign exchange and money market instruments.

Contributor or market-maker codes identify an organisation that contributes information to the Thomson Reuters network or a market-maker contributing quotes for a specific instrument. These codes are generally four upper-case characters in length. Exchange codes identify the exchange or trading platform for the instrument and consist of up to three upper- or lower-case characters.

Section 3: Miscellaneous Codes

This section examines two coding systems associated with the financial marketplace.

The first of these codes, country codes, was developed to establish an internationally recognised way of representing country names. ISO 3166 country codes are widely used by organisations such as national postal services, and in machine-readable passports. Similarly, ISO 4217, the international standard for currencies, the second code examined here, is widely used in global banking and financial markets for the publication and display of exchange rates, amongst other things.

Country codes (ISO 3166)

In brief

ISO 3166 is the international standard for countries and their subdivisions. The country names in ISO 3166 come from United Nations sources. New names and codes are added automatically when the United Nations publishes new names in either the Terminology Bulletin Country Names or in the Country and Region Codes for Statistical Use, both maintained by the United Nations Statistics Divisions. Names for subdivisions are taken from relevant official national information sources.

The country codes found in ISO 3166-1 are used by many organisations, businesses and governments. For example, national postal organisations worldwide exchange international mail in containers bearing a country code for identification. In machine-readable passports, the ISO 3166-1 codes are used to determine the nationality of the user. In addition, internet domain-name systems use the codes to define top-level domain names such as "fr" for France, "au" for Australia and "br" for Brazil.

Country code maintenance agency
c/o International Organization for Standardization
Chemin de Blandonnet 8
CP 401
1214 Vernier, Geneva
Switzerland
Tel: +41 22 749 01 11
Email: customerservice@iso.org
www.iso.org/iso/country_codes

History

ISO 3166 was developed to establish internationally recognised codes for the representation of names of countries, territories or areas of geographical interest, and their subdivisions. It does not establish the names of countries, only the codes that represent them.

Country codes (ISO 3166)

Originally published in 1974, ISO 3166-1 was expanded into three parts in 1997 to include the codes for subdivisions and the codes for names of countries that are no longer in use. Of the three parts, ISO 3166-1 alpha-2 is the most frequently used.

An additional standard, ISO 3166-2, first published in 1998, provides an international standard of short and unique alphanumeric codes to represent the relevant administrative divisions and dependent territories of all countries allowing unique identification of a country subdivision in a global context.

Currently, more than 4,000 codes are defined in ISO 3166-2. For some countries, codes are defined for more than one level of subdivisions.

Structure

ISO 3166 defines three sets of country codes:

ISO 3166-1 alpha-2: two-letter country codes which are the most widely used of the three, and used most prominently for the internet's country code top-level domains (with a few exceptions).

ISO 3166-1 alpha-3: three-letter country codes which allow a better visual association between the codes and the country names than the alpha-2 codes.

ISO 3166-1 numeric: three-digit country codes which are identical to those developed and maintained by the United Nations Statistics Division, with the advantage of script (writing system) independence, and hence useful for people or systems using non-Latin scripts.

ISO 3166-2: consists of two parts, separated by a hyphen. The first part is the ISO 3166-1 alpha-2 code of the country. The second part is a string of up to three alphanumeric characters, which is usually obtained from national sources and stems from coding systems already in use in the country concerned, but may also be developed by the ISO itself.

Code list

Country	A2	A3	Numeric
Åland Islands	AX	ALA	248
Afghanistan	AF	AFG	4
Albania	AL	ALB	8
Algeria	DZ	DZA	12
American Samoa	AS	ASM	16
Andorra	AD	AND	20
Angola	AO	AGO	24
Anguilla	AI	AIA	660
Antarctica	AQ	ATA	10
Antigua & Barbuda	AG	ATG	28
Argentina	AR	ARG	32
Armenia	AM	ARM	51
Aruba	AW	ABW	533
Australia	AU	AUS	36
Austria	AT	AUT	40
Azerbaijan	AZ	AZE	31
Bahamas	BS	BHS	44
Bahrain	BH	BHR	48
Bangladesh	BD	BGD	50
Barbados	BB	BRB	52
Belarus	BY	BLR	112
Belgium	BE	BEL	56
Belize	BZ	BLZ	84
Benin	BJ	BEN	204
Bermuda	BM	BMU	60
Bhutan	BT	BTN	64
Bolivia	BO	BOL	68
Bonaire, Sint Eustatius & Saba	BQ	BES	535
Bosnia & Herzegovina	BA	BIH	70
Botswana	BW	BWA	72
Bouvet Island	BV	BVT	74
Brazil	BR	BRA	76
British Indian Ocean Territory	IO	IOT	86

Country codes (ISO 3166)

Country	A2	A3	Numeric
Brunei Darussalam	BN	BRN	96
Bulgaria	BG	BGR	100
Burkina Faso	BF	BFA	854
Burundi	BI	BDI	108
Cambodia	KH	KHM	116
Cameroon	CM	CMR	120
Canada	CA	CAN	124
Cape Verde	CV	CPV	132
Cayman Islands	KY	CYM	136
Central African Republic	CF	CAF	140
Chad	TD	TCD	148
Chile	CL	CHL	152
China	CN	CHN	156
Christmas Island	CX	CXR	162
Cocos (Keeling) Islands	CC	CCK	166
Colombia	CO	COL	170
Comoros	KM	COM	174
Democratic Republic of Congo	CD	COD	180
Congo	CG	COG	178
Cook Islands	CK	COK	184
Costa Rica	CR	CRI	188
Ivory Coast	CI	CIV	384
Croatia	HR	HRV	191
Cuba	CU	CUB	192
Curacao	CW	CUW	531
Cyprus	CY	CYP	196
Czech Republic	CZ	CZE	203
Denmark	DK	DNK	208
Djibouti	DJ	DJI	262
Dominica	DM	DMA	212
Dominican Republic	DO	DOM	214
Ecuador	EC	ECU	218
Egypt	EG	EGY	818
El Salvador	SV	SLV	222

Country codes (ISO 3166)

Country	A2	A3	Numeric
Equatorial Guinea	GQ	GNQ	226
Eritrea	ER	ERI	232
Estonia	EE	EST	233
Ethiopia	ET	ETH	231
Falkland Islands	FK	FLK	238
Faroe Islands	FO	FRO	234
Fiji	FJ	FJI	242
Finland	FI	FIN	246
France	FR	FRA	250
French Guiana	GF	GUF	254
French Polynesia	PF	PYF	258
French Southern Territories	TF	ATF	260
Gabon	GA	GAB	266
Gambia	GM	GMB	270
Georgia	GE	GEO	268
Germany	DE	DEU	276
Ghana	GH	GHA	288
Gibraltar	GI	GIB	292
Greece	GR	GRC	300
Greenland	GL	GRL	304
Grenada	GD	GRD	308
Guadeloupe	GP	GLP	312
Guam	GU	GUM	316
Guatemala	GT	GTM	320
Guernsey	GG	GGY	831
Guinea	GN	GIN	324
Guinea-Bissau	GW	GNB	624
Guyana	GY	GUY	328
Haiti	HT	HTI	332
Heard & McDonald Islands	HM	HMD	334
Honduras	HN	HND	340
Hong Kong	HK	HKG	344
Hungary	HU	HUN	348
Iceland	IS	ISL	352

Country codes (ISO 3166)

Country	A2	A3	Numeric
India	IN	IND	356
Indonesia	ID	IDN	360
Iran	IR	IRN	364
Iraq	IQ	IRQ	368
Ireland	IE	IRL	372
Isle of Man	IM	IMN	833
Israel	IL	ISR	376
Italy	IT	ITA	380
Jamaica	JM	JAM	388
Japan	JP	JPN	392
Jersey	JE	JEY	832
Jordan	JO	JOR	400
Kazakhstan	KZ	KAZ	398
Kenya	KE	KEN	404
Kiribati	KI	KIR	296
North Korea	KP	PRK	408
South Korea	KR	KOR	410
Kuwait	KW	KWT	414
Kyrgyzstan	KG	KGZ	417
Laos	LA	LAO	418
Latvia	LV	LVA	428
Lebanon	LB	LBN	422
Lesotho	LS	LSO	426
Liberia	LR	LBR	430
Libya	LY	LBY	434
Liechtenstein	LI	LIE	438
Lithuania	LT	LTU	440
Luxembourg	LU	LUX	442
Macau	MO	MAC	446
Macedonia	MK	MKD	807
Madagascar	MG	MDG	450
Malawi	MW	MWI	454
Malaysia	MY	MYS	458
Maldives	MV	MDV	462

Country codes (ISO 3166)

Country	A2	A3	Numeric
Mali	ML	MLI	466
Malta	MT	MLT	470
Marshall Islands	MH	MHL	584
Martinique	MQ	MTQ	474
Mauritania	MR	MRT	478
Mauritius	MU	MUS	480
Mayotte	YT	MYT	175
Mexico	MX	MEX	484
Micronesia	FM	FSM	583
Moldova	MD	MDA	498
Monaco	MC	MCO	492
Mongolia	MN	MNG	496
Montenegro	ME	MNE	499
Montserrat	MS	MSR	500
Morocco	MA	MAR	504
Mozambique	MZ	MOZ	508
Myanmar	MM	MMR	104
Namibia	NA	NAM	516
Nauru	NR	NRU	520
Nepal	NP	NPL	524
Netherlands	NL	NLD	528
Netherlands Antilles	AN	ANT	530
New Caledonia	NC	NCL	540
New Zealand	NZ	NZL	554
Nicaragua	NI	NIC	558
Niger	NE	NER	562
Nigeria	NG	NGA	566
Niue	NU	NIU	570
Norfolk Island	NF	NFK	574
Northern Mariana Islands	MP	MNP	580
Norway	NO	NOR	578
Oman	OM	OMN	512
Pakistan	PK	PAK	586
Palau	PW	PLW	585

Country codes (ISO 3166)

Country	A2	A3	Numeric
Palestinian Territory	PS	PSE	275
Panama	PA	PAN	591
Papua New Guinea	PG	PNG	598
Paraguay	PY	PRY	600
Peru	PE	PER	604
Philippines	PH	PHL	608
Pitcairn Island	PN	PCN	612
Poland	PL	POL	616
Portugal	PT	PRT	620
Puerto Rico	PR	PRI	630
Qatar	QA	QAT	634
Reunion	RE	REU	638
Romania	RO	ROU	642
Russia	RU	RUS	643
Rwanda	RW	RWA	646
St. Barthelemy	BL	BLM	652
St. Helena, Ascension, Tristan da Cunha	SH	SHN	654
St. Kitts & Nevis	KN	KNA	659
St. Lucia	LC	LCA	662
French St. Martin	MF	MAF	663
St. Pierre & Miquelon	PM	SPM	666
St. Vincent & Grenadines	VC	VCT	670
Samoa	WS	WSM	882
San Marino	SM	SMR	674
Sao Tome & Principe	ST	STP	678
Saudi Arabia	SA	SAU	682
Senegal	SN	SEN	686
Serbia	CS	SCG	891
Seychelles	SC	SYC	690
Sierra Leone	SL	SLE	694
Singapore	SG	SGP	702
Sint Maarten	SX	SXM	534
Slovakia	SK	SVK	703
Slovenia	SI	SVN	705

Country codes (ISO 3166)

Country	A2	A3	Numeric
Solomon Islands	SB	SLB	90
Somalia	SO	SOM	706
South Africa	ZA	ZAF	710
South Georgia & South Sandwich Islands	GS	SGS	239
South Sudan	SS	SSD	728
Spain	ES	ESP	724
Sri Lanka	LK	LKA	144
Sudan	SD	SDN	736
Suriname	SR	SUR	740
Svalbard & Jan Mayen Islands	SJ	SJM	744
Swaziland	SZ	SWZ	748
Sweden	SE	SWE	752
Switzerland	CH	CHE	756
Syria	SY	SYR	760
Taiwan	TW	TWN	158
Tajikistan	TJ	TJK	762
Tanzania	TZ	TZA	834
Thailand	TH	THA	764
Timor-Leste	TL	TLS	626
Togo	TG	TGO	768
Tokelau	TK	TKL	772
Tonga	TO	TON	776
Trinidad & Tobago	TT	TTO	780
Tunisia	TN	TUN	788
Turkey	TR	TUR	792
Turkmenistan	TM	TKM	795
Turks & Caicos Islands	TC	TCA	796
Tuvalu	TV	TUV	798
Uganda	UG	UGA	800
Ukraine	UA	UKR	804
UAE	AE	ARE	784
UK	GB	GBR	826
USA	US	USA	840
US Minor Outlying Islands	UM	UMI	581

Country codes (ISO 3166)

Country	A2	A3	Numeric
Uruguay	UY	URY	858
Uzbekistan	UZ	UZB	860
Vanuatu	VU	VUT	548
Vatican City	VA	VAT	336
Venezuela	VE	VEN	862
Vietnam	VN	VNM	704
British Virgin Islands	VG	VGB	92
US Virgin Islands	VI	VIR	850
Wallis & Fortuna Islands	WF	WLF	876
Western Sahara	EH	ESH	732
Yemen	YE	YEM	887
Zambia	ZM	ZMB	894
Zimbabwe	ZW	ZWE	716

For more information

http://www.iso.org/iso/country_codes.htm

Currency codes (ISO 4217)

In brief

ISO 4217 is the international standard for currencies. ISO 4217 currency codes are used in the global banking and financial markets and for the publication and display of exchange rates in newspapers and banks. The codes are also used on airline tickets and international train tickets. SIX Interbank Clearing is responsible for the maintenance of the list of codes.

Currency code maintenance agency
c/o Currency codes RA/MA
SIX Interbank Clearing Ltd (acting on behalf of the Swiss Association for Standardization)
P.O. Box
Hardturmstrasse 201
8021 Zurich
Switzerland
Tel: +41 58 399 2999
Fax: +41 58 499 4550
Email: office@currency-iso.org
http://www.currency-iso.orgwww.currency-iso.org

History

In 1973, ISO Technical Committee 68 decided to develop codes for the representation of currencies and funds. Five years later, the related UN/ECE Group of Experts agreed that the three-letter alphabetic codes would be suitable for the representation of currencies and funds.

Over time, new currencies have been created and old currencies have been discontinued as a result of changes in governments (through war or a new constitution), treaties between countries standardising a currency e.g. the adoption of the euro by the Eurozone countries, or the revaluation of a currency due to excessive inflation.

Currency codes (ISO 4217)

Structure

The first two letters of the code are the two letters of ISO 3166-1 alpha-2 country codes (see previous chapter) and the third is normally the initial of the currency itself. For example, the currency code for the British pound (or sterling) is GBP, where GB is the country code for Great Britain and the "P" represents pound. Where a currency is revalued, the currency code's last letter is changed to distinguish it from the old currency. In some cases, the replacement third letter is the initial for the word "new" in that country's language, to distinguish it from an older currency that was revalued. For example, the currency code for the new Mexican peso is MXN where the "N" represents the Spanish word for new, "nuevo". Other letter changes have also been used, usually for alphabetic reasons. For example, the code for the Russian Ruble was changed from RUR to RUB, where the B is derived from the third letter of the word "ruble".

In addition a three-digit code number is assigned to each currency, in the same manner as there is also a three-digit code number assigned to each country as part of ISO 3166. This numeric code is usually the same as the ISO 3166-1 numeric code. For example, the US dollar (USD) has code 840, which is also the numeric code for the United States.

ISI 4217 also defines the relationship between the major currency unit and any minor currency unit. Usually, the minor currency unit has a value that is 1/100 of the major unit, but 1/1000 is also used. Some currencies do not have any minor currency unit at all. In others, the major currency unit has so little value that the minor unit is no longer generally used (e.g. the Japanese sen which represents 1/100th of a yen). This is indicated in the standard by the currency exponent. For example, USD has exponent 2, while JPY has exponent 0. Mauritania does not use a decimal division of units, setting 1 ouguiya (UM) = 5 khoums, and Madagascar has 1 ariary = 5 iraimbilanja.

Moreover, ISO 4217 defines codes for precious metals such as gold, silver, palladium and platinum (expressed per one troy ounce instead of per currency unit) and certain other entities used in international finance such as special drawing rights. There are also codes allocated for testing purposes (XTS) and to indicate no currency transactions (XXX). These codes all begin with the letter "X". The precious metals use "X" plus the metal's chemical/periodic table symbol. Hence silver is XAG and gold is XAU. Country currency codes never begin with "X" although "X" codes can be used for non-country-specific currencies.

Supranational currencies, such as the east Caribbean dollar, the CFP franc, the CFA franc BEAC and the CFA franc BCEAO are normally also represented by codes beginning with an "X". The euro is represented by the code EUR. Its predecessor, the European currency unit (ECU), had the code XEU.

Code list

Country or entity	Currency	Alphabetic code	Numeric code	Minor unit
Åland Islands	Euro	EUR	978	2
Afghanistan	Afghani	AFN	971	2
Albania	Lek	ALL	008	2
Algeria	Algerian dinar	DZD	012	2
American Samoa	US dollar	USD	840	2
Andorra	Euro	EUR	978	2
Angola	Kwanza	AOA	973	2
Anguilla	East Caribbean dollar	XCD	951	2
Antarctica	No universal currency			
Antigua & Barbuda	East Caribbean dollar	XCD	951	2
Argentina	Argentine peso	ARS	032	2
Armenia	Armenian dram	AMD	051	2
Aruba	Aruban florin	AWG	533	2
Australia	Australian dollar	AUD	036	2
Austria	Euro	EUR	978	2
Azerbaijan	Azerbaijanian manat	AZN	944	2
Bahamas	Bahamian dollar	BSD	044	2
Bahrain	Bahraini dinar	BHD	048	3
Bangladesh	Taka	BDT	050	2
Barbados	Barbados dollar	BBD	052	2
Belarus	Belarusian ruble	BYR	974	0
Belgium	Euro	EUR	978	2
Belize	Belize dollar	BZD	084	2
Benin	CFA franc BCEAO	XOF	952	0

Currency codes (ISO 4217)

Country or entity	Currency	Alphabetic code	Numeric code	Minor unit
Bermuda	Bermudian dollar	BMD	060	2
Bhutan	Ngultrum	BTN	064	2
Bhutan	Indian rupee	INR	356	2
Bolivia	Boliviano	BOB	068	2
Bolivia	Mvdol	BOV	984	2
Bonaire, Sint Eustatius & Saba	US dollar	USD	840	2
Bosnia & Herzegovina	Convertible mark	BAM	977	2
Botswana	Pula	BWP	072	2
Bouvet Island	Norwegian krone	NOK	578	2
Brazil	Brazilian real	BRL	986	2
British Indian Ocean Territory	US dollar	USD	840	2
Brunei Darussalam	Brunei dollar	BND	096	2
Bulgaria	Bulgarian lev	BGN	975	2
Burkina Faso	CFA franc BCEAO	XOF	952	0
Burundi	Burundi franc	BIF	108	0
Cambodia	Riel	KHR	116	2
Cameroon	CFA franc BEAC	XAF	950	0
Canada	Canadian dollar	CAD	124	2
Cape Verde	Cape Verde escudo	CVE	132	2
Cayman Islands	Cayman Islands dollar	KYD	136	2
Central African Republic	CFA franc BEAC	XAF	950	0
Chad	CFA franc BEAC	XAF	950	0
Chile	Unidades de fomento	CLF	990	0
Chile	Chilean peso	CLP	152	0
China	Yuan renminbi	CNY	156	2
Christmas Island	Australian dollar	AUD	036	2
Cocos (Keeling) Islands	Australian dollar	AUD	036	2
Colombia	Colombian peso	COP	170	2
Colombia	Unidad de valor real	COU	970	2
Comoros	Comoro franc	KMF	174	0
Congo	CFA franc BEAC	XAF	950	0
Democratic Republic of Congo	Congolese franc	CDF	976	2
Cook Islands	New Zealand dollar	NZD	554	2

Country or entity	Currency	Alphabetic code	Numeric code	Minor unit
Costa Rica	Costa Rican colon	CRC	188	2
Ivory Coast	CFA franc BCEAO	XOF	952	0
Croatia	Croatian kuna	HRK	191	2
Cuba	Peso convertible	CUC	931	2
Cuba	Cuban peso	CUP	192	2
Curacao	Netherlands Antillean guilder	ANG	532	2
Cyprus	Euro	EUR	978	2
Czech Republic	Czech koruna	CZK	203	2
Denmark	Danish krone	DKK	208	2
Djibouti	Djibouti franc	DJF	262	0
Dominica	East Caribbean dollar	XCD	951	2
Dominican Republic	Dominican peso	DOP	214	2
Ecuador	US dollar	USD	840	2
Egypt	Egyptian pound	EGP	818	2
El Salvador	El Salvador colon	SVC	222	2
El Salvador	US dollar	USD	840	2
Equatorial Guinea	CFA franc BEAC	XAF	950	0
Eritrea	Nakfa	ERN	232	2
Estonia	Euro	EUR	978	2
Ethiopia	Ethiopian birr	ETB	230	2
European Union	Euro	EUR	978	2
Falkland Islands	Falkland Islands pound	FKP	238	2
Faroe Islands	Danish krone	DKK	208	2
Fiji	Fiji dollar	FJD	242	2
Finland	Euro	EUR	978	2
France	Euro	EUR	978	2
French Guiana	Euro	EUR	978	2
French Polynesia	CFP franc	XPF	953	0
French Southern Territories	Euro	EUR	978	2
Gabon	CFA franc BEAC	XAF	950	0
Gambia	Dalasi	GMD	270	2
Georgia	Lari	GEL	981	2
Germany	Euro	EUR	978	2

Currency codes (ISO 4217)

Country or entity	Currency	Alphabetic code	Numeric code	Minor unit
Ghana	Ghana cedi	GHS	936	2
Gibraltar	Gibraltar pound	GIP	292	2
Greece	Euro	EUR	978	2
Greenland	Danish krone	DKK	208	2
Grenada	East Caribbean dollar	XCD	951	2
Guadeloupe	Euro	EUR	978	2
Guam	US dollar	USD	840	2
Guatemala	Quetzal	GTQ	320	2
Guernsey	Pound sterling	GBP	826	2
Guinea	Guinea franc	GNF	324	0
Guinea Bissau	CFA franc BCEAO	XOF	952	0
Guyana	Guyana dollar	GYD	328	2
Haiti	Gourde	HTG	332	2
Haiti	US dollar	USD	840	2
Heard & McDonald Islands	Australian dollar	AUD	036	2
Honduras	Lempira	HNL	340	2
Hong Kong	Hong Kong dollar	HKD	344	2
Hungary	Forint	HUF	348	2
Iceland	Iceland krona	ISK	352	0
India	Indian rupee	INR	356	2
Indonesia	Rupiah	IDR	360	2
International Monetary Fund (IMF)	Special drawing right	XDR	960	N.A.
Iran	Iranian rial	IRR	364	2
Iraq	Iraqi dinar	IQD	368	3
Ireland	Euro	EUR	978	2
Isle of Man	Pound sterling	GBP	826	2
Israel	New Israeli shekel	ILS	376	2
Italy	Euro	EUR	978	2
Jamaica	Jamaican dollar	JMD	388	2
Japan	Yen	JPY	392	0
Jersey	Pound sterling	GBP	826	2
Jordan	Jordanian dinar	JOD	400	3
Kazakhstan	Tenge	KZT	398	2

Currency codes (ISO 4217)

Country or entity	Currency	Alphabetic code	Numeric code	Minor unit
Kenya	Kenyan shilling	KES	404	2
Kiribati	Australian dollar	AUD	036	2
North Korea	North Korean won	KPW	408	2
South Korea	Won	KRW	410	0
Kuwait	Kuwaiti dinar	KWD	414	3
Kyrgyzstan	Som	KGS	417	2
Laos	Kip	LAK	418	2
Latvia	Latvian lats	LVL	428	2
Lebanon	Lebanese pound	LBP	422	2
Lesotho	Loti	LSL	426	2
Lesotho	Rand	ZAR	710	2
Liberia	Liberian dollar	LRD	430	2
Libya	Libyan dinar	LYD	434	3
Liechtenstein	Swiss franc	CHF	756	2
Lithuania	Lithuanian litas	LTL	440	2
Luxembourg	Euro	EUR	978	2
Macao	Pataca	MOP	446	2
Macedonia	Denar	MKD	807	2
Madagascar	Malagasy ariary	MGA	969	2
Malawi	Kwacha	MWK	454	2
Malaysia	Malaysian ringgit	MYR	458	2
Maldives	Rufiyaa	MVR	462	2
Mali	CFA franc BCEAO	XOF	952	0
Malta	Euro	EUR	978	2
Marshall Islands	US dollar	USD	840	2
Martinique	Euro	EUR	978	2
Mauritania	Ouguiya	MRO	478	2
Mauritius	Mauritius rupee	MUR	480	2
Mayotte	Euro	EUR	978	2
African Development Bank Group member countries	ADB Unit of account	XUA	965	N.A.
Mexico	Mexican peso	MXN	484	2
Mexico	Mexican Unidad de inversion (UDI)	MXV	979	2

Currency codes (ISO 4217)

Country or entity	Currency	Alphabetic code	Numeric code	Minor unit
Micronesia	US dollar	USD	840	2
Moldova	Moldovan leu	MDL	498	2
Monaco	Euro	EUR	978	2
Mongolia	Tugrik	MNT	496	2
Montenegro	Euro	EUR	978	2
Montserrat	East Caribbean dollar	XCD	951	2
Morocco	Moroccan dirham	MAD	504	2
Mozambique	Mozambique metical	MZN	943	2
Myanmar	Kyat	MMK	104	2
Namibia	Namibia dollar	NAD	516	2
Namibia	Rand	ZAR	710	2
Nauru	Australian dollar	AUD	036	2
Nepal	Nepalese rupee	NPR	524	2
Netherlands	Euro	EUR	978	2
Netherlands Antilles	Netherlands Antillean guilder	ANG	532	2
New Caledonia	CFP franc	XPF	953	0
New Zealand	New Zealand dollar	NZD	554	2
Nicaragua	Cordoba oro	NIO	558	2
Niger	CFA franc BCEAO	XOF	952	0
Nigeria	Naira	NGN	566	2
Niue	New Zealand dollar	NZD	554	2
Norfolk Island	Australian dollar	AUD	036	2
Northern Mariana Islands	US dollar	USD	840	2
Norway	Norwegian krone	NOK	578	2
Oman	Rial omani	OMR	512	3
Pakistan	Pakistan rupee	PKR	586	2
Palau	US dollar	USD	840	2
Palestinian Territory	No universal currency			
Panama	Balboa	PAB	590	2
Panama	US dollar	USD	840	2
Papua New Guinea	Kina	PGK	598	2
Paraguay	Guarani	PYG	600	0
Peru	Nuevo sol	PEN	604	2

Currency codes (ISO 4217)

Country or entity	Currency	Alphabetic code	Numeric code	Minor unit
Philippines	Philippine peso	PHP	608	2
Pitcairn Island	New Zealand dollar	NZD	554	2
Poland	Zloty	PLN	985	2
Portugal	Euro	EUR	978	2
Puerto Rico	US dollar	USD	840	2
Qatar	Qatari rial	QAR	634	2
Reunion	Euro	EUR	978	2
Romania	New Romanian leu	RON	946	2
Russia	Russian ruble	RUB	643	2
Rwanda	Rwanda franc	RWF	646	0
St. Barthelemy	Euro	EUR	978	2
St. Helena, Ascension, Tristan da Cunha	Saint Helena pound	SHP	654	2
St. Kitts & Nevis	East Caribbean dollar	XCD	951	2
St. Lucia	East Caribbean dollar	XCD	951	2
St. Martin (French)	Euro	EUR	978	2
St. Pierre & Miquelon	Euro	EUR	978	2
St. Vincent & Grenadines	East Caribbean dollar	XCD	951	2
Samoa	Tala	WST	882	2
San Marino	Euro	EUR	978	2
Sao Tome & Principe	Dobra	STD	678	2
Saudi Arabia	Saudi riyal	SAR	682	2
Senegal	CFA franc BCEAO	XOF	952	0
Serbia	Serbian dinar	RSD	941	2
Seychelles	Seychelles rupee	SCR	690	2
Sierra Leone	Leone	SLL	694	2
Singapore	Singapore dollar	SGD	702	2
Sint Maarten (Dutch)	Netherlands Antillean guilder	ANG	532	2
Sistema Unitario de Compensacion Regional de Pagos SUCRE	Sucre	XSU	994	n/a
Slovakia	Euro	EUR	978	2
Slovenia	Euro	EUR	978	2
Solomon Islands	Solomon Islands dollar	SBD	090	2
Somalia	Somali shilling	SOS	706	2

Currency codes (ISO 4217)

Country or entity	Currency	Alphabetic code	Numeric code	Minor unit
South Africa	Rand	ZAR	710	2
South Georgia & South Sandwich Islands	No universal currency			
South Sudan	South Sudanese pound	SSP	728	2
Spain	Euro	EUR	978	2
Sri Lanka	Sri Lanka rupee	LKR	144	2
Sudan	Sudanese pound	SDG	938	2
Suriname	Surinam dollar	SRD	968	2
Svalbard & Jan Mayen Islands	Norwegian krone	NOK	578	2
Swaziland	Lilangeni	SZL	748	2
Sweden	Swedish krona	SEK	752	2
Switzerland	WIR euro	CHE	947	2
Switzerland	Swiss franc	CHF	756	2
Switzerland	WIR franc	CHW	948	2
Syria	Syrian pound	SYP	760	2
Taiwan	New Taiwan dollar	TWD	901	2
Tajikistan	Somoni	TJS	972	2
Tanzania	Tanzanian shilling	TZS	834	2
Thailand	Baht	THB	764	2
Timor-Leste	US dollar	USD	840	2
Togo	CFA franc BCEAO	XOF	952	0
Tokelau	New Zealand dollar	NZD	554	2
Tonga	Pa'anga	TOP	776	2
Trinidad & Tobago	Trinidad & Tobago dollar	TTD	780	2
Tunisia	Tunisian dinar	TND	788	3
Turkey	Turkish lira	TRY	949	2
Turkmenistan	Turkmenistan new manat	TMT	934	2
Turks & Caicos Islands	US dollar	USD	840	2
Tuvalu	Australian dollar	AUD	036	2
Uganda	Uganda shilling	UGX	800	0
Ukraine	Hryvnia	UAH	980	2
UAE	UAE dirham	AED	784	2
UK	Pound sterling	GBP	826	2
USA	US dollar	USD	840	2

Currency codes (ISO 4217)

Country or entity	Currency	Alphabetic code	Numeric code	Minor unit
USA	US dollar (next day)	USN	997	2
USA	US dollar (same day)	USS	998	2
US Minor Outlying Islands	US dollar	USD	840	2
Uruguay	Uruguay peso en unidades indexadas (URUIURUI)	UYI	940	0
Uruguay	Peso Uruguayo	UYU	858	2
Uzbekistan	Uzbekistan sum	UZS	860	2
Vanuatu	Vatu	VUV	548	0
Vatican City	Euro	EUR	978	2
Venezuela	Bolivar	VEF	937	2
Vietnam	Dong	VND	704	0
British Virgin Islands	US dollar	USD	840	2
US Virgin Islands	US dollar	USD	840	2
Wallis & Futuna	CFP franc	XPF	953	0
Western Sahara	Moroccan dirham	MAD	504	2
Yemen	Yemeni rial	YER	886	2
Zambia	Zambian kwacha	ZMW	967	2
Zimbabwe	Zimbabwe dollar	ZWL	932	2
ZZ01 Bond Markets Unit European EURCO	Bond markets unit European composite unit (EURCO)	XBA	955	n/a
ZZ02 Bond Markets Unit European_EMU-6	Bond markets unit European monetary unit (EMU-6)	XBB	956	n/a
ZZ03_Bond Markets Unit European_EUA-9	Bond markets unit European unit of account 9 (EUA-9)	XBC	957	n/a
ZZ04_Bond Markets Unit European_EUA-17	Bond markets unit European unit of account 17 (EUA-17)	XBD	958	n/a
ZZ05_UIC-Franc	UIC-franc	XFU		n/a
ZZ06_Testing_Code	Codes specifically reserved for testing purposes	XTS	963	n/a
ZZ07_No_Currency	The codes assigned for transactions where no currency is involved	XXX	999	n/a
ZZ08_Gold	Gold	XAU	959	n/a
ZZ09_Palladium	Palladium	XPD	964	n/a
ZZ10_Platinum	Platinum	XPT	962	n/a
ZZ11_Silver	Silver	XAG	961	n/a

Currency codes (ISO 4217)

For more information

http://www.iso.org/iso/home/standards/currency_codes.htm

APPENDIX

Endorsed Pre-LOUs of the Interim Global Legal Entity Identifier System (GLEIS)

LEIs issued by pre-LOUs that have been endorsed by the ROC or accredited by the Global LEI Foundation are accepted by ROC authorities requiring the use of a common identifier (see LEI Uses). From 7 October 2015, new institutions that wish to become LEI issuers need to be accredited by the GLEIF, which will monitor their compliance with the standards of the Global LEI System. Pre-LOUs endorsed by the ROC will also have to be accredited by the GLEIF, as part of the ongoing monitoring of compliance with the standards of the system. Pre-LOUs endorsed by the ROC will continue to be able to issue and maintain LEIs even before they are accredited by the GLEIF, until end-2017.

Date of endorsement	Pre-LOU	Sponsor	Prefix	Endorsement note	Pre-LOU website
3 October 2013	WM Datenservice	Bundesanstalt für Finanzdienstleistungsauf sicht	5299	http://www.leiroc.org/publications/gls/lou_20131003.pdf	https://www.geiportal.org
3 October 2013	Institut National de la Statistique et des Etudes Economiques	French Ministry for Economy and Finance	9695	http://www.leiroc.org/publications/gls/lou_20131003.pdf	https://lei-france.insee.fr
3 October 2013	CICI utility[1]	U.S. Commodity Futures Trading Commission	5493	http://www.leiroc.org/publications/gls/lou_20131003.pdf	https://www.cici-utility.org
11 November 2013	Takasbank	Capital Markets Board of Turkey	7890	http://www.leiroc.org/publications/gls/lou_20131111.pdf	http://www.takasbank.com.tr/en/Pages/LEI.aspx

1. a set of approximately 3,000 codes that are not certified but that have been used for CFTC reporting purposes (*Uncertified Used CICIs*, identified as 'NOT CURRENT' in the CICI Utility database); these codes are not globally recognized.

Date of endorsement	Pre-LOU	Sponsor	Prefix	Endorsement note	Pre-LOU website
11 November 2013	London Stock Exchange	UK Financial Conduct Authority	2138	http://www.leiroc.org/publications/gls/lou_20131111.pdf	http://www.lseg.com/LEI

Endorsed Pre-LOUs of the Interim Global Legal Entity Identifier System

Date of endorsement	Pre-LOU	Sponsor	Pre-fix	Endorsement note	Pre-LOU website
7 December 2013	Irish Stock Exchange	Central Bank of Ireland	6354	http://www.leiroc.org/publications/gls/lou_20131207.pdf	https://www.isedirect.ie
27 December 2013	Russia National Settlement Depository (NSD)	Central Bank of Russian Federation	2534	http://www.leiroc.org/publications/gls/lou_20131227.pdf	https://www.nsd.ru/en/services/lei
27 December 2013	Poland Krajowy Depozyt Papierów Wartościowych S.A. (KDPW)	Polish Financial Supervisory Authority	2594	http://www.leiroc.org/publications/gls/lou_20131227.pdf	http://www.kdpw.pl/en/business/LEI/Pages/default. aspx
7 January 2014	Dutch Chamber of Commerce (KvK)	Netherlands Authority for the Financial Markets	7245	http://www.leiroc.org/publications/gls/lou_20140107.pdf	http://www.kvk.nl/english/how-to-register-deregister-and-report-changes/legal-entity-identifier-lei/
7 January 2014	National Board of Patents and Registration of Finland (PRH)	Financial Supervisory Authority, Finland	7437	http://www.leiroc.org/publications/gls/lou_20140107.pdf	http://www.prh.fi/en/uutislistaus/2013/P_1048.html
6 February 2014	Centrální depozitář cenných papírů, a.s	Czech National Bank	3157	http://www.leiroc.org/publications/gls/lou_20140206.pdf	http://www.centraldepository.cz/index.php/en/lei-pre-lei-legal-entity-identifier
7 February 2014	Unione Italiana per le Camere di Commercio, Industria, Artigianato e Agricoltura	Banca d'Italia and Commissione Nazionale per le Società e la Borsa	8156	http://www.leiroc.org/publications/gls/lou_20140207.pdf	https://lei-italy.infocamere.it/leii/Home.action
5 March 2014	Registro Mercantil del Reino de España	Banco de España	9598	http://www.leiroc.org/publications/gls/lou_20140305.pdf	https://www.lei.mjusticia.gob.es/es/Paginas/home.as px
21 May 2014	Centrálny depozitár cenných papierov SR, a.s. (Central Securities Depository: Slovakia)	National Bank of Slovakia	0979	http://www.leiroc.org/publications/gls/lou_20140521.pdf	https://www.cdcp.sk/english/lei/lei_general.php

Endorsed Pre-LOUs of the Interim Global Legal Entity Identifier System

Date of endorsement	Pre-LOU	Sponsor	Pre-fix	Endorsement note	Pre-LOU website
21 May 2014	Bundesan-zeiger Verlag GmbH (Bun-desanzeiger)	Bundesanstalt für Finanzdienstleistung-sauf sicht	3912	http://www.leiroc.org/pub-lications/gls/lou_20140521.pdf	https://www.ceireg.de/banzlei/cust
6 June 2014	Brønnøysund Register Centre	Royal Norwegian Min-istry of Trade, Industry and Fisheries	5967	http://www.leiroc.org/pub-lications/gls/lou_20140606.pdf	http://www.glei.no/
22 July 2014	Japan Exchange Group/Tokyo Stock Ex-change (JPX/TSE)	Financial Services Agency of Japan (JFSA)	3538	http://www.leiroc.org/pub-lications/gls/lou_20140722.pdf	https://www.jpx.co.jp/lei/en/index.html
10 August 2014	Central Secu-rities Clearing System Plc of Nigeria	Nigerian Securi-ties and Exchange Commission	0292	http://www.leiroc.org/pub-lications/gls/lou_20140810.pdf	https://www.cscsnige-riaplc.com/home/legalentity1
26 August 2014	LuxCSD	Banque Centrale du Luxembourg	2221	http://www.leiroc.org/pub-lications/gls/lou_20140826-1.pdf	http://www.luxcsd.com/luxcsd-en/
9 October 2014	Korea Securi-ties Deposito-ry (KSD)	Korea Financial Ser-vices Commission	9884	http://www.leiroc.org/pub-lications/gls/lou_20141009-1.pdf	https://lei-k.com/websquare/control.jsp?w2xPath=/LEI/eng.x ml
20 October 2014	China Finan-cial Stand-ardization Technical Committee (CFSTC)	People's Bank of China	3003	http://www.leiroc.org/pub-lications/gls/lou_20141020-1.pdf	www.leichina.org
28 January 2015	Registro de Identificación de Entidades del BCRA (Central Bank of Argentina pre-LOU)	Central Bank of Argentina	5791	http://www.leiroc.org/pub-lications/gls/lou_20150128-1.pdf	www.bcra.gov.ar Direct link: http://200.70.35.103/weblei/
5 March 2015	Central Depository & Settlement Co Ltd (CDS), Mauritius	Financial Servic-es Commission, Mauritius	1325	http://www.leiroc.org/pub-lications/gls/lou_20150305-1.pdf	http://www.stockex-changeofmauritius.com/cds-lei

Endorsed Pre-LOUs of the Interim Global Legal Entity Identifier System

Date of endorsement	Pre-LOU	Sponsor	Pre-fix	Endorsement note	Pre-LOU website
22 April 2015	Clearing Corporation of India Limited (CCIL)2	Reserve Bank of India		http://www.leiroc.org/publications/gls/	https://www.ccilindia-lei.co.in/
22 April 2015	Zagreb	Croatian Financial Services Supervisory Agency		http://www.leiroc.org/publications/gls/	http://lei.zse.hr/
20 July 2015	Saudi Arabian Credit Bureau (SACB/ MOA'RIF)	Saudi Arabian Monetary		http://www.leiroc.org/publications/gls/	https://www.leiarabia.com
3 September 2015	APIR Systems Limited	Australian Securities and Investments Commission (ASIC)		http://www.leiroc.org/publications/gls/	http://lei.apir.com.au/
18 December 2015	Strate (Pty) Ltd	Financial Services Board, South Africa		http://www.leiroc.org/publications/gls/	http://lei-strate.co.za/LegalEntityIdentifier/
20 January 2016	Central Securities Clearing Corporation (Centralna klirinško depotna družba d.d. – KDD), Slovenia	Bank of Slovenia		http://www.leiroc.org/publications/gls/	Slovenian: https://storitve.kdd.si/lei/ English: https://storitve.kdd.si/lei/en/index
10 February 2016	Instituto de Registos e Notariado (IRN)	Banco de Portugal		http://www.leiroc.org/publications/gls/	www.irn.mj.pt

2. LEI activities are now conducted by Legal Entity Identifier India Limited (LEIL), a wholly owned subsidiary of The Clearing Corporation of India Ltd. LEIL was accredited by GLEIF.

Date of issuance	Sponsor	Pre-LOU	Prefix	Operational status
8 November 2012	U.S. Commodity Futures Trading Commission	DTCC/SWIFT CICI	5493	Operational
20 November 2012	Bundesanstalt für Finanzdienstleistungsaufsicht	WM Datenservice	5299	Operational
20 December 2012	Central Bank of Ireland	Irish Stock Exchange	6354	Operational
20 December 2012	Palestine Capital Market Authority	Palestine Securities Exchange	1392	
11 January 2013	Capital Markets Board of Turkey	Takasbank	7890	Operational

Endorsed Pre-LOUs of the Interim Global Legal Entity Identifier System

Date of issuance	Sponsor	Pre-LOU	Prefix	Operational status
1 March 2013	Central Bank of Russian Federation (Federal Financial Markets Services, Russia)	National Settlement Depository	2534	Operational
18 March 2013	French Ministry for Economy and Finance	Institut National de la Statistique et des Etudes Economiques	9695	Operational
6 June 2013	UK Financial Conduct Authority	London Stock Exchange	2138	Operational

3. All pre-LOUs issuing codes are required to comply with all the principles to be observed by Pre-LOUs that have been specified by the ROC and the FSB. For the purpose of the Uniqueness and Exclusivity check, all operational pre-LOUs must perform Uniqueness and Exclusivity checks against all pre-LEIs issued by operational pre-LOUs as indicated in Table above.

Date of issuance	Sponsor	Pre-LOU	Prefix	Operational status
14 June 2013	Netherlands Authority for the Financial Markets	Dutch Chamber of Commerce	7245	Operational
12 August 2013	People's Bank of China	China Financial Standardization Technical Committee	3003	Operational
14 August 2013	Central Bank of Argentina	Registro de Identificación de Entidades del BCRA (Central Bank of Argentina pre- LOU)	5791	Operational
19 August 2013	Polish Financial Supervisory Authority	Krajowy Depozyt Papierów Wartościowych S.A.	2594	Operational
23 August 2013	Banca d'Italia and Commissione Nazionale per le Società e la Borsa	Unione Italiana per le Camere di Commercio, Industria, Artigianato e Agricoltura	8156	Operational
8 October 2013	Financial Supervisory Authority, Finland	National Board for Patents and Registration (PRH)	7437	Operational
9 November 2013	Bundesanstalt für Finanzdienstleistungsaufsicht	Bundesanzeiger Verlag GmbH (Bundesanzeiger)	3912	Operational
23 November 2013	Banco de España	Registro Mercantil del Reino de España	9598	Operational
27 November 2013	Czech National Bank	Centrální depozitář cenných papírů, a.s.	3157	Operational

Endorsed Pre-LOUs of the Interim Global Legal Entity Identifier System

Date of issuance	Sponsor	Pre-LOU	Prefix	Operational status
8 January 2014	Reserve Bank of India	Clearing Corporation of India Limited (CCIL)	3358	Operational
26 January 2014	Royal Norwegian Ministry of Trade, Industry and Fisheries	Brønnøysund Register Centre	5967	Operational
10 February 2014	Saudi Arabian Monetary Agency	Saudi Credit Bureau	5586	Operational
18 February 2014	National Bank of Slovakia	Centrálny depozitár cenných papierov SR, a.s. (Central Securities Depository Slovakia)	0979	Operational
12 March 2014	Financial Services Board, South Africa	Strate (Pty) Limited	3789	Operational
14 April 2014	Banco de Portugal	Instituto de Registos e Notariado – IRN	5798	
14 April 2014	Banque Centrale du Luxembourg	LuxCSD	2221	Operational
14 April 2014	Financial Services Agency of Japan (JFSA)	Japan Exchange Group/ Tokyo Stock Exchange (JPX/TSE)	3538	Operational
12 May 2014	Korea Financial Services Commission	Korea Securities Depository (KSD)	9884	Operational
16 May 2014	Securities & Exchange Commission of Nigeria	Central Securities Clearing System Plc of Nigeria	0292	Operational
28 May 2014	Australian Securities and Investments Commission	APIR Systems Limited	2617	Operational
4 August 2014	Ontario Securities Commission (OSC)	CDS Clearing and Depository Services Inc. (CDS)	9278	

Endorsed Pre-LOUs of the Interim Global Legal Entity Identifier System

Date of issuance	Sponsor	Pre-LOU	Prefix	Operational status
8 September 2014	Financial Services Commission, Mauritius	Central Depository & Settlement Co Ltd (CDS), Mauritius	1325	Operational
22 April 2015	Croatian Financial Services Supervisory Agency	Zagreb Stock Exchange (ZSE)	7478	Operational
20 January 2016	Bank of Slovenia	Central Securities Clearing Corporation (Centralna klirinško depotna družba d.d. – KDD), Slovenia	4851	Operational

Take the next step to high quality data

EXCHANGE DATA INTERNATIONAL

Who We Are?

We bring you affordable

Securities Reference Data

EDI helps the global financial and investment community make informed decisions through the provision of fast, accurate and affordable data reference services. EDI's extensive database includes worldwide equity and fixed income, corporate actions, dividends, static reference data, closing prices and shares outstanding, delivered via data feeds and the Internet.

Why Choose Us?

With more than 20 years experience, we offer comprehensive and complete securities reference data for equities and fixed income instruments around the globe. Currently, EDI supplies corporate actions, pricing and reference data for over 1,000,000 global securities collated from 400+ sources of information.

Our Services

Reference Data
Manage compliance and operational risk with high quality securities reference data.

Corporate Actions
Make informed investment decisions based on timely and accurate worldwide corporate actions data.

End-of-Day-Price
Get access to closing price data gathered from 170 exchanges worldwide including all emerging and frontier markets.

Initial Public Offering
Find out if a target company has declared its intention of going public, then use that information to set up the security in your reference database.

5 Highgate Road | London, NW51JY | +44 207 324 0020 | info@exchange-data.com

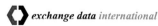

www.exchange-data.com